ECONOMIC COLLAPSE, ECONOMIC CHANGE

ECONOMIC COLLAPSE, ECONOMIC CHANGE

GETTING TO THE ROOTS OF THE CRISIS

Arthur MacEwan and John A. Miller

M.E.Sharpe
Armonk, New York
London, England

Arthur MacEwan dedicates this book to his grandchildren
Milo, Cyrus, and Olive, and to any future grandchildren who join them.

John A. Miller dedicates this book to his partner Ellen and his son Sam.

Library of Congress Cataloging-in-Publication Data

MacEwan, Arthur.
  Economic collapse, economic change : getting to the roots of the crisis / Arthur MacEwan
and John A. Miller.
    p. cm.
  Includes bibliographical references and index.
  ISBN 978-0-7656-3067-4 (hbk. : alk. paper) — ISBN 978-0-7656-3068-1 (pbk. : alk. paper)
  1. United States—Economic conditions—2009– 2. United States—Economic
  policy—2009– 3. Recessions—United States. 4. Financial crises—United States.
  5. International economic relations. I. Miller, John A., 1948 Nov. 10– II. Title.

  HC106.84.M33 2011
  330.973—dc22   2010053890

Printed in the United States of America

The paper used in this publication meets the minimum requirements of
American National Standard for Information Sciences
Permanence of Paper for Printed Library Materials,
ANSI Z 39.48-1984.

∞

IBT (c)   10   9   8   7   6   5   4   3   2   1
IBT (p)   10   9   8   7   6   5   4   3   2   1

Contents

List of Table, Figures, and Boxes

Preface

Over the last several years, as economic conditions deteriorated so seriously in the United States and in many other countries, we have been increasingly presented with questions about what has been happening. We addressed many of these questions in our classes and in *Dollars & Sense* magazine, for which we have both been writing for many years. We felt, however, that our answers were inadequate, too brief to deal with the many aspects of the economic crisis that has developed. Also, if one tries to treat important issues too briefly, the result is often an opaque and confusing explanation.

So we decided to write this book. Our intention was to do three things. First, we wanted to provide a widely accessible account of the economic collapse of recent years. Economic events, especially financial events, are usually presented in an unnecessarily complex manner, leaving many people feeling that the economic world is beyond their understanding. So we have tried to explain things in a language that will enlighten people rather than confuse them.

Second, we wanted to go beyond a description of what has happened in recent years and provide a deeper explanation of the economic crisis that has emerged. This has meant a focus on the way economic inequality, elite (undemocratic) control of power, and a perverse leave-it-to-the-market ideology have been so important in bringing about the crisis. Also, we have found it important to provide a historical context for understanding the current situation, and we have therefore explained important changes that have occurred over the last several decades.

Third, what we really care about is how economic conditions can be improved. So we have built upon our "deeper explanation" to suggest the kinds of changes that must be undertaken to bring about better, more stable economic conditions—and such changes would also mean more democratic conditions. The changes we suggest, while not ignoring immediate efforts to repair the economy, would bring about broader changes in economic and social relations. We do not have a blueprint for how to fix things, but we do have some ideas.

Our hope is that this book will contribute to the efforts of many people, working through an array of social movements, to bring about progressive change.

In writing this book, we have benefited from the advice, questions, and comments of many people. Our students and the readers of *Dollars & Sense* have been helpful in many ways. Advice from the editors of *Dollars & Sense*, Amy Gluckman and Chris Sturr, have been valuable at many points, as have the suggestions from other members of the *Dollars & Sense* collective. Important comments and advice have been provided by various friends and colleagues—including John Gildea, Arjun Jayadev, and Itai Lourie. Jim Campen was extremely helpful in reading large parts of an early draft of the manuscript, correcting our errors, and pushing us in useful directions. Also, we very much appreciated Kate Davies' work in preparing the graphs, and we are grateful to Apostolos Koutropoulos for making the diagram in Chapter 6 look nice. None of these people, of course, bear any responsibility for the errors that remain.

We are, in addition, especially grateful and indebted to Margery Davies and Ellen Lapowsky, who encouraged us as we labored through this project.

Part I
Economic Crisis, Causes, and Cures

1

What Ails the U.S. Economy?

Understanding Causes to Find Cures

Once upon a time, not so very long ago, we in the United States pretended that our economic situation was pretty good. The doldrums of the 1970s and early 1980s were ancient history. Yes, there was a recession in the early 1990s, but then we had a decade of economic growth, and many people saw new technology—computers followed by the advent of biotechnology—as ushering in an era of prosperity. The dot-com bust and another recession just after the turn of the twenty-first century put a damper on the enthusiasm, but then the economy started to grow again. Not very fast, but after all, there had been the events of September 11, 2001, and, the government claimed, it was necessary to fight the so-called war on terror. Besides, with housing prices soaring, lots of ordinary people were getting rich—or so they thought.

"Housing prices soaring." There was the clue that something was wrong—if anyone had cared to notice. The rapid rise in housing prices during the early part of the new millennium was a speculative "bubble." People were paying more and more for houses because they believed that prices would continue to go up and up. Manipulations by banks and mortgage companies along with a perverse set of government policies had encouraged the inflation of the bubble. When the bubble burst, as all bubbles eventually do, the impact spread economic disaster far and wide. A virtual collapse of the financial system followed and led into a general economic crisis.

Yet the housing bubble and its inevitable bursting were only symptoms of much deeper maladies in the U.S. economy. Most important, even while the economy was growing and average incomes were rising, many, many people were being left out. The United States had become a very unequal society, with a small group at the top getting most of the benefits of economic growth. For others, wages were stagnant and the number of people living in poverty was growing. This rising inequality was at the center of the economic fiasco that the country was to experience.

Inequality, however, was not the lone cause of the economic crisis that began in 2007. Rising inequality was tied up with a greater and greater concentration of economic and political power in the hands of the wealthy and with the ascendance of a pernicious leave-it-to-the-market ideology, which was an instrument of that power. Inequality, power, and ideology worked together, reinforcing one another and forming a vicious circle, creating the conditions that generated the economic crisis. Several other factors were involved, all very important, including: the housing bubble, the growing role of debt in the whole economy, the general deregulation of financial markets (as well as other markets), and a lack of coordination and regulation of the global economy. These factors, however, are best understood as transmitters of our economic problems, arising from the inequality-power-ideology nexus that lay at the core of the current crisis.

A main purpose of this book is to elaborate this point, to develop the argument that the economic crisis, which is causing such hardships in the United States and, in fact, around the world can best be understood as arising from the conditions of inequality, power, and ideology that have dominated life in the United States in recent decades. Understanding the origins of the crisis is an issue of substantial practical importance if we are to have any hope of dealing with it and overcoming the economic hardship.

An economic crisis might be likened to an infectious disease, and economics is a bit like medicine. In medicine, until we gained an understanding of the way bacteria and viruses cause various infectious diseases, it was virtually impossible to develop effective cures. Of course, dealing with many diseases is complicated by the fact that germs, genes, diet, and the environment establish a nexus or intertwined set of causes. The same is true in economics. Without an understanding of the causes of the current crisis, we are unlikely to develop a solution; certainly we cannot create a solution with lasting impact. And determining the causes is complicated because several intertwined factors are involved.

As doctors are concerned with the causes of disease in order to find cures, we are concerned with the causes of economic crisis in order to find cures. If we focus on the wrong factors, the symptoms rather than the underlying disease, we will have no more success than the doctor who treats a serious illness by focusing on the headache and providing only aspirin. The aspirin may provide some short-term relief, which can be a good thing, but the underlying disease is still there. Even antibiotics may do little good if the patient, cured of the immediate illness, continues to face a nexus of deeper, underlying problems—a weak immune system; a germ-infested, polluted environment; and poor dietary habits (and smoking)—that create a risk for recurrence of the ailments.

So the ultimate purpose of this book is to suggest cures and to get others to think about cures for what ails our economic lives—cures that make sense in relation to what we argue are the fundamental causes of the crisis. Economic stimulus; a program to deal with the limited liquidity (i.e., the limited availability of funds) in the financial sector; mortgage support for stressed home owners (and parallel programs for renters); effective regulation of the financial sector; and new approaches to international economic relations are all necessary steps. They can help—just as aspirin and antibiotics can help a sick person—but they do not deal with the whole nexus of deeper, underlying problems. Moreover, like a doctor prescribing a dosage that is too small to be effective, the U.S. government has been far too timid with its economic stimulus package and its new regulations for financial institutions. Worse yet, like the doctor's prescription of an insufficient dose of antibiotics that then generates resistant and dangerous bacteria, the financial bailout that originated with the Bush administration and was continued by the Obama administration is likely to reinvigorate the perverted financial operations that wreaked such havoc on people's lives (to say nothing of the way the bailout transferred more wealth to the financial nabobs who brought us to this point).

Our approach is very different and follows from our analysis of the economic crisis. Because we identify the inequality-power-ideology nexus as the cause of the crisis, we believe that changes in income and wealth distribution, in who has power in our society, and in the ideology of how we view the operation of the economy are at the center of a lasting solution to the problems of our economic lives. Moreover, these are changes that build a more democratic society. Taken together, they can generate a wider sharing of political authority, giving greater substance to the essential forms of democracy (elections and civil liberties). So, if we are able to change income and wealth distribution, power, and ideology, we can get two good things: better economic lives and a more democratic society.

But how are such changes to be accomplished?

Unfortunately, we have no magic pills that will bring a quick cure. We do, however, have some ideas. We think that our analysis of the economic crisis suggests some ways to begin to bring about positive change. As we will argue, an important cause of greater inequality, greater power for the wealthy, and greater reliance on the myth of the market has been the weakening of labor unions. In significant part, this weakening of unions has been a political phenomenon, and we believe unions can in turn be strengthened by political action. We will also argue that social policies—such as universal, single-payer health care, universal child care, environmental protection and repair, full-employment programs, and extensive housing support—not only provide direct benefits to the recipients, but also contribute to greater economic equality and a more democratic distribution of power. They also tend to bring about a shift in ideology.

We do not pretend that it is easy to strengthen labor unions or establish more extensive social programs. After all, a large part of the reason for the weakness of unions and the inadequacy of social policies is the unequal distribution of power in our society. So one might ask how we propose to strengthen the role of unions or improve social policy while the structure of power is not altered. Our answer is that these changes provide particular places to start altering the structure of power. As we have said, inequality, power, and ideology form a vicious circle, each reinforcing the other. The problem is finding openings where we can break into this circle, transforming it to a virtuous circle of change. We think this is possible, but it is not easy.

Furthermore, and especially important, the current economic crisis and the economic structures out of which it developed are international—or, to use the in-vogue term, global. Just as the crisis is global, so are the conditions that led to the crisis. Issues of income distribution, power, and ideology operate around the world, not just in the United States. And the global nature of economic relations has had a major role in shaping social, political, and economic relations in the United States. For example, one of the reasons labor unions have been weakened in recent decades is that U.S. workers have been placed in direct competition with much more poorly paid workers elsewhere in the world. We think there are ways that political action in the United States, when focused on conditions and policy within the country, can bring about positive changes in the structure of international economic relations. Still, it will be hard to increase the power of U.S. labor unions or to greatly improve the distribution of income and wealth in the United States without also achieving the much needed improvement in the conditions of workers elsewhere in the world.

All this sounds like a Herculean task—if not an impossible task! And we would probably see it as impossible if we believed it to be an all-or-nothing proposition—that is, if we believed that without a complete, all-or-nothing change in our economic conditions and structures of power there could be no progress. Yet we think that experience shows something quite different: that progress can be made short of a complete solution. After all, the U.S. and world economies have not always been in crisis or on the brink of crisis, income and wealth distribution has not always been as unequal as it is now, power has not always been so badly distributed, and the myth of the market has not always been so dominant. So we are optimistic.

Where We Are Going

In Chapter 2, we are going to do a few more things to set the stage for the discussion and analysis in the rest of the book. We first provide a description of some of the central aspects of economic conditions existing at the time of this writing. We make no pretense of being able to forecast the immediate course of the U.S. and world economies—if the worst has passed, how long the doldrums will continue, or if another setback is in the near offing. Other economists have sufficiently embarrassed themselves through that pretense, and we do not wish to join their ranks. Some brief description of how things have been moving, however, will help to establish a basis for the analysis and arguments we want to present in later chapters.

We then explain just what we mean by the term "economic crisis," and in doing so we intend to make clear why the economic downturn that began in 2007 has been different than other downturns. A crisis is not simply an exceptionally bad recession. It is that, but it is something more. A crisis is a disruption not only of output and employment, but also of both the basic organizational structures of the economy and the way people think about their economic lives. Thus, when a crisis develops, it opens up opportunities for substantial changes. The changes are by no means automatic, and they can be of very different sorts. There is no guarantee that something good will emerge from a period of crisis. Things can revert to the pre-crisis situation or even lead to something much worse (as the European experience of the 1930s demonstrated). But at least there are possibilities for positive change. The problem is how to make the most of those possibilities.

The Core of Our Analysis

In Parts II and III we present the core of our analysis of the development of the economic crisis within the United States. First, in Part II, we examine the changes in recent decades of the inequality-power-ideology nexus, and then, in Part III, we explain how those changes led into the current economic disarray.

In Part II (Chapters 3 and 4) we trace the evolution of economic relations from the structures that came out of the Great Depression and World War II to a significantly different set of structures in the new millennium. In the earlier years, the focus of Chapter 3, there was substantial income and wealth inequality in the United States, but less than had existed before the 1930s. Power, too, was disproportionately in the hands of the wealthy, but the dramatic political and social changes of the 1930s and war years had shifted the balance of power a bit in favor of the labor movement in particular and popular forces in general. A complex of factors in this period created, for example, the basis for the advance of the civil rights and the women's movements. The ideology that guided economic affairs, shaped very much by the experience of the Great Depression, was more accepting of government intervention than it had been in an earlier era and than it would become in subsequent decades. The War on Poverty, in spite of its shortcomings, seemed to establish the principle that the government had a responsibility to improve the conditions of those people economically worst off. And both economists and politicians generally accepted the idea that the government could and should use fiscal policy as well as monetary policy in an active manner to avoid recessions or severe inflation. Employing an active fiscal policy came to be known as Keynesian economics, after the British economist John Maynard Keynes whose writings explained and justified this approach. At the end of 1965, *Time* magazine titled a major article on the economy "The Economy: We Are All Keynesians Now," and at the beginning of the 1970s, the conservative Republican president Richard Nixon would declare, "I am now a Keynesian in economics."[1]

Beginning in the mid-1970s, it became apparent that things were changing. The economic relations of the post–World War II era had broken down, and economic life was severely disrupted in those years. The changes that emerged out of this period are examined in Chapter 4. In response to the economic problems that were emerging, large firms and wealthy individuals set out to establish a new set of economic relations. They engaged in what we might call a "power grab." In the ensuing years, through the 1980s, 1990s, and the first decade of the new millennium, the success of this power grab was most evident in the changes in taxation—not only at the federal level, but also at the state and local levels. Indeed, perhaps the first noteworthy success of these changes was the passage in 1978 of Proposition 13 in California, an amendment to the state's constitution that greatly limited both local property taxes and the state government's ability to increase taxes. The attack on taxation reached its high point—or, from our perspective, its low point—with the substantial reduction of taxes on the wealthy during the early years of George W. Bush's administration.

Yet while tax issues were perhaps the most apparent feature of the power grab, it had equally important manifestations in deregulation of business (especially financial business), major changes in social welfare legislation, and steps that weakened the role of labor unions. Republicans took the lead in these changes, and it was during the reign of Ronald Reagan in the 1980s that the process gained full momentum. However, Democrats also played a large role, with crucial deregulation of the financial sector and major alteration of social welfare programs ("the end of welfare as we know it") during the Clinton administration (though the years of Democratic control of the White House seem to have been somewhat better, or less bad, for labor unions).

The power changes of these years were accompanied, both as cause and effect, by ideological changes and rising inequality. Not only was there an onslaught against taxes, with tax rates for the rich being cut most substantially, but conservative forces succeeded in establishing the dominance of a full-blown anti-tax ideology. Virtually nowhere in the country could a politician succeed without declaring her or his commitment to "no new taxes." George H.W. Bush underscored the approach with his famous 1988 campaign statement, "Read my lips: no new taxes." Then, after implementing some tax increases during his administration, he lost his bid for re-election in 1992.

Antitax rhetoric was closely linked to a more general antigovernment ideology. Conservatives portrayed government as bureaucratic, inept, corrupt, and just plain bad. In economic affairs, they avowed, it was best just to "leave things to the market." Unfettered, unregulated market activity was virtually deified as providing the basis for innovation, economic growth, and the spread of good times for everyone. The prevailing ideology was summed up in the old aphorism, "That government is best which governs least." While the ideology was not always expressed in these simplistic terms, it was in fact often reduced to such slogans. Moreover, the U.S. government and its allies were able to spread this ideology into—or perhaps it is better to say that they were able to impose it on—international economic affairs.

The facts on the ground, however, didn't quite fit with claims of this free-market ideology. In particular, it did not spread good times for everyone—far from it. From the mid-1970s on, income and wealth in the United States became more and more unequally distributed. Wages stagnated and most families were able to achieve some increase in their overall incomes only by sending more family members into the paid workforce, working longer hours, or both. At the same time, the incomes (and the wealth) of the very rich soared. Those at the very top, the richest one percent of families, took the lion's share of income increases, and those near the top also did pretty well. But for most people, improvement was very limited if it took place at all. The numbers, which we will present as we tell the story, are shocking.

In Part III (Chapters 5 and 6), we explain how the economic crisis emerged out of these structures of inequality, elite power, and perverse ideology. The stage was set for crisis by the great changes that took place in the financial industry, changes that had begun in the 1970s. The power of business leaders and the wealthy, expressed in the antigovernment ideology, was the basis for the reduction of government controls on economic activity (i.e., deregulation) that, especially in the financial sector, was so important in generating the crisis.

Unregulated bankers are dangerous. Failing to regulate them is a bit like failing to regulate automobile drivers in that they put the rest of us at risk. Competition leads unregulated banks to take on greater and greater risks.

The winners in this competition become bigger and bigger—so big, in fact, that their failure jeopardizes the operation of the whole economy. They are too big to be allowed to fail. Then, knowing that the government will bail them out if their risky operations turn sour, they take on even greater risks. (If the jeopardy of the whole economy is not sufficient to persuade the government to intervene and prevent the bank failures, the banks can use their direct political power to bring about the bailouts.)

Deregulation alone did not cause the financial crisis, and some regulations did exist. Yet because of the antigovernment ideology that prevailed in the early 2000s, existing regulations were often ignored by both the firms and the government regulators. For example, banks and mortgage companies approved home-purchase loans for people who did not meet the basic, required standards. Some of these loans were just plain fraudulent. Then, of course, there is the infamous Bernard Madoff case, where regulators apparently ignored warnings that Madoff was running the largest Ponzi scheme of all time. It increasingly appears, however, that fraud in the financial system was limited to neither the bottom level of the system where mortgages are issued nor to strange cases like the Madoff affair. De facto, if not always de jure, fraud appears to have permeated the financial system, as witness the early 2010 case of fraud brought by the government against Goldman Sachs, one of the country's largest and most prestigious financial firms. As the whole deregulation-nonregulation story illustrates, power operates on many levels—having impacts on legislation, influencing the application of policy, and generating fraud. Also, increasingly the power to subvert regulation has found thorough support in ideology.

Furthermore, as we describe in Chapter 5, government policies in the early years after 2000 facilitated the housing bubble that, when it burst, was the catalyst for the whole crisis. Under the leadership of its long-time chairman Alan Greenspan, the Federal Reserve Board (the Fed) pursued an excessively loose monetary policy. Moreover, Greenspan continually denied the existence of a housing bubble (as he had denied the existence of a stock market bubble in the late 1990s) and virtually acted as cheerleader for the financial practices that fueled the crisis. While the roots of the crisis may lie, as we argue, deep within structures of the U.S. and global economies, Greenspan and several others bear a great deal of responsibility for the dire economic conditions that emerged in 2007 and 2008.

In Chapter 6 we turn to the unfolding of the crisis, tracing the connections between how the deep structures of the inequality-power-ideology nexus generated the particular steps that caused the economic implosion. Inequality, in particular, was a central part of the foundation on which the huge edifice of consumer debt was constructed—including the vast increase in mortgage debt. Put simply, with their incomes growing very slowly if at all, most people could meet their economic needs only by borrowing. Also, because most people's incomes were limited, economic growth was always threatened by the potential of a weakening of consumer demand. So the government—that is, the Fed—kept interest rates low, encouraging borrowing to maintain consumer demand.

The excessive expansion of debt would not have taken place and would not have had such a destructive impact if not for the deregulation of the financial sector. As we demonstrate in Chapter 6 with the aid of a (we hope not overly complex) diagram, inequality on the one hand and elite power and perverse ideology on the other were the bases on which the particulars of the crisis unfolded.

Although the argument of Parts II and III is based on the view that there is a close connection between wealth and political power, we do not explain how that connection operates. In Appendix A, however, we do provide some brief comments on the relationship between wealth and power. While a full examination of this relationship is beyond the scope of this book, we hope that Appendix A will at least provide some useful discussion of the issue.

Global Issues in the Emergence of Crisis

In Part IV (Chapters 7 and 8) we turn our attention to the international economy. The current era in international economic affairs is usually characterized by the term "globalization," and we describe the long history of this phenomenon in Chapter 7. Globalization is often described as involving an intrinsic link between the increase of economic activity across international boundaries and the reduction of direct regulation of international commerce. Yet there is no such intrinsic link, and international economic integration—or globalization—has taken many different forms: colonialism, various regulatory regimes, and, in the current era, deregulation. In each era, globalization has brought some great gains and, to use Adam Smith's term, "dreadful misfortunes." The deregulated system of global commerce, often described as a free trade system, has created problems in international economic relations that parallel the problems that deregulation has created in the U.S. economy—and those problems contributed to the emergence of the economic crisis.

Neither the extent nor the form of globalization just "happened." As we explain in Chapter 7, the structure of the global system, the deregulation, and the central role of the United States in the system were the results of political efforts by the U.S. government. While those efforts have a long history, they became most apparent during and following World War II, when planning and actions by the U.S. government and private interests began to build the institutional framework for the operation of the postwar global economy. That framework facilitated a rapid increase in international trade, the enhanced role of multinational firms, and the expansion of global investment. It also pushed nations toward greater openings for free trade and the unregulated movement of finance. While the U.S. government and U.S. business could not simply work their will in structuring international commerce, the direction of their efforts has been consistent from World War II onward—namely to create a more open international economy, a free trade economy.

While the direction of U.S. international economic policy has been consistent for at least the last seventy years, events of the 1980s gave new impetus to the push toward more openness. The emergence of the debt crisis of the 1980s created an opportunity for the U.S. government—largely through the International Monetary Fund and the World Bank (important parts of that "institutional framework" created after World War II)—to pressure other countries to yield to greater openness. Also, the advent of leave-it-to-the-market ideology in the United States and the power shift that took place in this country and in Great Britain gave greater intensity to the push of more openness. This direction of change continued through the 1990s and into the new millennium, and was reflected in the creation of the World Trade Organization and in several bilateral and multilateral trade pacts between the United States and other countries.

Financial openness was an important part of the emerging, less-regulated international economy. The impact of the freer movement of finance appeared in the Mexican financial crisis of 1994, and then, with greater force, in the East Asian financial crisis of 1997. These events foreshadowed the problems that were to arise in the early 2000s, problems that contributed to the emergence of the economic crisis.

Contrary to the widespread effort among economists and policy makers to claim that great benefits are being obtained from free trade, much of Chapter 7 involves an implicit critique of free trade. In this book we do not directly or fully engage in the debates surrounding this claim, but we have included Appendix B, which examines and eviscerates some of the principal arguments that are used to justify "free trade globalization." In addition to providing an addendum to Chapter 7, Appendix B also strengthens an argument that runs throughout the entire book—namely that unregulated markets, so-called free markets, do not serve the interests of most people.

In Chapter 8 we focus on the reemergence of China as a great economic power and on the economic relationship between China and the United States. This relationship alone is not responsible for the international factors that contributed to the economic crisis, but an examination of this relationship helps clarify those factors. It turns out that the U.S. housing bubble and subsequent mortgage foreclosures in Las Vegas, South Florida, and elsewhere are closely connected to the production of socks in Datang, China (a connection we will explain in Chapter 8—and, yes, that's socks, not stocks!). Chinese policies, however, are not in some sense to blame for economic problems in the United States—a charge that has been advanced from many quarters. In fact, the playing out of those policies was part of a relationship of codependency or symbiosis between China and the United States. It was a relationship that served interests on both sides of the Pacific—for a while. Yet, in the context of a deregulated global economy—the structure that had been advanced by the United States for decades—this relationship interacted with events in the United States to bring about the crisis.

What to Do About the Crisis

It is one thing to explain an economic crisis, another thing to figure out what to do about it. Explaining a crisis, however, is an important step in figuring out what to do about it. In Part V (Chapters 9 and 10)) we attempt to build on the analysis of the earlier chapters; first, to examine the steps that the government has taken to deal with the crisis, and, second, to explain some directions of change that would address the more fundamental causes of the crisis, the underlying inequality-power-ideology nexus.

We argue that the government's responses to the crisis have been insufficient and sometimes very harmful. Nonetheless, government actions—the bailout of the banks, the stimulus of aggregate demand, and the enactment of legislation to regulate the financial industry—have involved dramatic departures from the policy line that Washington has followed for the last few decades. With these actions, the government engaged in a high degree of direct involvement in economic affairs, dropping even the façade of leaving things to the market. Thus, policy developments from late 2008 onward demonstrated how an economic crisis can generate significant changes. While we believe the changes have been inadequate and sometimes harmful, they do suggest that the economic crisis of recent years has created opportunities for extensive and perhaps more meaningful change.

In general, as we explain in Chapter 9, the government's efforts to stimulate aggregate demand have been insufficient. This was especially true during the Bush administration. Having failed to recognize the inflation of the housing bubble, members of the Bush administration seemed also incapable of recognizing the economic debacle that was developing as the bubble started to deflate. It was as though government decision makers were wearing ideological blinders, guided by a faith that markets would be self-correcting and that there was little if any need for government intervention.

As 2008 proceeded and the potential dissolution of the financial sector became more apparent, ideology began to give way to reality. With the trauma of Bear Stearns, Lehman Brothers, Fannie Mae and Freddie Mac, and the American International Group (AIG), the government (the Fed and the U.S. Treasury) began to intervene heavily and directly. In October 2008 the Troubled Assets Relief Program (TARP) was established to provide funds to large financial institutions with severe problems. Government officials believed that several of the largest financial institutions—Bank of America, Goldman Sachs, J.P. Morgan Chase, and others—were "too big to fail." The failure of even one of them could have had far-reaching negative impacts; and the failure of one could lead to the failure of others, generating an economic disaster. By providing funds to the firms (which were effectively subsidies for their operations) the government did appear to avoid a full-scale financial "meltdown."

Even if one accepts the government's argument that a failure to support the financial system would have resulted in economic disaster, there were at least three major problems with TARP. First, it involved a huge transfer of wealth, not simply to the banks but to the bankers—the individuals who had steered us into crisis. Second, in supporting the banks and the bankers when their risk taking led to failure, TARP encouraged the continuation of excessively risky behavior. Third, and most important, there were alternatives available; the operation of the financial sector could have been maintained without bailing out the bankers or encouraging risky behavior. Because better alternatives were available, which we explain in Chapter 9, TARP must be seen as extremely costly, bad policy. At the same time, however, TARP involved a massive government intervention in the economy, a striking departure from longstanding government ideology and practice.

The economic stimulus package that was enacted at the outset of Barack Obama's presidency was also a major departure from past practice, a rejection of anti-deficit mania and a forceful recognition of the value, under certain circumstances, of large government fiscal deficits. With a combination of expenditures and tax cuts that totaled $787 billion, the stimulus package was supposed to provide the lift to aggregate demand that would significantly lessen the depth of the downturn and curtail the rise of unemployment. As described in Chapter 9, however, while the 2009 stimulus package did move things in a positive direction, it was too small and poorly structured. The appraisal of the package's size requires some calculations that we explain in Chapter 9. The problems with its structure are easily seen: far too reliant on tax reductions—which are often saved instead of spent—the 2009 stimulus had limited impact.

Conservative critics of the 2009 stimulus package claim that it was bad policy because it brought about a large government deficit. We point out, however, that the government's large deficit was primarily a result of the economic downturn itself and of policies adopted in earlier years. The stimulus package and TARP, taken together, accounted for a relatively small portion of the deficit. Moreover, a large federal budget deficit is exactly what is needed in a severe economic downturn.

Finally in Chapter 9, we comment on the 2010 Dodd-Frank Wall Street Reform and Consumer Protection Act, which established a number of new regulations on the financial industry. On the one hand, Dodd-Frank is another demonstration of the dramatic change that can emerge from an economic crisis, a reversal—small but nonetheless real—of the direction of government regulatory policy. On the other hand, while the legislation contains some useful gains, Dodd-Frank was an inadequate response to the crisis.

The most clearly positive feature of Dodd-Frank is its establishment of a consumer protection agency to restrict some of the particular abuses of borrowers that became so common in the decades leading up to and contributing to the crisis. In other areas, however, the new legislation is either weak or virtually nonexistent. The act does set up a procedure for dealing with large financial firms that become insolvent (resolution authority) and creates a high-level commission to monitor financial risk, but the effectiveness of these provisions is questionable. There are some new restraints on the risky practices of financial institutions; they will be required to keep more capital in reserve, and their trading in high-risk "derivatives" will be somewhat limited. These restraints, however, are not likely to alter substantially the operations of those institutions, and are not likely to prevent the sorts of risky activities that led to the crisis. In the realm of limiting the size of financial institutions—dealing with the too-big-to-fail problem—the Dodd-Frank does nothing. Likewise, two other factors that were central to the development of the crisis are unlikely to be substantially affected by the 2010 legislation: the role of the rating agencies and the salary and bonus practices in financial firms. Taken together, these shortcomings suggest that this new legislation will not substantially alter the way financial firms do business.

Even if these new financial regulations were more thoroughly in line with what is needed, the problem of their implementation would remain. The details of the broad regulations contained in the Dodd-Frank Act are to be filled in by the regulating agencies and will then have to be enforced. In both of these realms, the power of the industry and the ideology of nonregulation will continue to be major obstacles to effective change. Ultimately, the issues of power and ideology, and the closely connected issue of economic inequality, need to be addressed in order to bring about changes that would seriously limit the likelihood that the financial industry will lead the country into another crisis.

So in Chapter 10 we turn in a different direction, giving attention to the deeper story, the structures of inequality, power, and ideology that provided the foundation for economic instability in general and the current crisis in particular. Changing these structures is a long-term project, and we can only suggest some directions for moving ahead. Steps that have relatively immediate impacts—implementing a federal economic stimulus program and ensuring the availability of credit—are probably necessary and desirable. If they simply move the economy back to where it was before the crisis, that would alleviate the terrible hardships that are being experienced by millions of people. But even if the steps being taken in Washington were much better than what we describe in Chapter 9, they would not deal with the underlying problems at the foundation of the crisis.

Our focus in Chapter 10 is not on government policy, but on how popular movements might push things in a different direction, toward a more stable and sustainable economy. We will explain how an effective response to the crisis lies in the effort to expand social programs, especially universal social programs, and in the struggle to redevelop the labor movement. Furthermore, a full response to the economic crisis will require changes in the structure of the international economy and, ultimately, improvements to the economic conditions of people around the world. None of this can be accomplished immediately or even over a few years. We are advocating a direction of change, not an impossible leap to some ideal situation.

From our perspective, universal social programs, best exemplified by universal availability of childcare or a universal health care program (what has come to be known as "Medicare for all" or a single payer system), are good things in themselves. In the context of economic crisis, however, the value of such programs lies not only in their intrinsic desirability but in the role they can play in altering the structures of inequality, power, and ideology. For example, providing everyone with health care through a public program would have a profound impact on the distribution of income—directly by providing people with this real benefit and indirectly by protecting people against the huge income losses that can accompany serious illness. Also, such a universal program tends to redistribute power in society because it provides people with options that would otherwise be lacking—for example, the option of switching jobs without risking the loss of health care. Furthermore, a universal health care program that operates largely outside of the market helps to develop the acceptance of solving problems through shared responsibility rather than through "ability to pay." What is true of a universal health program is also true of other social programs.

Likewise, labor unions have the potential of making a major contribution to a favorable shift in income distribution, power, and ideology. In the United States, as in many other parts of the world, the labor movement has played a major role in providing working people with direct income improvements, better social programs, and greater political power. Labor unions have also contributed to an ideology that favors collective social action, rather than a simplistic reliance on the market, as a means of social progress. Thus the decline of the labor movement over the last half century has been associated with those structural shifts that we identify as the bases of the economic crisis. And, as we elaborate in Chapter 10, a restoration of the role of labor unions would be an important element in the creation of a stable and sustainable economy.

In part, the decline of the labor movement has been the result of "objective factors," major changes in the organization of the economy—the decline of manufacturing employment, for example, and the globalization of production—that appear to be beyond the control of direct political decisions. However, the position of unions has also been the consequence of political action, choices that have been made at various levels of government. Moreover, the "objective factors" themselves are not so objective, not outside of the political realm, but have also been shaped by government decisions. It would be folly to suggest that the labor movement of fifty years ago can be recreated simply through political action, but it would also be folly to assume that "objective" economic phenomena have ruled out a major role for labor unions in the United States.

Figuring out how to bring about changes in the international economic system is especially difficult, because there is no effective means of coordinating national policies in a way that would regulate the international system. Indeed, this incongruence between the economic system (global) and political systems (national) is a large part of the problem of instability and conflict in the world economy. There are some useful steps that have been proposed by a special commission established by the United Nations. While we are skeptical that the proposals put forth by this commission will be adopted, we review them in Chapter 10 for what they tell us about things that should and could be done to bring greater stability.

Even while reform of the global economy may be a distant goal, there are things that can be done within national economies, especially within the United States, that can both change the relationship between national economies and the global economy and influence the structure of the global economy. Such efforts, we argue, begin with the recognition that "globalization" is not one thing. If we think of globalization as the increasing integration of commerce across international boundaries, then, as we have pointed out, this integration can take place in various ways—indeed, it has taken place in various ways over the course of history. Globalization need not be the dismantling of national and international regulation of commerce through the adoption of so-called free trade. In the same way that a national economy needs regulation, so too does a well-functioning global economy. Efforts to move in this direction can be initiated on the national level, and the national efforts we emphasize—to establish universal social welfare programs and to redevelop the labor movement—are good places to start.

Nonetheless, there is the inescapable problem of the vast differences that exist in the global economy, the fact, in particular, that workers in the United States face competition from much, much more poorly paid workers elsewhere. How can we integrate the global economy and gain all the benefits of such integration without sacrificing the well-being of workers in the United States and other high-income countries? A partial, short-term answer to this question lies in establishing appropriate ways to regulate integration, and better social welfare program and stronger unions can be important pillars of that regulation. In the long-term, however, effective globalization needs to include a program for improving the material conditions of life in low-income countries. We do not pretend to have such a program. This shortcoming of our work, we plead, should be tolerated because our focus is on the United States. We cannot do everything in one book.

Chapter 10 does not focus on *how* things should be done but on *what* should be done. That is, we argue that universal social programs and a stronger labor movement are important foundations for a stable and sustainable economy, and they can play positive roles in reforming the global economy. We do not attempt, however, to lay out political strategies for accomplishing these ends. Strategies need to be worked out by those who are engaged in the struggles for these goals. Likewise in the global realm, we point to things that need to be done, but we are not going to attempt to define a strategy to alter the mode of globalization. If we can persuade our readers that the changes we are advocating are needed to deal with the economic crisis, we will have achieved something worthwhile.

Note

1. *Time,* December 31, 1965, www.time.com/time/magazine/article/ 0,9171,842353,00.html. The Nixon statement is reported to have been made to the ABC commentator Howard K. Smith; see, for example, the *Christian Science Monitor* article of October 1, 2007, "Supply-siders Take Some Lumps," www.csmonitor. com/2007/1001/p15s01-wmgn.html.

2

Where Are We Now?
Why Is This a "Crisis"?

It has become a frequent refrain of recent years: "The worst crisis since the Great Depression of the 1930s." Ever since the deteriorating economic situation in the United States became widely evident in 2007, the specter of the 1930s has hung over discussions among policy makers and analysts. The parallel to the Great Depression lies not only in the severity—and the apparent potential severity—of events unfolding in 2007 and 2008. The virtual collapse of the financial sector also underscored the similarities to that earlier era. As major financial institutions failed, firms and individuals were unable to obtain loans to advance or maintain their activity—and the economic decline spread and spiraled downward.

Furthermore, as in the Great Depression, the severe economic downturn that began in the United States quickly became an international phenomenon. Japanese and European exporters suffered steep declines in output. In the developing world, previously hot stock markets tanked and economic growth slowed, although less dramatically than in the high-income countries. However, export-dependent economies, such as Mexico in the western hemisphere and Thailand and Malaysia in Southeast Asia, suffered sharp declines in output. Even in China, the powerhouse and export giant of the developing world, economic growth slowed. Global job losses reached levels not seen since the 1930s as U.S. autoworkers, European and U.S. finance workers, Japanese electronics workers, Chinese garment workers, and Indian software workers were sent packing.

Over and over we hear comparisons to the economic and political changes of the Great Depression, the policy errors, the human suffering, and the lessons, both real and imagined. These refrains, however, beg several questions: How bad is the current economic situation? How does it compare with conditions in other economic bad times—not just the 1930s, but also other periods of economic downturns in more recent decades? And why is this period a "crisis"?

Where Are We Now?

In the United States, the economic downturn—defined in terms of the drop-off in total output, gross domestic product (GDP)—actually began in December 2007. By June 2009 when GDP started to grow again, the Great Recession, as it is now called, had lasted longer than any downturn since the Great Depression. The recurring refrain of "worst since the 1930s" was correct. The duration and severity of the Great Recession set records for the post-1930s era.

The *crisis,* however, by no means ended with the formal end of the Great Recession when GDP began to grow again in the second half of 2009. As we write in the early autumn of 2010, the U.S. and global economies remain in the doldrums—very slow economic growth, high unemployment, lack of investment, and continued uncertainty prevail. Indeed, it seems that each day brings some new indication of economic troubles: a revision downward of economic growth figures for an earlier period; a sharp decline in the stock market; a U.S. unemployment rate stuck near 10 percent; the financial crisis in Greece threatening the stability of Europe; the specter of a similar crisis in Spain or Portugal, or Italy; further weakening of the Japanese economy; and even a faltering of growth in the powerhouse Chinese economy.

The U.S. government has not been able (some might say has not tried) to enact a sufficient policy response, actions that would initiate significant reductions in unemployment and more substantial economic growth. Other governments have done no better, and, in fact, many European governments have pursued policies of austerity, which will almost surely worsen conditions. As we write, the talk is of a "double-dip" recession. Whether or not the U.S. and global economies soon sink downward, there is no expectation of any imminent restoration of strong growth.

The duration and severity of the Great Recession set the stage for these continuing troubles. As we said, its duration was longer than any other downturn since the 1930s; lasting eighteen months, it was almost twice as long as the ten months average of the ten recessions since the 1930s.[1] Its severity appears in several measures as shown in Table 2.1 (see page 22).[2]

To begin with, the boom-bust of the U.S. housing market, which triggered the financial panic of 2008 and the Great Recession, far exceeded the housing price swings of earlier periods of instability, including that of the Great Depression. Housing prices (adjusted for inflation) rose by 84.5 percent in the decade up to 2006, and then fell off by 33.1 percent by the middle of 2009. (Relatively stable over the following year, housing prices would likely fall again before any lasting stability is established in the real estate market.)[3] In the Great Depression, housing prices fell by only 12.6 percent.

The most severe falls before the current period were those associated with the 1981–82 recession (13.9 percent) and the economic slowdown at the beginning of the 1990s (14.1 percent).

The decline of output during the Great Recession was also larger than in any other recession since the 1930s:

- The cumulative drop in real GDP of 4.1 percent was more than twice the average of post-1930 recessions.
- Industrial production—which includes hard-hit manufacturers of automobiles, home electronics, and construction supplies—fell by 14.5 percent, surpassing the previous post-1930s high of a 12.2 percent decline in the mid-1970s.
- Retail sales, usually one of the more buoyant sectors in an economic downturn, dropped off dramatically, by 11.5 percent as compared to the 2.7 percent average recession decline (though the mid-1970s saw an 11.8 percent fall).

But lost jobs were the hallmark of the Great Recession. From December 2007, when the recession began, to December 2009, when employment hit bottom, total employment in the United States fell by 8.4 million jobs. Both the absolute number of jobs lost and the 6.1 percent decline of total employment were far greater than in any other post–World War II recession. The official unemployment rate hit a peak of 10.1 percent in October 2009, and, although declining slightly in subsequent months, remained close to 10 percent through the time of this writing. In 1982–83, the unemployment rate peaked at 10.8 percent and remained over 10 percent for ten months. However, the drop in total employment in those years was much less than in the 2007 through 2009 period.

The unemployment situation in recent years has actually been a good deal worse than indicated by the official unemployment rate. The official unemployment figures do not include as unemployed those workers who want a job but have not looked for a job in the last month, and counts as fully employed those people who want full-time work but are only able to obtain part-time jobs (underemployed workers). If the unemployment rate is recalculated, counting marginally attached workers (workers who have not looked for a job in the last month but have looked in the last year) as unemployed and also counting underemployed workers, the unemployment rate for October 2009 rises to 17.4 percent. No bout of unemployment since the last years of the Great Depression would have produced a comparable number (and thus the official figures showing a higher unemployment rate in the early 1980s yield a misleading comparison between those years and the more recent period).[4]

Table 2.1

Sizing Up the Great Recession

	2007–2009 Great Recession	Average for 10 Recessions since 1948	1974–75 Recession	1981–82 Recession	Great Depression (1929–1933)[a]
Length of Downturn	18 months	10 months	16 months	16 months	43 months
Change of Output (GDP– inflation adjusted)	–4.1%	–1.9%	–3.2%	–2.9%	–26.5%
Change of Industrial Production Index	–14.5%	–4.0%	–12.2%	–9.3%	–52.9%
Change of Retail Sales (inflation adjusted)	–11.5%	–2.7%	–11.8%	–7.4%	–31.5%
Change of Employment (non-farm)	–6.1%	–2.7%	–1.9%	–3.1%	–24.6%
Peak Unemployment Rate	10.1%	7.3%	8.9%	10.8%	24.9%
Rise in Unemployment Rate	5.7 percentage points	2.9 percentage points	4.1 percentage points	3.4 (5.1) percentage points[b]	21.7 percentage points
Long-term Unemployment (% of unemployed)[c]	46.0%	18.9%	21.0%	26.0%	62%
Housing Price Decline[d]	33.1%	—	5.4%	13.9%	12.6%

Notes: (a) Figures for the Great Depression are derived from annual data, while figures for other recessions are derived from monthly data. (b) Figure in parentheses is unemployment increase over the two recessions of the early 1980s. (c) Long-term unemployment is the highest percentage of unemployed workers who had gone more than 26 weeks without a job, during or immediately after recession. Long-term unemployment data not available for the Great Depression; figure is for men in Massachusetts without a job for 52 weeks or more. (d) The periods of decline of housing prices for the four recessions shown individually are 1925–1932, 1972–1976, 1979–1984, and 2006–2009. The decline for the early 1990s, referred to in the text but not shown in this table, is 1989–1997.

Sources: Data on housing prices from Robert Shiller's index, online at www.econ.yale.edu/~shiller/data.htm. Data on average loss of output and employment are from Federal Reserve Bank of Minneapolis, "The Recession and Recovery in Perspective," online at www.minneapolisfed.org/publications_papers/studies/recession_perspective/ (click on "View Data"). Data on the Great Depression are from *Historical Statistics of the United States*, Series D 85–86, Series D 127–141, Series T 79–196, and Series E 135–166. Data on industrial production are from Economic Research Federal Reserve Bank of St. Louis, research.stlouisfed.org/fred2/graph/?graph_id=15871 and Industrial Production Index: Total index; 2002=100; SA, online at www.economagic.com/em-cgi/data.exe/frbg17/b50001_ipsa. Data on retail sales are from Real Retail and Food Services Sales; Economic Research Federal Reserve Bank of St. Louis, Industrial Production Index online at research.stlouisfed.org/fred2/graph/?graph_id=16071, and Real Retail Sales (Discontinued Series): Millions of Dollars: SA available at www.economagic.com/em-cgi/data.exe/fedstl/rsales. Data on employment loss after 1969 are from Bureau of Labor Statistics: Table A-1. Employment status of the civilian population by sex and age, Employed, seasonally adjusted, online at ftp.bls.gov/pub/suppl/empsit.cpseea1.txt. Earlier data are from Bureau of Labor Statistics, Employment Level: 16 years and over; Thousands; SA, online at http://www.economagic.com/em-cgi/data.exe/blsln/lns12000000:%28rev%29. Data on unemployment rates after 1969 are from Bureau of Labor Statistics: Table A-1. Employment status of the civilian population by sex and age, Unemployed, percentage of the labor force, seasonally adjusted, online at ftp.bls.gov/pub/suppl/empsit.cpseea1.txt. Earlier data are from Bureau of Labor Statistics, Unemployment Rate: Percent; 16 years and over, online at www.economagic.com/em-cgi/data.exe/blsln/lns14000000:%28rev%29. Data on long-term unemployment rates are from the Bureau of Labor Statistics, Table A-12. Unemployed persons by duration of unemployment, online at ftp.bls.gov/pub/suppl/empsit.cpseea12.txt and A-37 Unemployed persons by occupation, industry, and duration of unemployment, online at ftp.bls.gov/pub/suppl/empsit.cpseea37.txt; earlier data are from Bureau of Labor Statistics, Of Total Unemployed; Unemployed; Percent; 16 years and over; 27 weeks and over; Percent of unemployed within group; SA available at www.economagic.com/em-cgi/data.exe/blsln/lns13025703; Linda Levine, "The Labor Market during the Great Depression and the Current Recession," Congressional Research Service, June 19, 2009.

Furthermore, in the current period long-term unemployment is more pervasive than any time since the Great Depression. In May 2010, nearly one half (46.0 percent) of the unemployed had been without work for more than the 26 weeks traditionally covered by unemployment benefits, the highest level of long-term unemployment since 1948 (the first year for which such data are available).

The impact of the high and lasting unemployment that emerged in 2008 and 2009 was all the greater because the employment situation leading up to the Great Recession was already poor. From late 2001 through late 2007, the United States experienced a relatively long period of economic expansion, but it was not an expansion that did much to improve the lives of most people. To begin with, the growth of GDP was anemic, averaging just 2.7 percent per year, far below the 4.3 percent annual average of expansions in the previous half century.[5] Sluggish economic growth left employers with little need for new hires. From 2001 to 2007 the economy added jobs only at about one-third the rate of the typical expansion since World War II. Not surprisingly, the expansion also did less to lift incomes, to improve wages, and alleviate poverty than did any of those earlier expansions. Just how much of the population had missed out on the benefits of economic growth, however, was surprising. The income of the top one percent of households increased 10.1 percent per year from 2002 to 2007, accounting for two-thirds of the real income gains generated by the expansion. In contrast, the bottom 90 percent of households saw their real incomes grow just 0.8 percent annually over those years.[6]

This lopsided growth during the years of expansion meant that the hardship people experienced when the recession hit—real suffering for many—was all the more intense. With few new jobs, especially few full-time jobs, the number of workers who had given up looking for work or had been forced to accept part-time positions was already quite high at the onset of the recession. As their incomes stagnated, many people were taking on more and more debt simply to get by—an issue we will return to in later chapters. As the recession hit, households were dedicating a larger share of their after-tax income to debt-service payments than at any time since 1980 (the first year for which data are available).[7]

Looking back on the last ten years from the perspective of 2010, most people viewed the period as a lost decade—or, as the economist and *The New York Times* columnist Paul Krugman put it, "the zero decade." Job creation for the decade was basically zero. Zero economic gains for the typical family during the decade. A decade of zero gains for home owners. And a decade of zero gains on the stock market.[8]

As the second decade of the twenty-first century began, there were virtually no signs of significant improvement in the U.S. economy—or, for that matter, most of the global economy. Quite the contrary:

- In 2010, growth of U.S. GDP continued to be weak, running at an annual rate of only 2.8 percent since the recovery began in June 2009—a rate about half that for similar periods in other recoveries.[9] Continued high growth rates in China and India may have pulled the growth rate for the world economy to 4 percent in 2010, but even these two rapidly growing economies were starting to show signs of slow-down. Among the high-income countries, virtually all were expected to show even slower growth than the United States in 2010.[10]
- The housing crisis, which had been the catalyst to the Great Recession, remained unresolved. In mid-2010, housing prices were still well above their historic trend, indicating that the housing market was yet to hit bottom and stabilize. Moreover, forecasts indicated that foreclosures were continuing unabated, with the expectation that as many as a million families would be turned out of their homes in 2010—ten times the historic rate.[11]
- With continuing high unemployment rates and wages virtually frozen, there was no reason to expect the U.S. economy to be pulled upward by consumer spending.
- Slow growth and no expectation of a coming economic surge led firms to hold back on investment. Although corporate profits had picked up in 2009 and 2010, nonfinancial firms were sitting on their money. At the end of March 2010, nonfinancial corporations held $1.84 trillion in cash—an amount that was 7 percent of all their assets, the highest level since 1963.[12]
- Lending was weak. In 2009 total outstanding loans at Federal Deposit Insurance Corporation (FDIC) insured banks had dropped 7.4 percent, the sharpest decline in lending in 67 years. Partly because financial institutions were cautious and partly because consumers and investors were not spending, lending remained anemic in 2010. Indeed, consumers in general were taking steps to reduce their debt burden.[13]

Most of all, however, it was the continuing employment disaster that generated the poor economic prognosis for the second decade of the century. In spite of the return of economic growth in the second half of 2009, by mid-2010 the employment level had shown no significant pick-up, and 7.4 million fewer workers had jobs than when the recession began in December 2007. Indeed, in June, July, and August of 2010, total employment levels were below the levels of employment for each of these same months in 2009.[14] In August 2010, for every job opening, there were 4.6 officially unemployed workers looking for jobs—and many more who had given up looking.[15] In July of 2010, the plague of long-term unemployment had led Congress to extend jobless benefits to a maximum of 99 weeks in states with high unemployment, but the number of jobless people who exhausted their 99 weeks of unemployment insurance benefits continued to grow. These "99ers," as they have been called by some journalists, had reached a record 1.4 million people in June 2010. (Moreover, jobless benefits were only extended until November 2010.)[16]

A pick-up of employment usually lags behind the improvement of economic growth in the recovery from a recession. Employers are reluctant to add to their workforces until they are confident that a post-recession expansion will last. Also, employers tend to use the shock of a recession to reorganize work processes to save labor costs over the long term. Yet the pick-up of employment following the Great Recession has been worse than usual. Why?

The simple answer is that the recession has been worse than usual. The sharp and extreme decline of output and employment that we have described has meant a lack of demand—that is, people have not had money to buy things. As of October 2010, there were 14.8 million people looking for work, 5.9 million who wanted a job but who were not currently looking for work, and 9.1 million who wanted full-time work but could only find part-time jobs.[17] In addition to these 29.8 million unemployed and partially unemployed people, millions more who saw their plight said to themselves, "There but for luck go I." Without a steady source of sufficient income or in fear of falling into such conditions, these many millions of people curtailed their spending. And those who did have sufficient income often chose to reduce their debt rather than increase their spending. With the resulting lack of sales, businesses were, quite rationally, not willing to either invest or hire; and this meant a continuing lack of demand.

The problem was not a lack of profits. Unlike employment, in late 2009 and early 2010 corporate profits rose sharply; by the middle of 2010, corporate profits (adjusted for inflation) were about 60 percent above their low point at the end of 2008, well on their way back to the peak level of mid-2006.[18] Also, as we have pointed out, in early 2010 nonfinancial firms were sitting on almost $2 trillion in cash. There was no lack of ability to invest and hire, but there was a lack of incentive to invest and hire—that is, a lack of an expectation that demand (sales) would rise. Yet by failing to invest and hire, businesses were ensuring that demand would continue to be weak. As is well known, small businesses have generally accounted for a disproportionately large share of employment increases. Yet, since the onset of the Great Recession, small business owners have consistently identified poor sales as their single most important problem—and thus, presumably, what prevented them from expanding employment.[19]

Some analysts have argued that the reason for the persistent high rate of unemployment is not the lack of demand. Instead, they allege that high unemployment continues because many workers who lost their jobs in the Great Recession lack the skills that are needed in today's economy. This "mismatch" between the skills people have and the skills that are needed by employers, they say, explains most of today's unemployment.[20] Yet workers with a diverse set of skills have lost jobs—in manufacturing, professional and business services, leisure and hospitality, transportation and utilities, and information industries among others. Moreover, there remains a substantial backlog of experienced workers looking for jobs or more hours in their existing part-time jobs in major industries that have begun hiring—including education, health care, durable goods manufacturing, and mining.[21] There is no reason to believe that most of these workers have lost their skills or that production activity has changed in a few short years to require dramatically new skills. The reality of the situation—the widespread job losses and the continuing job searches of experienced workers—makes it clear that the heart of the employment problem is not enough jobs rather than a lack of skills among those looking for work. Most important, the extreme lack of demand, continuing into 2010, and probably continuing well into the future, offers sufficient explanation for the employment woes. (Of course, skill deficiencies are a problem for many workers, but there is no reason to think that these skill deficiencies increased sharply and suddenly in recent years.)

This lack of sufficient consumer and business spending, this lack of demand, creates a compelling case of additional government spending that would boost sales and lead firms to increase hiring. If large enough, government spending could reestablish an expansion of consumer spending that would sustain economic growth. Yet, the economic stimulus that the government has provided has been inadequate, too small to do the job. (We will examine government efforts to stimulate demand in some detail in Chapter 9.) While inadequate, however, the U.S. government's actions have been major departures from the policy directions of previous decades. More than anything else, the great social costs of high unemployment and an increasing awareness of the extreme increases in economic inequality have begun to open up the possibilities for doing things differently.

Why Is This a "Crisis"?

When a car runs out of gas, the solution to the problem is straightforward. Refill the gas tank, and the driver can restart the engine and drive away. Inconvenient and perhaps costly, but not a big problem. With the tank refilled, the car can run again as it did before. No major overhaul of the engine is needed, and certainly there is no need to get a new car.

The car-running-out-of-gas scenario is a bit like a "normal" recession. For whatever reasons, consumer and business spending (demand) falls off, production declines, and unemployment rises. Perhaps the situation will be self-correcting: with less output, resource costs and maybe even labor costs will fall a bit, profits will be restored, businesses will start hiring again. If government action is needed the monetary authorities might lower interest rates, inducing businesses and consumers to take out loans, spend more, and increase demand. Or the government might bolster demand by cutting taxes or increasing its spending. Even a "normal" recession can lead to real suffering for those who lose their jobs, and the disruption of economic activity can have lasting and nasty impacts on many families and communities. Nonetheless, with demand restored, like the car that ran out of gas and had its tank refilled, the economy can run again as it did before.

But what if the car did not run out of gas and stalled for some other reason? What if, for example, the car ran out of oil, the lubricant that allows the mechanical parts of an engine to run smoothly? Without oil, the dry metal parts of the engine rub against each other, generating extreme heat and severely harming, if not destroying, the engine. Putting more gas in the tank will not help. Even putting in more oil will not help. At the very least a major engine overhaul will be required.

The financial panic of 2008, the Great Recession, and the lingering economic malaise have been more like a car running out of oil than running out of gas. In the panic, credit—the lubricant of the economic system—dried up. Manufacturing companies, software firms, farmers, and every other kind of firm, large and small, were hard pressed to obtain the funds they needed to operate their businesses—to meet payroll, to finance inventory, or to make new investments. And consumers found it difficult, often impossible, to get loans to pay for cars, houses, college tuition, or much else. The problem was not simply an insufficient amount of credit—an insufficient amount of lubricant. Pumping in more credit (more lubricant), which the government did, would not solve the problem. Something was amiss, deeply amiss, with the whole financial system—and the problems had spread to the rest of the economy. It was time to start thinking about an engine overhaul.

In part, the current era is a crisis because, as we have demonstrated, it has seen an especially severe recession. It is an era that began with the emergence of recession at the end of 2007 and the financial panic of 2008, and continues as the economy limps along with minimal growth and high rates of unemployment, foreclosures, and business failures. The severity of economic conditions suggests that something more than just running out of gas is going on. This situation is what makes the current period one of crisis—the engine of our economy is broken, there is need for an overhaul, and this need is widely recognized.

The American Heritage Dictionary of the English Language, tells us that crisis means: "(a) A crucial or decisive point or situation; a turning point; (b) An unstable condition, as in political, social, or economic affairs, involving an impending abrupt or decisive change." So the term seems an apt description of the current period—one where change is needed and is likely to come because that need is so generally apparent. Hitting the restart button, as some have put it, will not deal with the serious economic problems that currently confront us. Something else, something quite different, needs to be done. There are, then, opportunities to set things right, opportunities for what we define as progressive change.

Opportunities for change, however, do not guarantee that change will take place. It is possible that economic arrangements could muddle along pretty much as they have, and that we would continue to experience economic instability, stagnation, and further severe recessions. Moreover, even if significant change takes place, the direction of that change is by no means predetermined. Consider the two previous crises to strike the U.S. and global economies in the last eighty years, the Great Depression of the 1930s and the period of inflation and recessions (stagflation) of the 1970s and early 1980s. In each case the economy that emerged from the crisis was very different from what had existed in the preceding years, but the changes coming out of those crises were quite different, essentially opposites of one another.

The severity of the Great Depression is well recognized (and some aspects of that severity are shown in Table 2.1). The Depression, and the war that followed, led to major changes in the distribution of income and wealth, ideology, and power in the United States. The power shift greatly enhanced the position of labor and popular forces. Part of that shift was a much greater role for government in regulating business (finance in particular), supporting overall economic stability, and providing a social safety net. The structure of the economy was dramatically altered from its relatively free-market operation of earlier years. What's more, these changes set in motion by the crisis of the 1930s led to an era of general prosperity in the decades following World War II—an era of substantial growth, the benefits of which were widely shared. (In Chapter 3 we will set out and explain these changes; understanding them is an important part of understanding the current situation.)

By the mid-1970s, however, the post–World War II expansion had given out. With the stagflation of the 1970s and early 1980s, the United States experienced what, at that time, were the two longest and deepest recessions since the Great Depression (see Table 2.1), and it was again apparent that the economy needed an overhaul. This overhaul was characterized by a strong attack on the gains that had been won in previous years by labor and other social movements. It was also characterized by an effort to reduce the government's various roles in the economy, a shift toward a greater role for the unregulated, unfettered operation of markets—both in the domestic economy and in the relations of the U.S. economy to the global economy. Overall, the changes coming out of the crisis of the 1970s and early 1980s altered income and wealth distribution, power, and ideology in the opposite direction from what had come out of the Great Depression. The following years saw moderate or relatively slow economic growth, with those at the top taking most of the benefits that the growth generated. The changes coming out of the 1970s-80s crisis and the experience of subsequent years set the stage for the current crisis.

In the wake of the crises of the 1930s and 1970s–80s, shifts in the balance of economic and political power, in government policy, and in ideology brought radical changes in the levels of inequality and labor market conditions, for the better in one case and for the worse in the other. With much of today's U.S. and global economies out of order, the current crisis presents an opening for change that might push things back in a progressive direction. Yet the obstacles to bringing about progressive change are formidable, and the direction of the change that is afoot is uncertain. Perhaps the understanding of the current period and the ideas for change that we present in the rest of this book will contribute to positive developments.

Notes

1. See "Business Cycle Dating Committee, National Bureau of Economic Research," September 20, 2010 announcement of June 2009 business cycle trough marking the end of the last recession, www.nber.org/cycles/sept2010.html.

2. Sources of data discussed in this chapter are as provided in Table 2.1 unless otherwise indicated in the endnotes.

3. The statement about housing price stability for the year after the middle of 2009 is based on data in Standard & Poor's "Case-Shiller Home Price Indices," www.standardandpoors.com/indices/sp-case-shiller-home-price-indices/en/us/?indexId=spusa-cashpidff—p-us——.

4. For the October 2009 adjusted unemployment rate, the U-6 seasonally adjusted, see Bureau of Labor Statistics (BLS), "Table A-12 Alternative measures of labor underutilization," in "Employment Situation News Release," January 8, 2010, www.bls.gov/news.release/archives/empsit_01082010.htm. Data for 1967 to 2002 using a related but now discontinued measure are available as "Special unemployment rate: U-6; SA," www.economagic.com/em-cgi/data.exe/blslf/lfs2401. For a

discussion of the adjusted unemployment rate in the 1982 recession, see John E. Bregger and Steven E. Haugen, "BLS Introduces New Range of Alternative Unemployment Measures," *Monthly Labor Review,* October 1995, www.bls.gov/opub/mlr/1995/10/art3abs.htm.

5. The 2.7 percent growth for the 2001 to 2007 expansion is for the fourth quarter 2001 to the fourth of 2007 and is calculated from Bureau of Economic Analysis, "Real Gross Domestic Product, Chained Dollars [Billions of chained (2005) dollars] Seasonally adjusted at annual rates (quarterly), www.economagic.com/em-cgi/data.exe/nipa/Q10106-A191RX. For the average growth rate for expansions since 1949 see Aviva Aron-Dine, Chad Stone, and Richard Kogan, "How Robust Was the 2001–2007 Economic Expansion?" Center on Budget and Policy Priorities, January 14, 2008, www.cbpp.org/cms/?fa=view&id=575.

6. See Avi Feller and Chad Stone, "Top 1 Percent of Americans Reaped Two-Thirds of Income Gains in Last Economic Expansion," Center on Budget and Policy Priorities, September 9, 2009, online at www.cbpp.org/cms/index.cfm?fa=view&id=2908. The data are from detailed Internal Revenue Service micro-files complied by Thomas Piketty and Emmanuel Saez, which we describe in Box II.1 on page 35.

7. See Federal Reserve Board, "Household Debt Service and Financial Obligations Ratios," www.federalreserve.gov/releases/housedebt/.

8. See Paul Krugman, "The Big Zero," *The New York Times,* December 27, 2009, www.nytimes.com/2009/12/28/opinion/28krugman.html.

9. Authors' calculation from Bureau of Economic Analysis, Table 1.1.6. "Real Gross Domestic Product, Chained Dollars [Billions of chained (2005) dollars] Seasonally adjusted at annual rates (quarterly)," www.economagic.com/em-cgi/data.exe/nipa/Q10106-A191RX.

10. International Monetary Fund, "IMF Raises Forecast for Global Growth, Sees Multispeed Recovery," April 21, 2010, www.imf.org/external/pubs/ft/survey/so/2010/RES042110A.htm.

11. See Alex Veiga, "Foreclosure Rate: Americans on Pace for 1 MILLION Foreclosures In 2010," *Huffington Post,* July 15, 2010, www.huffingtonpost.com/2010/07/15/foreclosure-rate-american_n_647130.html. The article reports that Rick Sharga, a senior vice president at RealtyTrac, told the *Huffington Post* that a million foreclosures in 2010 "would be unprecedented," and that "lenders have historically taken over about 100,000 homes a year."

12. The $1.84 trillion figure is from Justin Lahart, "U.S. Firms Build Up Record Cash Piles," *Wall Street Journal,* June 10, 2010, online.wsj.com/article/SB100014 24052748704312104575298652567988246.html. Cash holding levels were higher in the entire period from 1952 to 1963 (before which these data are not available). These years were not a bad time for the U.S. economy (although they included two mild recessions), and one can only speculate why the levels were so high. Perhaps the larger role of manufacturing created a basis for higher cash levels to finance inventories; perhaps in the years leading up to 1963 firms' cash holding policies were still influenced by the memories of the 1930s; or perhaps innovations in financial arrangements allowed cash holdings to come down after the early 1960s.

13. See Michael R. Crittenden and Marshall Eckblad, "Lending Falls at Epic Pace," *The Wall Street Journal,* February 24, 2010, online.wsj.com/article/SB1000 1424052748704188104575083332005461558.html.

14. The 2009 data are from the *Economic Report of the President 2010*, Table B-36. The 2010 data are available from the Bureau of Labor Statistics, "Employment Situation Summary Table A: Household Data, Seasonally Adjusted," bls.gov/news.release/empsit.a.htm.

15. Bureau of Labor Statistics, "Job Openings and Labor Turnover Survey, Highlights, August 2010," www.bls.gov/web/jolts/jlt_labstatgraphs.pdf.

16. See Michael Luo, "99 Weeks Later, Jobless Have Only Desperation," *New York Times*, August 2, 2010, www.nytimes.com/2010/08/03/us/03unemployed. html. For a description of workers who have gone a year without a job see, Bureau of Labor Statistics, "Ranks of those unemployed for a year or more up sharply," *Issues in Labor Statistics*, Summary 10–10, October 2010, www.bls.gov/opub/ils/pdf/opbils87.pdf.

17. For the number of officially unemployed: Bureau of Labor Statistics (BLS) "Table A-1 Employment status of the civilian population by sex and age, Employed, seasonally adjusted," ftp.bls.gov/pub/suppl/empsit.cpseea1.txt. For the number of individuals who wanted jobs but were not looking, see BLS, "Persons not in the labor force and multiple jobholders by sex, not seasonally adjusted," www.bls.gov/news.release/empsit.t16.htm. For the number forced to work part time for economic reasons, see BLS, "Employed persons by class of worker and part-time status," www.bls.gov/news.release/empsit.t08.htm.

18. See Bureau of Economic Analysis, National Income and Product Accounts Table, Table 6.16D, "Corporate Profits by Industry," bea.gov/national/nipaweb/TableView.asp?SelectedTable=239&Freq=Qtr&FirstYear=2008&LastYear=2010; and the *Economic Report of the President 2010*, Table B-90.

19. See Catherine Rampell, "What's Holding Back Small Businesses?" *The New York Times*, September. 14, 2010, economix.blogs.nytimes.com/2010/09/14/whats-holding-back-small-businesses/. Also see William C. Dunkelberg and Holly Wade, *NFIB Small Business Economic Trends*, National Federation of Independent Business, October 2010, p. 18 Table "Single Most Important Problem," www.nfib.com/Portals/0/PDF/sbet/SBET201010.pdf.

20. For example of this argument see the August 17, 2010, speech given by Narayana Kocherlakota, president of the Minneapolis Federal Reserve Bank, "Inside the FOMC," Marquette, Michigan, www.minneapolisfed.org/news_events/pres/speech_display.cfm?id=4525. For a detailed response to this argument see Lawrence Mishel, Heidi Shierholz, and Kathryn Edwards, "Reasons for Skepticism About Structural Unemployment: Examining the Demand-Side Evidence," Economic Policy Institute, September 22, 2010, www.epi.org/publications/entry/bp279/.

21. See Arjun Jayadev and Mike Konczal, "The Stagnating Labor Market," The Roosevelt Institute, September 19, 2010, especially Figure 11, www.rooseveltinstitute.org/sites/all/files/stagnant_labor_market.pdf.

Part II
How We Got Here
The Changing Terrain of Inequality, Power, and Ideology

On March 25, 1968, in the midst of the Vietnam War, as the U.S. government's policies were coming under increasing attack from a broader and broader segment of the population, President Lyndon Johnson addressed the Conference of the Building and Construction Trades Department of the AFL-CIO. Seeking support for his foreign war policies by touting the economic situation at home, Johnson looked out at his friendly audience and said, "I am not saying you never had it so good. But that is a fact, isn't it?"[1]

Johnson was right. Not about the war, of course, but about the economic situation of most people in the United States in the late 1960s. Between 1948, when the economy began to move out of a brief post–World War II recession, and 1968, real (i.e., adjusted for inflation) national output had more than doubled; real per capita income after taxes had risen by almost 60 percent.[2] Especially for those who had experienced the Great Depression of the 1930s, which included a large segment of those in Johnson's audience, the 1950s and 1960s were a period of remarkable prosperity.

What was most significant about this era was that the prosperity was widely shared. Wages rose along with increases in productivity (that is, with increases in output per time worked), and the incomes of those at the bottom rose as rapidly—if not more rapidly—than the incomes of those at the top. Moreover, changes during the Great Depression and World War II had brought about a sharp shift toward greater equality in the distribution of income and wealth. One pair of figures stands out as summing up the change: in 1928 the 1 percent of families with the highest incomes obtained 24 percent of all income, but in 1948 the share of this top group had halved to 12 percent. (The rest of the top 10 percent of families also saw their share of income decline, but their decline was not nearly so great.) The shift in the distribution of wealth was similar: On the eve of the Great Depression the richest 1 percent of households held almost 50 percent of the country's assets; twenty years later, this figure was about 30 percent.[3] (The wealth figures are for net worth, including primary residences. Financial wealth—stock, bonds, and other assets, but excluding primary residences—was, and is, distributed even more unequally and shifted in the same way.)

The income and wealth distribution changes are shown at the end of Chapter 3 in Figures 3.1, 3.2, and 3.3. Box II.1 ("Measuring Income Inequality") explains issues in measuring income inequality and Box 3.1 explains the income and wealth concepts.

Through the 1950s and 1960s and into the early 1970s, the share of income going to the very, very rich, the top 1 percent, fell somewhat further, from about 12 percent of total income at the end of World War II to about 9 percent in the mid-1970s. Most of this loss of income share by the very, very rich was simply shifted to the very rich and the rich. Nonetheless, the share of income going to the bottom 60 percent of families appears to have inched up slightly between the late 1940s and the 1970s, from about 34 percent of the total to about 35 percent of the total. The leveling off that had been brought about by the shocks of the Great Depression and World War II was maintained for the next quarter century. All income groups seemed to share in the prosperity of that era. The move toward equality in this postwar era was sharper in terms of the distribution of wealth; by the end of the 1970s, the richest 1 percent held only slightly more than 20 percent of all assets.[4]

The "leveling" between the 1920s and the late 1940s was a result of the major economic and political changes of the Depression and war years. Poor white farmers and African American sharecroppers in the South had left the land and moved into the urban centers and factories of the North, especially during the war years. In those factories and urban centers, labor unions had made substantial gains in membership and strength. And underlying these changes was a profound shift in national politics, as the Roosevelt administration established the National Labor Relations Act (NLRA) and the Social Security system, and through these and other legislative acts committed the government to providing a social safety net. The Great Depression had also had a severe negative impact on the incomes of the very richest families, much of whose income came from owning businesses. Many firms failed during the 1930s, and, at the depth of the Depression, total corporate profits after taxes were negative (i.e., corporations as a groups were losing money). The progressive income tax and the highly progressive estate tax probably limited the extent to which the incomes at the top could be quickly restored.

In the 1950s and especially the 1960s there was even an improvement in the incomes of African Americans as a group relative to European Americans. While the median income of black families was about 51 percent of

Box II.I

Measuring Income Inequality

The data on increasing income inequality here and in subsequent chapters are taken from two sources. One of these is the work of economists Thomas Piketty and Emmanuel Saez. Using Internal Revenue Service data from federal income tax returns, Piketty and Saez provide a good picture of the incomes of the top income groups—the top 10 percent and smaller groups within the top 10 percent. They capture the doubling of the income share of the richest 1 percent of families over the last three decades, missed in the traditional Census Bureau data on income inequality. The Piketty-Saez data are available at http://elsa.berkeley.edu/~saez/.

Tax return data are superior to those compiled by the Census Bureau for two reasons. First, respondents to the Census Bureau's survey of income, the Current Population Survey (CPS), underreport their income relative to the income that appears on their tax returns. Second, the CPS has a "top coding" restriction on very high incomes. If a survey respondent has an income greater than $999,999, it is recorded simply as $999,999. Also, top coding limits the maximum capital gains income reported in the CPS to $99,999. These procedures result in census data missing the extraordinary gains in income going to the very high-income groups in recent decades.

However, while the Piketty-Saez data show the relation between the incomes of the rich and the very rich to the rest of society, they do not provide information on the relative incomes of groups below the very rich—for example, their data do not tell us what has happened to the bottom 20 percent or the bottom 40 percent in relation to other income recipients. To get this more complete, if less accurate, picture, we have used the Census Bureau data as our second source, available at www.census.gov/hhes/www/income/data/historical/families/f02AR.xls. Throughout the book, these sources are used without further reference for statements about overall income inequality.

the median income of white families in 1947, it had risen to 61 percent in 1970.[5] No, the situation was not one of racial equality; both direct racial discrimination and a legacy of centuries of racial oppression continued to keep African Americans on the bottom. Yet in terms of relative income, there appears to have been some improvement.

As the continuing racial inequality makes clear, the era following World War II was not some sort of fine time, "good old days" that we should long for. Similarly, severe inequality between the pay of men and women continued in the era, and the gap between the rich and the poor, while a far cry from the extreme inequality of the 1920s, was still substantial. Yes, compared to earlier years, most people in this country had, as Lyndon Johnson proclaimed, "never had it so good." And compared to what was to come, that era looks pretty decent. Yet for many people things were not good at all. In 1962, Michael Harrington's book *The Other America*[6] revealed what should have been long recognized: that poverty was severe and widespread in the United States. From the hollows of Appalachia to urban ghettos in the north and rural backwaters around the country, millions of people continued to survive on a bare minimum. Harrington's book provided the impetus for the War on Poverty, which, however limited, reflected the belief that the government had some responsibility to address the plight of those who were being passed by in the "normal" operation of economic life—and this belief was an important part of the ideology of the period.

Notes

1. The Johnson speech is online at www.presidency.ucsb.edu/ws/index.php?pid=28754.

2. U.S. Bureau of the Census, *Historical Statistics of the United States Colonial Times to 1970,* Part I, Series F 1–5 (Washington DC: U.S. Department of Commerce, 1975), Chapter F.

3. Wealth distribution figures are from Edward N. Wolff, *Top Heavy: The Increasing Inequality of Wealth in America and What Can Be Done About It* (New York: The New Press, 2002), Figure 3.1.

4. For income figure sources, see Box II.1. Wealth data are from Wolff, *Top Heavy.*

5. Data on families by race are from the U.S. Census Bureau, "Race and Hispanic Origin of Householder—Families by Median and Mean Income," www.census.gov/hhes/www/income/data/historical/families/index.html.

6. Michael Harrington, *The Other America: Poverty in the United States* (New York: Macmillan, 1962).

3

Ideology and Power in the Post–World War II Era

In 1935, the National Labor Relations Act (NLRA) was passed by Congress and signed into law by President Franklin D. Roosevelt. The final paragraph of first section set out is the act's motivating principles:

> It is declared to be the policy of the United States to eliminate the causes of certain substantial obstructions to the free flow of commerce and to mitigate and eliminate these obstructions when they have occurred by encouraging the practice and procedure of collective bargaining and by protecting the exercise by workers of full freedom of association, self-organization, and designation of representatives of their own choosing, for the purpose of negotiating the terms and conditions of their employment or other mutual aid or protection.[1]

The NLRA set out procedures by which a majority of workers could establish a union. The act protected workers engaged in efforts to form a union from being fired (or other retribution by an employer), and it required an employer (and the union) to bargain in "good faith." It also established the National Labor Relations Board (NLRB) to enforce the provisions of the act.

For decades leading up to the 1930s, labor unions had fought against fierce opposition from business firms and political authorities. They had had some substantial organizing success, had won some major victories, and in 1920 over 11 percent of the civilian labor force was unionized. Yet by 1930 only 7 percent of the civilian labor force was union members, and the figure had fallen slightly to 6.9 percent by the time the NLRA was enacted. Five years later, however, 15.7 percent of the civilian labor force was in unions, and at the end of World War II the figure was 26.6 percent (see Figure 10.1).[2]

The government's political support for unions, as embodied in the NLRA, was an important part of the story of organized labor's growth during the 1930s and the subsequent war years. It was, however, not simply the passage of the NLRA that transformed the position of labor unions in this period. The conditions of the Great Depression lay at the root of both the important political shifts, which the legislation represented, and the ascendency of organized labor. In the early 1930s, with a quarter of the labor force unemployed and with the dismal conditions of business (those negative corporate profits), the very existence of the economic system was called into question. Workers themselves responded, organizing unions in mines and factories and demanding change. The labor movement shifted from its relative emphasis on the crafts and building trades, the organizations of skilled workers, to industrial unionism. In auto, in steel, in coal, there was a great upsurge of activity. Still, the accomplishments of unions would have been limited without the political support they received—in statements by political officials, in acts such as that of Michigan's Governor Frank Murphy who refused to call out the National Guard when workers took over auto plants in the famous 1936–37 sit-ins, and in the NLRA and its creation of the NLRB.

The great change in unionization that took place during the 1930s and through the war years marked a shift in both power and ideology. The power shift was relatively obvious: workers had a greater say over what took place on the job. Collective bargaining resulted in higher wages and improved working conditions for unionized workers and protected their job security. Also, representing a much larger portion of the workforce, unions gained some political clout. This clout operated most clearly in elections, where union support often made a significant difference. Workers who were not in unions were indirect beneficiaries of the unions' strength, as wages and working conditions generally were improved because of both unions' gains in the workplace and their political successes.

Equally important, unions had become an accepted part of the nation's life. Fierce opposition to unionization remained in many segments of industry, especially in the South where wages were low and industrial production was both less extensive than elsewhere in the country and more labor intensive (as in the textile factories that had moved south over the first half of the century). Yet in the large and increasingly important industries such as auto, steel, tires, and electronics, company executives accepted unionization—generally a begrudging acceptance, but an acceptance nonetheless.

The new role for unions in U.S. political and economic life, however, came at a price. Unions essentially abandoned efforts—which had played a significant role in earlier union activity—to alter the organization of the economy. In exchange for their acceptance and a general increase of wages along with productivity advances, unions ceded to management control over the organization of production, investments, and prices. This implicit "accord" between labor and management was perhaps most clearly set in the outcome of the 1946 strike in the auto industry. The autoworkers' union had demanded higher wages and also that the higher wages not be passed on to consumers as higher prices. The union lost, and the issue of unions' part in price determination and in many other realms of management played no substantial role in subsequent years.

Also, while unions had gained a great deal during the Depression and World War II, with the passage of the NLRA as the fulcrum of change, legislation of the late 1940s moved things in the other direction. In particular, in 1947, overriding President Truman's veto, Congress enacted the Taft-Hartley Act. The act placed numerous restrictions on union activities (e.g., prohibiting secondary boycotts and solidarity strikes), restricted union shops and allowed states to pass "right to work" laws, and required union officers to sign non-communist affidavits. Nonetheless, while Taft-Hartley and the political reversal that it represented were a setback for union power, the changes that had taken place during the 1930s and the war years continued to have significant impacts on economic and political life.

The Rising Role of Government

In any case, the new role for unions in the post–World War II era was just one part of a shift in power and ideology. Another change of great importance was a substantially increased economic role for the government. The apparent failure of the "free market" during the 1930s had generated an increasing belief that government had to play a larger role in economic affairs in order to maintain prosperity. This larger role for government had three features: using the government's spending and taxation powers to regulate total demand—an active fiscal policy; providing an extended social safety net for low-income people; and regulating business activity.

This importance of an active fiscal policy found its formal expression in the writings of the famous British economist John Maynard Keynes. In his landmark 1936 book, *The General Theory of Employment, Interest and Money,* Keynes had argued that in a market economy there was a chronic tendency toward insufficient demand—that is, insufficient private spending to maintain full employment—and this tendency could become severe, as it had in the 1930s. In such times, Keynes argued, government needed to intervene through fiscal policy to increase aggregate demand by running a budgetary deficit (spending more than it taxed and filling the gap by borrowing). Subsequently, the practice of adopting an active fiscal policy to regulate demand came to be called Keynesianism.

In the United States during the era following World War II:[3]

- Government became bigger in terms of its spending in relation to national output. Before the Depression, in 1927, total government spending—local, state and federal—was 11.8 percent of GNP. By 1940, with the expansion of government programs and the weak growth of GNP during the intervening decade, the figure was 20.5 percent. In subsequent years, the increase continued: to 24.7 percent in 1950, 30 percent in 1960, and 34.1 percent in 1970. (A large portion of the increase was accounted for by Social Security and Medicare outlays, which rose from 2 percent of federal outlays in 1950, to 13 percent in 1960, to 19 percent in 1970. By 2007, Social Security and Medicare outlays would rise to 35 percent of federal government expenditures.)
- Federal spending as a share of government spending at all levels (federal plus state and local) rose dramatically. Before the Depression, federal spending had accounted for roughly one-third of the total, but by the 1950s the relation was reversed with the federal government accounting for about two-thirds of total government spending (and then dropped down to about 60 percent of the total in the 1970s and subsequent years).
- With this larger federal spending role, government fiscal policy became more important in regulating the overall operation of the economy. Indeed, the large role of federal government spending was a necessary condition for the effective operation of an active fiscal policy. Throughout the 1950s and 1960s, government spending and taxation policies were seen as a key element in maintaining aggregate demand. Military spending, in particular, provided a major stimulus. In the (relatively mild) recession of the early 1960s, the Kennedy administration cut taxes to stimulate demand, providing the first explicitly conscious use of Keynesian policy.
- Military spending provided a major boost to the economy in the early post–World War II years, jumping from about 5 or 6 percent of total government spending before the Depression to about 25 percent in the 1950s and 1960s. However, government spending on social programs—from education to housing to health to Social Security—became increasingly important, rising from about 25 percent of total government spending in 1950 (roughly the same percentage as in the 1920s) to 40 percent in 1970, largely but not entirely due to Social Security increases.

Both the practice of a larger economic role for government and the acceptance of this practice—that is, the incorporation of this practice into the dominant ideology of the era—grew out of the experience of the 1930s and the war. The economic collapse of the Great Depression and the role of the government in bringing the country back from the abyss—largely, in the end, through massive spending for World War II—had generated the belief that government had to play a larger role in economic affairs in order to maintain prosperity. This belief became a central part of the ideology of the post–World War II era—among the general public, among political authorities, among business executives, and among economists. By the beginning of the 1970s, as we noted in Chapter 1, Republican President Richard Nixon would declare: "I am now a Keynesian in economics."

While Keynes's economic ideas had focused on fiscal policy, Keynesianism came to represent the more general growing economic roles of the government, including its roles in providing a social safety net and regulating economic affairs. While social programs, though limited, had existed in earlier years, the 1930s and postwar years saw a new wave of public social programs. The most far reaching of these was Social Security, enacted through the Social Security Act of 1935. Along with later amendments— for example, the establishment of a cost of living adjustment in the early 1970s—the act has had an extensive impact in reducing poverty among the aged and incapacitated. The 1935 act also created Aid to Dependent Children, which later became Aid to Families with Dependent Children (AFDC), providing income support to low-income families with children. Though Social Security and many other programs were important parts of the country's social welfare system—with Social Security by far the largest program—it was AFDC that was widely viewed as the nation's "welfare" program (until it was replaced in 1997 by the Temporary Assistance for Needy Families program—TANF). Medicare (medical care for the elderly), a major program in terms of size and impact, was added to the Social Security system in 1965. In 1938 the Fair Labor Standards Act (FLSA) established the minimum federal wage, the 40-hour work week, premium pay for overtime, and restrictions on child labor and work at home. In 1939 Congress enacted the Federal Unemployment Tax Act, which provided for unemployment insurance—and, not incidentally, in providing unemployment insurance, ensured an automatic expansion of government spending in an economic downturn, as called for in Keynes's fiscal prescriptions.

Also in 1938, the federal government intervened in the housing market through the creation of the Federal National Mortgage Association, generally known as Fannie Mae. The Depression had severely undermined the housing industry. Not only was demand for housing weak because incomes were low, but in addition private financial institutions were not supplying sufficient credit to reestablish the expansion of home ownership. So Fannie Mae was created as a government financial institution to make credit more readily available to low-income families. Fannie Mae would purchase and then hold or re-sell mortgage loans that had been originated by private lenders, and, importantly, Fannie Mae would guarantee payments on these mortgages. As a government institution, Fannie Mae could borrow funds at a lower rate than private firms. It could therefore make credit available through the private firms at a lower rate than would otherwise have been the case.

Fannie Mae would play a substantial role in the post–World War II housing boom, and, along with Federal Home Loan Mortgage Corporation (Freddie Mac), which was created in 1970, would come to dominate the secondary mortgage market—that is, buying, packaging into "bundles," and reselling mortgages. (This bundling will be explained in Chapter 5.) Although Fannie Mae was transformed into a private corporation in 1968 and Freddie Mac was created as a private corporation, both retained the implicit backing of the federal government, allowing them to continue to borrow and provide credit to the housing market at relatively low rates. With their central role in the housing market, these two entities were, as we shall see, major players in the economic crisis that started to appear in 2007.

Immediately after the war, the Employment Act of 1946 formally assigned responsibility for stabilizing the economy to the federal government. While initially a *full* employment bill, the final passage still avowed that: "Congress hereby declares that it is the continuing policy and responsibility of the federal government to use all practicable means . . . to promote maximum employment, production, and purchasing power." The Employment Act can be seen as marking the formal ascendancy of Keynesianism to official policy.

All of these increases of the government's social welfare role had their organizational counterparts in administrative expansion of the federal government. In 1953, the Department of Health, Education, and Welfare came into existence, overseeing a broad range of social services; in 1980 it was divided into the Department of Education and the Department of Health and Human Services. The Department of Housing and Human Development was created in 1965. And the War on Poverty was initiated in 1964 by the Economic Opportunity Act, involving programs in several departments and agencies.

The rising role of the government in regulating economic activity also spawned new departments and agencies. In this regulatory upsurge that began during the 1930s and continued after World War II, the government built upon the regulatory activism that emerged in the Progressive era in the first part of the twentieth century. For example, while the U.S. Food and Drug Administration (FDA) was created by the Pure Food and Drug

Act of 1906, its authority was expanded in 1938 by the Food, Drug, and Cosmetic Act (FDC), and further extended by several amendments to the FDC in the postwar years. Regulation of the airline industry had begun in the 1920s, but it was only in 1958 that the Federal Aviation Agency (FAA) was created, putting in place extensive regulation of the industry. The Motor Carrier Act of 1935 had given the Interstate Commerce Commission (ICC) authority to regulate interstate trucking, and the ICC used that authority to set uniform rates. June 1948 saw the first water pollution control act in the United States, and 1967 brought the Air Quality Act. This increasing regulatory role of government continued into the 1970s, even with the Republican administration of Richard Nixon, as both the Environmental Protection Agency (EPA) and the Occupational Safety and Health Administration (OSHA) were created in 1970.

Regulating Finance

All of these regulatory actions, and the controversies surrounding them, played important roles in the evolution of the U.S. economy. The role of government in regulating finance, however, requires elaboration because it is such an important issue in relation to the crisis that emerged in 2007 and 2008. In the wake of the financial failures at the center of the market crash of 1929 and the Great Depression, the Roosevelt administration had put in place a number of programs designed to ensure that the type of financial failure that precipitated the Depression would not recur.

Of special importance was the Glass-Steagall Act of 1933, which required the separation of commercial banks and investment banks. Commercial banks take deposits in various forms (e.g., checking accounts, savings accounts, certificates of deposit) and make loans to individuals and businesses. Investment banks manage corporate mergers and acquisitions. They also act as underwriters, handling the sales of stocks and bonds on behalf of the corporations and governments issuing these securities. In requiring the separation of these two categories of banking, Congress sought to create a "firewall" between the different segments of the financial industry to reduce the spread of a crisis that began in one segment. This separation also had some impact on limiting the size of banks, thus limiting the "too big to fail" problem. In addition, enactment of Glass-Steagall was motivated by concern about a conflict of interest between investment banking and commercial banking, whereby, for example, an integrated bank could use its deposits to support its underwriting activities, placing the interests of the depositors at risk. (The potential for conflicts of interest would become even greater later in the twentieth century, as investment banks started trading on their own accounts. That is, they used their own capital, often combined with a high degree of borrowed funds, to make various investments, sometimes highly risky investments.)

Glass-Steagall also created the Federal Deposit Insurance Corporation (FDIC). By insuring depositors' accounts in commercial banks, the FDIC greatly limited "runs" on banks—that is, with a rumor, based on fact or fiction, of a bank's problems, uninsured depositors would rush ("run") to get their funds out before the bank failed. Such a "run"all but assured that a bank in trouble would in fact fail. The FDIC increased depositors' confidence in the banking system and virtually eliminated the problem of "runs." In addition, when a bank does become insolvent, the FDIC manages its orderly demise, often by arranging for it to be taken over by another bank. (However, as we will see, with banks that are considered too big to fail, the situation is handled differently.) As with the separation of commercial and investment banking, the creation of the FDIC generated a high degree of confidence in the U.S. banking system.

This confidence and the financial stability, for which the regulation embodied in Glass-Steagall was a foundation, were important bases of the long and relatively rapid post–World War II economic expansion. In the latter part of the twentieth century things turned in the other direction, and deregulation of financial institutions became an important factor leading into the crisis that emerged in 2007 and 2008 (see Chapters 5 and 6). This deregulation, however, did not include elimination of the FDIC, which continues to play its essential roles.

The regulation of finance, the more general regulation of business, the extension of social welfare programs, and the government's active engagement in fiscal policy were central characteristics of economic life in the United States in the decades following World War II. They did not solve all the problems of the era, not by a long shot. Nor were these steps taken by the U.S. government as extensive as similar steps taken by governments in other high-income countries, by the European social democracies in particular. But they did make a difference in people's lives. Along with the substantial role of organized labor in that era, they contributed to a less unequal distribution of income and wealth, a more democratic distribution of power, and an ideology that saw a major role for government in economic life. (See Box 3.1 on income and wealth.)

On November 4, 1968, Paul Samuelson, perhaps the most renowned economist of the post–World War II generation, writing in his *Newsweek* column, represented the "conventional wisdom" with this paean for the "New Economics," by which he meant an active, Keynesian economic role for government: *"The New Economics really does work.* Wall Street knows

Box 3.1

Income and Wealth

People's income and wealth are two related measures of their economic well-being. Income is the amount of money—or, more generally, purchasing power—that one obtains in a particular period of time. For most people, wages and salaries are the main components of their incomes. But there are several other sources of income—for example, profits and dividends, rents, and interest payments. Wealth is the amount of assets that one has at any moment in time. Assets include, for example, the equity in one's home, stocks and bonds, other property, cash, and the value of pension funds. Thus income is a "flow" and wealth is a "stock." If your flow of income in a year is $50,000 and you spend only $45,000, your stock of wealth will have increased by $5,000.

Wealth is much more unequally distributed than income. For example, in 2007, the richest 5 percent of households held 63 percent of assets including primary residences. The ownership of assets excluding primary residences is even more unequally distributed, with 72 percent held by the richest 5 percent in 2007. In that year the 5 percent of households with the highest incomes obtained "only" 39 percent of all income.[4]

The two measures of economic well-being move roughly similarly over time because wealth at any point in time is an accumulation of previous income (less spending). By both measures, as noted at various points in the text and shown in the graphs at the end of this chapter, economic inequality was very great at the end of the 1920s, became significantly reduced over the period of the Great Depression and World War II, continued to reduce slightly until sometime in the 1970s, and then increased sharply in the 1980s. After the 1980s, however, while income inequality continued to increase, wealth inequality changed little. The appearance of stability in wealth inequality masked various countervailing shifts in stock values and housing values since 1990, features of the economic instability of the period.

While income tells us about people's economic well-being at a particular time, wealth gives us a better picture of their security and their long-run economic well-being. Even people with relatively good incomes can easily get in difficulties if they do not have substantial wealth. Also, and especially important for our purposes, wealth is probably a better indicator of political and social power. It is the fund which people can draw on to exercise influence.

it. Main Street knows it. The accountants who chalk up record corporate profits know it. The children of the workingmen do not know it: but their mothers do, and so do the school nurses who measure the heights and weights of this generation and remember the bony structure of the last" (emphasis in original).

Things Fall Apart

Then things changed. Keynesian policies—Samuelson's "New Economics"—were not the panacea for economic ills that many had claimed. There is no doubt that judicious use of fiscal policy can often attenuate fluctuations of economic activity. There are, however, various factors that can interfere. One of these is that other considerations often come into conflict with the policies that would be appropriate based on narrow economic considerations. On a sometimes mundane, day-to-day level, it is often in the particular political interest of those in office to keep spending on favored programs but to avoid the taxation needed to pay for these programs. On a grander level but representing the same pattern, in the late 1960s the particular circumstances of the Vietnam War and its political unpopularity led the government to pursue damaging fiscal policies—as we will explain shortly. The second and fundamental factor limiting the effectiveness of expansion-promoting fiscal policy is that it can conflict with the maintenance of profits. Expansionary policy promotes a high level of employment that can shift power in favor of labor and lower profits. The interests of business then come into conflict with the continued use of fiscal policies to maintain an economic expansion.

Furthermore, Keynesian policies alone, while they can help maintain stable growth, do not provide the foundations for a long period of expansion. The economic growth of the post–World War II period had other important foundations. These other foundations, unlike fiscal policies, are not subject to direct manipulation by government. By the late 1960s, several pillars in the foundation of economic expansion began to crumble. The 1970s saw slower economic growth and considerable instability in the form of recessions and inflation. These economic changes in turn precipitated important political changes, political changes that amounted to a "power grab" by business and wealthy citizens.

The economic success of the quarter century following World War II was based on special circumstances. In part, the success was a consequence of the war. The war—or, more precisely, war spending—had finally brought an end to the depression of the 1930s. In the five years from 1938 to 1943, the unemployment rate plummeted from 19 percent to 1.9 percent.[5] Because of the diversion of production to war materials, however, the higher incomes generated in the war years could not be spent to meet consumer wants—not on houses, not on cars, and not on myriad other goods. (The government used wage-price controls and rationing of some goods to deal with the shortages.) Thus at the end of the war there was a huge backlog of consumer demand, funds available in the pockets of consumers, and consumer spending was an important factor pushing the economy upward. In addition, the war had spawned a surge of technological changes that contributed to the long economic expansion of the era—everything from aeronautics to medicine to electronics had been altered by the war.

The international situation also provided an important basis for the economic expansion. As countries in Europe and Asia recovered from the damage of the war, their growth—promoted actively by the U.S. government through the Marshall Plan and other aid programs—established markets for U.S. goods and opportunities for U.S. investors. Furthermore, while business firms in the other high-income capitalist countries had been devastated by the war, U.S. firms had been strengthened and were therefore in an extremely good competitive position in the international economy. Their position was further bolstered by the unchallenged power of the U.S. government among capitalist countries. A particular manifestation of this power was the set of arrangements for the international financial system that had been established as the war came to an end. That system placed the dollar at the center of international commerce, an arrangement that provided stability for economic expansion and facilitated the international operations of U.S. firms (see Chapter 7). Also, and important, the diplomatic and military power of the United States provided a backdrop for the international expansion of U.S. business.

The conditions of consumer demand and technological change engendered by the war, the international situation, and the rising role of the government in economic affairs were the pillars on which the long economic expansion was built. But the positive economic impacts of the war waned over time, and the international situation changed. As a result, the U.S. government became over-burdened.

On the international front, by the 1970s U.S. firms began to lose their position of unchallenged dominance among capitalist countries. Firms in Europe and Japan had reestablished themselves, both in their home markets and in the international arena, and were mounting a challenge to their U.S.-based competitors. Things were also changing in countries that had long been on the periphery of the world economy. Most notable was the rising power of the oil-exporting countries. The long economic expansion leading up to the 1970s had meant strong demand for oil and had created the opportunity for oil-exporting countries, which had organized themselves into the Organization of Petroleum Exporting Countries (OPEC), to push up prices. And then there was the war in Vietnam.

The Vietnam War turned out to be much more difficult militarily than the U.S. government had anticipated. This created some substantial economic problems, in no small part because of the opposition to the war among the U.S. populace. On the one hand, the increasing military difficulty of the war demanded more government spending. On the other hand, the unpopularity of the war made the government unwilling to increase taxes to cover this higher level of spending. With the government already spending heavily on domestic programs, including the War on Poverty, this expansion of war spending without an expansion of taxes meant a growing federal government budgetary deficit that reached almost 3 percent of GNP in 1968—not huge by later standards, but the largest deficit to that point in the post–World War II era. A government deficit had been an important factor contributing to aggregate demand in previous years—in the recession at the beginning of the 1960s, for example. But when the war-related deficit began to grow in the mid-1960s, the economy was already near full employment. The result was even lower unemployment, which created greater power for labor in bargaining with management, downward pressure on profits, and upward pressure on prices.

Thus the economic change in the United States at the end of the 1960s and the beginning of the 1970s was the consequence of a number of inter-related factors—the giving-out of the favorable economic impetus that had been created by the World War II, the weakening competitive position of U.S. firms in the international economy, a rise in the price of oil and other natural resources, the pressures on labor markets created by the Vietnam War and other government spending, and the political instability generated by the war itself. While periods of economic expansion always give way to slow-downs or recessions, this constellation of factors made the instability and disruption more substantial than a "normal" business cycle downturn.

The favorable conditions of the expansion in the previous twenty-five years had provided a basis for the de facto accord between big business and labor. By and large, as we have said, major firms in central U.S. industries had accepted unionization. What's more, the owners and managers of these firms, the very wealthy members of society, had largely accepted the major role that the government had played in economic affairs—Keynesianism in its broadest sense. The Great Depression was still fresh in their minds, and this broad Keynesian approach seemed to be working. During these post–World War II years, businesses had been able to make profits while, in effect, sharing the benefits of growth with workers through rising wages and with society in general through government expenditures on social programs. By

Figure 3.1 **Share of Income Going to the Highest-Income One Percent and the Highest-Income Ten Percent of Families, 1917–2008**

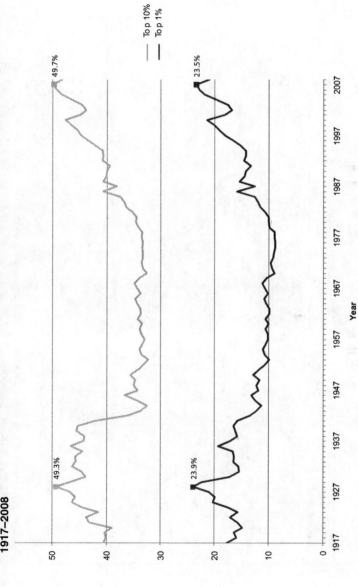

Source: Piketty and Saez, http://elsa.berkeley.edu/~saez/

Note: Discussed in Box II.1.

Figure 3.2   Income of the Highest-Income Five Percent of Families as a Percentage of the Income of the Lowest-Income Forty Percent of Families, 1947–2009

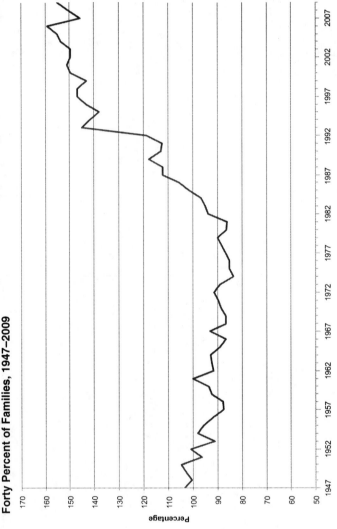

Source: U.S. Census Bureau, Current Population Survey, Annual Social and Economic Supplements, http://www.census.gov/hhes/www/income/data/historical/families/f02AR.xls.

Note: Discussed in Box II.1

Figure 3.3   **Shares of Wealth (Net Worth) Held by Most Wealthy One Percent and Most Wealthy Five Percent of Households, 1922–2007**

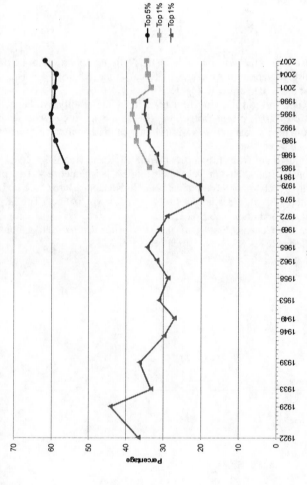

Source: For most weatlhy one percent 1922–1998 data, Edward N. Wolff, *Top Heavy: The Increasing Inequality of Wealth in America and What Can Be Done About It,* New York: The New Press, 2002, Appendix Table A-1. For most wealthy one percent and most wealthy five percent 1983–2007, Edward N. Wolff, "Recent Trends in Household Wealth in the United States: Rising Debt and Middle-Class Squeeze — An Update to 2007," Working Paper No. 589, Levy Economics Institute of Bard College, March 2010, Table 2, available online at http://www. levyinstitute.org/pubs/wp_589.pdf.

the early 1970s, however, Keynesianism and sharing the benefits of growth were no longer working. Moreover, even while things had worked in terms of economic growth, the relative position of those at the top in terms of income and wealth distribution had, as we have noted, been ebbing. From the perspective of business and those people in the highest income brackets, it was time for a change.

Notes

1. The full text of the NLRA is available on the National Labor Relations Board website, www.nlrb.gov/about_us/overview/national_labor_relations_act.aspx.

2. Sources for these data are with Figure 10.1.

3. The data cited in the following four paragraphs are readily available from U.S. Bureau of Census, *Historical Statistics of the United States Colonial Times to 1970* and, for more recent years, from various issues of the *Economic Report of the President*, www.gpoaccess.gov/eop/.

4. The wealth data are from Edward N. Wolff, "Recent Trends in Household Wealth in the United States: Rising Debt and Middle-Class Squeeze—An Update to 2007," Working Paper No. 589 (Annandale-on-Hudson, NY: Bard College, Levy Economics Institute, 2010), www.levyinstitute.org/pubs/wp_589.pdf. The income data are from Piketty and Saez (see Box II.1).

5. U.S. Bureau of Census, *Historical Statistics of the United States Colonial Times to 1970*, Series D 85–86.

4

The Turnaround

Change in the Last Quarter
of the Twentieth Century

Major change took place in the U.S. economy in the last quarter of the twentieth century, and that change was fully evident by the late 1980s. It can most readily be charted in the data on the distribution of income. As we have emphasized, as compared with the pre-1930s era, the distribution of income and wealth was notably less unequal in the post–World War II era, and what's more, over this era there was a slow and slight movement toward even greater equality. This direction of change toward greater equality, however, was reversed in the 1970s, and was clearly evident in the data by the late 1980s. (See Figures 3.1, 3.2, and 3.3.)

At the end of World War II, in 1946, the highest income families—the top 1 percent—obtained 13 percent of all income and the top 10 percent obtained 37 percent. By the mid-1970s, as we have pointed out, the share of the top 1 percent had fallen to about 9 percent, while the share of the entire top 10 percent had fallen to one-third of total income. A decade later, in 1986, these top groups had gained a great deal, with most of the gain going to that small group at the very top: the top 1 percent was getting 16 percent of all income, while the top 10 percent was obtaining 41 percent. The available data do not allow a precise comparison of other segments of the population with these elite groups. (See the Box II.1 for an explanation.) However, using the Census Bureau's data, which understate the income of those at the top, the shift is striking: according to those data, in the mid-1970s the top 5 percent of families obtained 16 percent *less* income than did the bottom 40 percent of families, but by the end of the 1980s that top 5 percent was obtaining 18 percent *more* than the bottom 40 percent.

The upward shift in income distribution would continue through the 1990s and into the new millennium. By 2000, the top 1 percent was obtaining 21.5 percent of income and the top 10 percent was getting 48 percent. By 2007, as the crisis emerged, the most elite group had virtually reattained its peak pre-1930s share of 24 percent; the top 10 percent got 50 percent of the total in that year. Interestingly, however, the pattern of wealth distribution does not correspond fully to these income distribution shifts. The 1980s did see a sharp rise of inequality in the distribution of wealth. At the end of the 1970s, the share of wealth ("net worth" including primary residences) in the hands of the top 1 percent of households stood at about 22 percent, and by 1987 the figure had risen to 37 percent. In subsequent years, however, there does not appear to have been a further concentration of wealth, in spite of the continuing rise in income inequality. (This is true whether or not primary residences are included in the wealth measure.)[1]

This turnaround, marked by the changing distribution of income and wealth in the 1980s, went deep. It involved major changes in political power and economic structures and was accompanied by an ideological shift. The clearest manifestation of the shift in political power was the election of Ronald Reagan to the presidency in 1980, and the accompanying rise of the right wing of the Republican Party. But the political changes were well underway before Reagan's election.

The rising conservative movement gained its first victories with the antitax movement that emerged in the 1970s. The most famous of these victories was the passage of Proposition 13 in California in 1978, a referendum that amended the state's constitution. Its best-known section limited property taxes to 1 percent of the value of the property and limited annual increases in the assessed value of property to 2 percent, severely restricting the ability of local jurisdictions to raise revenue. The resulting reduction in the revenues of local governments both reduced their ability to finance services—schools, in particular—and created a greater reliance on the state government to provide the funds for local services. However, Proposition 13 also contained provisions that required a two-thirds vote in both houses of the state legislature in order to raise taxes and a two-thirds vote in local elections for local governments to raise taxes. The limit on the ability of the state government to raise taxes became especially important in California in 2009, when the state entered into a severe fiscal crisis— probably the worst such crisis of any state, though many other states were in similar binds.

Proposition 13 was followed in several other states by similar initiatives, many of which (though not all) were successful in placing significant limits on state and local governments' ability to raise revenue. Overall, these efforts were touted as a "taxpayer revolt." This "revolt" had a dual foundation. On the one hand, it was a reaction to the real economic problems that faced many people in the 1970s. People could not vote against slower economic growth, inflation, or stagnant real wages. But they could cast a vote for curtailing taxes, a vote that would positively affect their incomes—at least in the short run. So the revolt was able to gain a popular base.

On the other hand, the taxpayer revolt was fueled by a conservative response to the major economic role of government that had emerged in the post–World War II era. Faced with the pressures that had developed in the late 1960s and early 1970s that undermined their profits, many business executives and others who obtained their income from investments defined the source of their difficulties as excessive government programs—fiscal deficits, social programs, excessive taxes, and overregulation. The general instability of the 1970s—the leap upward of oil prices, the recession at mid-decade, general inflation, higher unemployment—created a basis on which they could gain some popular support and begin to push back against "big government."

When Ronald Reagan ascended to the presidency, these efforts, which had begun at the local and state level, moved to the national stage. Reagan championed the anti–big-government agenda, especially in rhetoric but also in practice. He defined the government as "The Problem," and he demeaned social programs with an image of the "Welfare Queens," the myth that welfare programs were supporting women having too many children, driving Cadillacs, and living in luxury and laziness. It was, however, his practice rather than his rhetoric that had the clearest impacts.

In 1981, the president was able to use the severe recession as a basis to push through an across-the-board cut in income tax rates. The change in the top rate from 70 percent to 50 percent (a 29 percent decrease) was a dramatic tax reduction for people with high incomes, and was supported by the classical arguments for "trickle-down economics." Tax breaks to the rich and directly to businesses would supposedly induce them to invest more and thus create jobs and raise incomes of those in the middle and at the bottom. (The famous economist John Kenneth Galbraith once referred to this as "horse and sparrow economics"—feed the horses well and there will be more droppings for the sparrows.) Over and over again, this approach to economic policy has produced poor results in terms of economic growth, but has been successful in raising the incomes of the rich and contributing to greater economic inequality. (At the bottom end, the 1981 tax cuts lowered the rate from 14 percent to 11 percent, a 21 percent decrease.)

The tax cuts of 1981 were not accompanied by reductions in government spending, and the resulting deficit contributed to the economic recovery that began the following year. However, the rationale that Reagan and his supporters offered for these tax cuts was not the Keynesian demand rationale. Instead they argued that high tax rates were inhibiting work and investment. With existing tax rates, they claimed, people were discouraged from working hard and from making investments because the taxes would reduce the gains so severely that the extra effort or extra risk would not be worthwhile. And they took the argument one step further, asserting that the lower tax rates would yield a higher level of revenue for the government as they induced more work and more investment and thus more income; the lower tax rate on more income would supposedly lead to more revenue than a higher tax rate on less income. The evidence did not support these arguments—either before or after the implementation of the tax cuts—and the tax package of 1981 represented the triumph of ideology over reality.

The 1981 Reagan tax cuts did not curtail "big government," if the term is defined to mean the amount of government spending as a share of total spending. During the 1980s, this figure was roughly constant. Discretionary spending on social programs (education and training, health, income security, transportation, and community development) declined, however, falling from 29.5 percent of government outlays in 1980 to 22.5 percent in 1990. The declining share of these social programs in total government spending in the 1980s is partly explained by the rising share spent on the military (about 1 percent more in 1990 as compared to 1980) and Social Security and Medicare (about 2 percent more). But the really big shift in the composition of government spending came in a category called "net interest payments." This is the interest government pays on its borrowing to cover the federal deficit. The combination of large government budget deficits in the 1980s and especially the high interest rates of the era meant that net interest payments jumped up from 8.9 percent of federal outlays to 14.7 percent.[2]

The high interest rates and the large federal deficit were not some sideshow to the general shift in government policies of this era. The high interest rates were the result of the implementation of extremely tight monetary policy by the Federal Reserve. The interest rate on three-month treasury bills averaged more than 10 percent in the period from 1979 to 1982, and peaked at the historically high rate of 16.3 percent in May 1981. This policy, initiated during a Democratic administration by a Federal Reserve chairman appointed by a Democratic president, was presented as the means by which to halt the high inflation rate of the late 1970s and early 1980s. The extremely high interest rates did curtail inflation, but only by generating a severe recession. The unemployment rate was above 10 percent for the ten-month period of September 1982 through June 1983, peaking at 10.8 percent in November and December of that year. For the entire decade, the unemployment rate averaged 7.3 percent, a rate not matched by any decade since the 1930s.[3]

A high level of sustained unemployment is usually the strongest measure that can shift the income distribution in favor of the wealthy (though, as we have discussed earlier, under certain circumstances and when high unemployment is a manifestation of severe crisis, things can be very different, as they were in the 1930s). In the short term, the incomes of those in the lower income groups—people who are laid off at the highest rates—are sharply reduced. Over the longer term, as unemployment remains high, a broad range of workers is affected, whether actually laid off or not. High levels and sustained unemployment undermine the bargaining power of all workers. Workers' alternatives are greatly reduced, and power depends on having alternatives. In the 1980s the political power shift had created an economic power shift in favor of employers and to the detriment of workers. The result: from their peak in 1977 to their nadir in 1992, inflation-adjusted average weekly earnings of workers in private, nonagricultural industries fell by 17 percent. In 1992 (as in the late 1980s) the income of the highest income 5 percent of families was 18 percent *more* than the income of the bottom 40 percent, and in 1993 this figure would leap to 45 percent. In the mid-1970s, as we noted earlier, the income of that top group had been 16 percent *less* than that of the bottom 40 percent. (And these are U.S. Census Bureau income distribution figures, which tend to understate the degree of inequality.)[4]

The attack on workers' power and incomes during the 1980s, however, did not operate only through the impact of high unemployment. Especially important, throughout the 1980s the federal minimum wage was not changed, standing at $3.35 an hour in 1981 and remaining at that level until the early 1990s. Inflation during that ten-year period reduced the buying power of the minimum wage by roughly one-third, so that in terms of 1981 buying power the 1991 minimum wage was worth only $2.24.

Reagan's most famous—or infamous, if one prefers—attack on organized labor was his firing of the air traffic controllers when they went on strike in 1981. The Professional Air Traffic Controllers Organization (PATCO) had been at odds with the Carter administration over multiple issues concerning pay, working conditions, and air traffic safety. Amidst this conflict with the Carter administration, PATCO gave its support in the 1980 campaign to Ronald Reagan. On October 20, 1980, shortly before the election, candidate Reagan wrote to the president of PATCO, saying, " . . . too few [air traffic controllers] working unreasonable hours with obsolete equipment has placed the nation's air travelers in unwarranted danger. In an area so clearly related to public safety the Carter administration has failed to act responsibly . . . I pledge to you that my administration will work very closely with you to bring about a spirit of cooperation between the President and the air traffic controllers."[5] Yet, when PATCO was unable to reach a contract agreement with the government and went on strike in 1981, President Reagan gave the air traffic controllers 48 hours to return to work. When they did not return, he fired them.

The PATCO event was a symbol of a new era in the government's relationship with organized labor. As a practical matter, while extremely important for PATCO and the workers who were fired, it was probably less important than the impact of Reagan's appointments to the National Labor Relations Board (NLRB). The antagonism toward organized labor that was expressed in the PATCO firings became the order of the day for the NLRB. On its website the NLRB states that the National Labor Relations Act "guarantees the right of employees to organize and to bargain collectively with their employers, and to engage in other protected concerted activity with or without a union, or to refrain from all such activity."[6] The guarantee of the right of employees to organize was interpreted during the Reagan era to mean very little. A 2009 study by the Center for Economic and Policy Research indicates that workers taking the lead in organizing unions in their places of employment had a 20 to 25 percent probability of being fired during the 1980s (and faced similar odds during both Bush presidencies). The NLRB was failing to do its job, and in this failure was providing a good illustration of the use of political power to affect economic power.[7]

The attack on workers also had an ideological element, illustrated by efforts to blame the unemployed themselves for their plight. Reagan played a direct, leading role. When asked during an interview about nonwhite unemployment in 1982, which rose to 18.9 percent in December of that year, the President pointed to the help wanted ads in *The Washington Post*. "I made it a point to count the pages of help wanted ads," Reagan stated. "In this time of great unemployment there were 24 full pages of classified ads of employers looking for employees. What we need is to make more people qualified to go and apply for those jobs."[8] However, of the 26 pages of ads (not 24), half were devoted to jobs openings for professionals, such as engineers and nurses, unlikely to be filled by the unemployed. The nature of the jobs aside, there were but 3,500 jobs advertised, while 85,000 people were unemployed in the Washington metropolitan area at the time.[9]

Continuing the Shift

Ronald Reagan did not begin the turnaround in inequality, power, and ideology. As we have pointed out, the shift emerged in the 1970s, as the post–World War II bases of economic progress waned and the economy entered a period of weakened profits, slow growth, and instability. That situation created the opportunity for a resurgence of conservative ideology and actions that began to achieve successes with the antitax movement of that decade. The achievement of the Reagan era was the consolidation of this conservative offensive. By the end of the 1980s, the ideology that Reagan had expounded—that government was The Problem, that less government involvement in economic life was best, that economic affairs should be left to the market as much as possible—had become the conventional wisdom. No longer would a president acknowledge the effectiveness of Keynesian policies, though such policies continued to be used. Taxes, unions, budget deficits, and welfare recipients were widely scorned.

Reagan's consolidation of conservative ideology and power was continued in the subsequent Bush administration, and it was also evident in the years of the Clinton presidency. The Clinton administration did make some substantial departures from the economic policies of its Republican predecessors. Perhaps most important, Clinton was willing to raise taxes. The Omnibus Budget Reconciliation Act of 1993, among other provisions, raised the tax rates slightly on people in the highest income brackets, increased the portion of Social Security benefits subject to taxation, and pushed up the federal gasoline tax by 4.3 cents per gallon. The 1993 act, while clearly involving a tax increase, also increased the Earned Income Tax Credit (EITC), providing low-income families with a larger tax refund, and only the gas tax change increased taxes on lower-income and middle-income families. The increased tax burden created by the act fell almost entirely on the very wealthy. Nonetheless, while a significant departure from Republican policy (and opposed by Republicans with the claim that it would stifle economic growth), the tax increases of 1993 were passed under the rubric of "deficit reduction." By embracing the mantra of "deficit reduction," Clinton and the Democrats had abandoned the rhetoric of Keynesianism in favor of conservative ideology. (Tellingly, while the Republicans opposed the Clinton tax increases claiming they would stifle economic growth, the remaining seven years of the Clinton era saw GDP grow at the relatively high rate of 4 percent annually.)

In addition to the tax increase for the wealthy, the Clinton era saw some shift in policy toward labor. This was evident in the operations of the NLRB. Whereas in the Republican years the probability of being fired while leading a union drive was 20 to 25 percent, this figure dropped below 10 percent by the late 1990s. This change did not lead to a rise in union membership, which was affected by several factors, but it did represent a shift from the 1980s.

Yet in spite of raising tax rates for the wealthy and establishing a more labor-friendly NLRB, economic policy in the Clinton era continued important trends established in the Reagan and Bush years. Indeed, on reducing the size of government and cutting the deficit, Clinton put the rhetoric of the Republicans into practice; by the end of the Clinton years, federal government spending relative to GDP was smaller than at any time since the mid-1960s. The decline in federal spending was in part a result of a decline in military spending, following the end of the Cold War. In addition, however, during the Clinton administration federal spending on education, natural resources, and income security all fell relative to GDP.[10] On welfare policies and deregulation, in particular, the Clinton administration appears to have been guided by the increasingly dominant leave-it-to-the-market ideology. Also, on international economic policy, which we will take up in Chapters 7 and 8, "free trade" continued to guide the agenda of the U.S. government.

Clinton's approach to welfare provides a clear illustration of the continuing power of conservative ideas and conservative power. Welfare policies in the United States, as represented most significantly by Aid to Families with Dependent Children (AFDC), have long been problematic. AFDC provided limited support, created substantial negative stigma on recipients, and involved heavy bureaucratic obstacles. Also, like many social support programs, AFDC created perverse incentives, with recipients losing the support as they took steps to improve their positions (a point to which we will return in Chapter 10). However, the conservative attack on AFDC as a drain on government resources had little merit: in the early 1990s, AFDC accounted for less than 1 percent of the federal budget and less than 3 percent of state budgets. Moreover, the idea that the system encouraged women to have more and more children was not supported by the facts: mothers on AFDC had on average fewer children than other mothers, and, once on AFDC, were less likely to have another child.[11]

Yet Clinton had adopted much of the conservative antiwelfare rhetoric, touting the slogan of "ending welfare as we know it" in his 1992 campaign. In 1996, the Personal Responsibility and Work Opportunity Reconciliation Act abolished AFDC and established the Temporary Assistance for Needy Families (TANF) program. TANF did yield a reduction in the number of people on the public assistance roles, with its emphasis on temporary assistance forcing many mothers into the labor force—including those who had been able under the previous system to go to school while on welfare. TANF places a lifetime cap of five years of assistance, but some states have limits as low as twenty-one months. As a result many women, mothers with children (and often without adequate child care support), entered the paid labor force, working in low-paying jobs that shifted them from welfare poverty to working poverty.

The creation of TANF in place of AFDC, beyond its impact on low-income mothers and their children, increased the ranks of people available to work at the bottom of the wage scale. TANF thus created more downward pressure on wages at or near the bottom. While not the largest factor affecting the distribution of income, the shift from AFDC to TANF contributed to the continuation of growing income inequality in the following years.

Beyond the direct practical implications of this change in welfare policy, its further significance lies in its implications about the powerful role of conservative ideology. The change reflected a belief—at least among the dominant political authorities in the country, Republican or Democrat—that there was something fundamentally illegitimate about social welfare. According to the ideology behind TANF, people in difficult economics situations were responsible for their own plights; their situations did not indicate a failure of the economic system; and it was up to them—through work in the marketplace—to solve their own problems. With rare exceptions, The Market was viewed as the solution to individuals' economic difficulties, and they should receive only temporary assistance from society (through the government).

The same ideological shift from the ideas behind the War on Poverty of the 1960s to the ideas that facilitated the creation of TANF in 1997 also appear in the move from the regulatory regime that guided the economy in the 1950s and 1960s to massive deregulation of business in the last quarter of the twentieth century. While ideology provided the rationale, behind the ideology was power, the power of businesses that would gain from the deregulation. Nowhere were the gains more apparent and the deregulation more significant than in the financial sector. What's more, the deregulation of finance was an essential factor setting the stage for the crisis that appeared in 2007 and 2008. In the next chapters, we will give full attention to that deregulation and its role in generating the crisis.

Rising Inequality and Slow Growth

Financial deregulation, however, played its role within the broader economic context, and a central part of that economic context at the end of the twentieth century was a continuation of the trend of rising inequality. In spite of the departures of the Clinton administration from its Republican predecessors (EITC, some tax increases, more reasonable treatment of unions), inequality in the distribution of income rose during the 1990s.

During the much-touted long economic expansion from 1991 to 2001, real national output (GDP) rose by 42 percent, and real per capita disposable personal income rose by almost 25 percent. By these crude figures, the 1990s might appear similar to the relatively "good times" of the 1950s or 1960s. But that was not the case. During the 1990s, wages were relatively stagnant, with real weekly earnings in the private sector rising by only 6.6 percent over the decade. Income distribution, in spite of the economic growth of the 1990s, became more unequal. Over the decade the 10 percent with the highest incomes increased its share from 40 percent to 48 percent of total income, with most of this increase going to the top 1 percent, which saw an increase from 14 to 21.5 percent. Census data, covering a broader swath of the population and understating the income of those at the top, show a less marked increase in inequality, but still an increase. As we have stated, in 1993 the income share going to the top 5 percent of families had jumped up to be 45 percent greater than the share of the bottom 40 percent. While the figure fluctuated in subsequent years, it stood at 50 percent in 2000, the last year of the Clinton administration.[12]

In terms of the average incomes of African American families relative to European American families, however, there was a slight improvement during the 1990s—but only a recovery of the ground that had been lost since the beginning of the 1970s. In 1971, the median income of African American families had been 61 percent of that of European American families; by 1991, the figure had fallen to 57 percent, but rose up to 62 percent in 2001. In spite of the overall trends, it would appear that on average African Americans gained a good deal from the growth and relatively high employment rates of the 1990s—though, again, the gain was only back to where things stood before the economic and political "turnaround" that began in the 1970s. Moreover, as with the population in general, the "on average" gains of African Americans mask increasing income inequality, which had become even greater among African Americans than among the whole population.[13]

Although economic growth in the 1990s continued for a long period, growth over the whole decade was not especially rapid. The 40 percent increase of GDP between 1990 and 2000 (3.4 percent annual average) was hardly better than the record of the two previous decades: 37 percent in the 1970s and 38 percent in the 1980s. It was, however, well below the roughly 51 percent (4.2 percent annual average) expansion seen in the 1960s. Though growth after 1993 was relatively rapid, at 4 percent per annum, even the rate of expansion in those years was less than that of the 1960s.[14]

Nonetheless, the relatively long expansion of the 1990s generated a substantial rise in the stock market, the so-called dot-com bubble, based in large part on exuberance over the rapid expansion of information technology and the formation of new firms based on applications of information technology. Between 1990 and 2000 the Dow Jones Industrial Average more that quadrupled: at its peak in September 2000, the Dow Jones was 4.3 times what it had been ten years earlier (with most of the increase taking place in the second half of the decade). In this same period, as we have just noted, the overall output of goods and services had risen only 40 percent.[15]

When this dot-com bubble burst in 2000 the Dow Jones dropped by more than a third over two years, and the NASDAQ, which includes a concentration of the "high-tech" firms, fell by an astounding 75 percent. This stock market crash was an ominous sign of the economic maladies that would appear in even more serious form a few years later. We can see in the 1990s many of the problems that were to increase substantially after the turn of the century. In the context of slow economic growth, the triumvirate of rising inequality, leave-it-to-the-market ideology, and highly concentrated power lay at the basis of the downturn in 2001. With the further evolution of all these forces after 2001, the deregulation of finance would work its full mischief.

Notes

1. The income and wealth distribution figures in the preceding two paragraphs are from Piketty and Saez and the Census Bureau (see Box II.1). The wealth distribution figures are from Edward M. Wolff, *Top Heavy: The Increasing Inequality of Wealth in American and What Can Be Done About It* (New York: The New Press, 2002), Figure 3.1, and from Edward N. Wolff, "Recent Trends in Household Wealth in the United States: Rising Debt and Middle-Class Squeeze—An Update to 2007," Working Paper No. 589, Levy Economics Institute (Annandale-on-Hudson, NY: Bard College, March 2010), www.levyinstitute.org/pubs/wp_589.pdf.

2. These data are from the *Budget of the United States for Fiscal Year 1996, Historical Tables*, www.gpoaccess.gov/usbudget/fy96/pdf/bud96h.pdf.

3. For data on the three-month treasury bills, see *Economic Report of the President 1983*, Table B-67; for unemployment data, Bureau of Labor Statistics, Unemployment Rate; Percent; 16 years and over, www.economagic.com/em-cgi/data.exe/blsln/lns14000000: percent28rev percent29.

4. The wage figures are from the *Economic Report of the President 2010*, Table B-47. The income distribution figures are the Census Bureau (see Box II.1).

5. Quoted in Frank Sepulveda, "P.A.T.C.O., the F.A.A., and Air Safety: A history on the specialists, their working conditions, and their removal," www.patcoairsafety.com/.

6. The NLRB website is www.nlrb.gov/.

7. John Schmitt and Ben Zipperer, *Dropping the Ax: Illegal Firings During Union Election Campaigns, 1951–2007* (Washington DC: Center for Economic and Policy Research, March, 2009), www.cepr.net/documents/publications/dropping-the-ax-update-2009-03.pdf.

8. Ronald Reagan, The President's News Conference, January 19, 1982, www.presidency.ucsb.edu/ws/index.php?pid=42476.

9. AFL-CIO Public Employee Department, REVENEWS, February 1982, as quoted in Herbert F. Spirer, Louise Spirer, and Abram J. Jaffe, *Misused Statistics*, 2d edition (New York: Marcel Dekker, Inc., 1998), p. 139.

10. These points on social spending and the data to support them are from Robert Pollin, *Contours of Descent* (London and New York: Verso Books, 2003), pp. 73–75.

11. See Randy Albelda and Chris Tilly, "It's A Family Affair: Women, Work and Poverty," in Ann Withorn and Diane Dujan, editors, *For Crying Out Loud: Women's Poverty in the United States* (Boston: South End Press, 1996), pp. 79–85.

12. Economic growth data are from the *Economic Report of the President 2010,* Tables B-2, B-31, and B-47. Income distribution figures are from the Piketty and Saez and U.S. Census sources (see Box II.1).

13. See the census data previously cited.

14. Growth data from the *Economic Report of the President 2010,* Table B-2.

15. Historical figures on the Dow Jones Industrial Average and the NASDAQ are available at finance.yahoo.com/q/hp?s=^DJI and finance.yahoo.com/q/hp?s=^IXIC, respectively.

Part III
The Emergence of Crisis in the United States

Driving a car is dangerous. It is dangerous for the driver and the car's passengers, but it is also dangerous for others on the road, both pedestrians and people in other vehicles. If we could count on all drivers to take full account of these dangers—these risks of driving—and operate their cars accordingly, we would not need much by way of regulations. Speed limits, for example, would be superfluous because no one would drive at an unsafe speed. In fact, most of the time most drivers will take account of the risks to themselves and exercise appropriate caution.

But what about the risks to others? Can we count on drivers to be as careful about the rest of us—other drivers and pedestrians—as they are about themselves? The answer is probably that some will and some won't. And the greater the pressures to get someplace fast, the fewer drivers we can count on to reduce the risks that they impose on the rest of us. So we establish rules and regulations—speed limits, stop signs, car safety inspections, and so on. We do so not to (or not only to) protect drivers from themselves, but to protect ourselves from the risks external to themselves, the risks that their driving imposes on the rest of society.

Economists have developed a term for the impact of people's decisions on others not involved in those decisions. For example, the decision to generate electricity by burning coal creates air pollution that affects everyone, not just those who are buying or selling either the coal or the electricity. This impact on the rest of us is called an "externality." Even the most ardent advocates of leaving economic affairs to the markets recognize that when an externality is large, some social (governmental) regulation is desirable. Without regulation, too much electricity would be generated by methods that produced pollution.

The risk that is imposed on the rest of us by the driver of a car is an externality. Without regulation, we would expect that drivers would tend to impose too much risk on us, just like the generator of coal-based electricity would impose too much pollution on the rest of us without regulation.

What about finance? When financial institutions make investments—issuing a loan, for example, or purchasing a bond or a stock or some other financial instrument—they are taking risks. If the loan is paid off on time or the stock or bond rises in value, then the investment pays off, they win, and the risk was worth taking. If the loan fails or the value of the stock or bond falls, they lose; it was a bad risk. If the only impact of failure were a loss for the financial institution, the rest of us would have little if any reason for concern about the riskiness of their investments. Like the risks involved with driving a car, however, the risks involved with financial investments can, and often do, have impacts on the rest of us. And like the driver of a car, the investor is unlikely to take sufficient account of the risks to the rest of us.

Indeed, the problem with the externality of risk in the financial system is a good deal worse than the problem of risk associated with driving a car. Most people do in fact take account of the dangers their driving imposes on others. That danger is direct and very tangible, and it can be quite severe. Driving too fast can lead to the killing of a child. The driver of a car can be led by the pressure of circumstances—the need to get to work on time, for example—to drive with excessive risk, but the risk externality will seldom be ignored because it is usually so direct and tangible and can be so severe.

The danger imposed by the risk externality of financial transactions, however, is very different from the risk involved in driving a car—neither direct nor tangible, and, when viewed in terms of the individual investment, not very severe. Not only does the risk appear less problematic, but the circumstances that generate risky behavior are often very substantial. Those circumstances are created in part by the pressure of competition that exists in financial activity. When investment opportunities appear, no bank or other financial firm wants to be left behind, allowing its competitors to get the new business unchallenged. If one firm moves, others tend to follow. A new stock or bond becomes available or a new financial instrument comes on the market. These new issues promise high returns, but only at high risk. Yet competitive pressures will lead firms to take these risks, for fear that the high returns will be garnered by their competitors and that they will be left out of a new, lucrative market. The result can be more and more risky investments, often beyond what is prudent from the point of view of the firm and certainly beyond what is prudent for the rest of us. (There is also the question of what the finance, safe or risky, is being used for—like the question of where the cars are going. But that is an issue for another day.)

Furthermore, this risk taking generated by competition is substantially exacerbated by the way salaries and bonuses of financial investors are determined. In brief, the decision makers in financial firms can derive very large personal gains from risky actions that yield quick profits; later, if those profits turn into losses, the decision makers generally do not suffer those losses themselves, in part because the government will bail them out.

No child will be killed, at least not directly, from a failed financial investment. Yet from the collection of financial failures that can emerge together, as in a general financial crisis, the external impact can be extremely severe, plunging the entire economy into crisis. This is roughly what happened in 2007–2008, as there was widespread failure due to excessive risks having been taken by financial firms and the consequent failures. Fearing things would get worse for them, banks greatly curtailed making loans, and without the regular flow of credit (those loans) many nonfinancial firms started to go downward. Output fell, unemployment rose, and a severe recession developed. In these circumstances, deaths do occur, though they can seldom if ever be linked to a particular risky investment. So we regulate financial firms to prevent the financial debacles that can be imposed upon the rest of us by excessively risky behavior.

Or at least we used to. The United States concluded the twentieth century with a spate of financial deregulation, beginning in the 1970s, developing momentum in the 1980s, and continuing through the passage of the Financial Services Modernization Act (Gramm-Leach-Bliley) in 1999 and the Commodity Futures Modernization Act in 2000. Not all the protections against banks' risky behavior were eliminated; the FDIC, in particular, was left in place. Yet, rationalized by the argument that the removal of regulations would make for a more efficient and robust economy, these steps of deregulation were analogous to taking down the stop signs and removing the speed limits, while expecting the "rational" behavior of drivers to lead to a good situation for society. Yes, some cars would get places faster, automobile activity would generally speed up, but disaster would be sure to strike sooner or later.

The U.S. financial system, in effect, entered the new millennium with the stop signs and speed limits removed. Disaster was not long in coming.

5

Setting the Stage

Loosening the Reins on Finance

The deregulation of the financial sector, which was part of a general trend toward the deregulation of business, was given its impetus by the economic instability of the 1970s and was carried along by the growing power of business and the free-market ideology that became increasingly ascendant in the 1980s. Also, technological developments—various aspects of the expansion of computerization—facilitated the changes in finance.

Up until the 1970s, the financial industry had been regulated so that it was highly compartmentalized.[1] Not only were commercial banks and investment banks separated from one another, as provided for by the Glass-Steagall Act, but almost all of the financial activity of households and small businesses was confined to commercial banks and thrift institutions (savings and loan associations, mutual savings banks, and credit unions). Only commercial banks offered checking accounts, and checking accounts could not pay interest. Commercial banks and thrift institutions offered savings accounts, but the interest rates on these accounts were strictly limited. Most mortgages were issued by thrift institutions, and were almost all long term with fixed interest rates; and thrift institutions were prohibited from engaging in most other forms of lending. Furthermore, most banks could operate only in one state, and many states confined banks to a single branch. (A single branch could still be very large in terms of its assets, especially those that specialized in corporate finance. Also, while not operating in more than one state, banks could still operate internationally and many, especially the larger ones based in New York City, did.)

The End of "Boring" Banking

The inflation that developed in the 1970s upset the relatively stable structure of U.S. banking, and regulators followed by allowing more and more variation from the standard rules. The problem for the existing system was that inflation generated interest rates that were higher than what commercial banks and thrifts were allowed to offer on savings accounts. At the same time, advanced computer and information technology made it possible for nonbank financial firms—such as Fidelity, Merrill Lynch, and T. Rowe Price—to create attractive personal investment alternatives. Money market mutual funds, which invested in short-term securities and offered checking accounts, grew rapidly, attracting funds that previously—before the period of inflation and rising interest rates—would have been placed in savings accounts. Only in the early 1980s did Congress eliminate the cap on bank interest rates.

One impact of these events was a major shift in the mortgage market. On the one hand, customers removed their funds from thrift institutions and commercial banks and, placed them in mutual funds and other institutions that paid higher interest rates; thus the traditional mortgage suppliers no longer had sufficient funds to meet the demand for new mortgages. On the other hand, the emergence of "securitization"—creating one of the new financial instruments of recent decades—facilitated the entrance of other financial firms into the mortgage market. (See Box 5.1 for an explanation of the term "financial instruments.") Securitization, or bundling, places a mortgage into a pool with a large number of other mortgages, perhaps a thousand or more, allowing the original lenders to sell this bundled package—or shares in the package—to investors who would reap the cash flow as the monthly payments on the mortgages flowed in. These packages of mortgages were called mortgage-backed securities (MBSs). They were regarded as relatively secure investments because, involving so many different mortgages, they were seen as embodying diversification. Furthermore, early securitization was undertaken by government-sponsored enterprises (GSEs), Fannie Mae and Freddie Mac, which guaranteed the repayment of the mortgages, and these enterprises had the implicit backing of the U.S. Treasury. Private financial institutions, however, also created MBSs. The MBSs became the foundation for the creation of collateralized debt obligations (CDOs), a more complicated form of security that played a major role in the financial crisis in 2007 and 2008. (See Chapter 6 for a detailed explanation of CDOs.) But because securitization of mortgages had been in existence for many years, through relatively good times as well as bad times, it should not in itself be viewed as the crucial causal element in the crisis.

With these various changes, the thrift institutions, which made three-fifths of all mortgages in the early 1970s, had fallen into third place behind mortgage companies and commercial banks by the mid-1990s. In addition, by the mid-1990s, mortgages were available in all shapes and sizes—with variable or fixed interest rates, different maturities, different down payments, and a variety of other features (about which more in the next chapter).

Box 5.1
Financial Instruments and Derivatives

The term "financial instruments" refers to a variety of financial arrangements that are traded on markets and involve claims on assets or claims
on payments associated with assets. A loan agreement (often a bond) that
can be bought and sold on a market is a financial instrument. Likewise,
equities (stocks) and cash are also financial instruments, as are various
forms of agreements to deliver or receive assets in the future (futures
contracts).

A "derivative" is a financial asset the value of which depends on the
value of some other financial asset. For example: a mortgage-backed
security (MBS) is a derivative because the value of an MBS depends on
the value of the mortgages that are contained in the MBS. Likewise, a collateralized debt obligation (CDO) is a derivative because its value depends
on the values of the MBSs on which it is based. Other examples include
credit default swaps and contracts whose values are based on the value
of a futures contract. As long as these derivatives can be bought and sold
on markets, they are financial instruments. When, however, the sale of a
derivative takes place directly between two parties (an over-the-counter,
or OTC, transaction), that derivative would not be a financial instrument.
OTC arrangements are often the case with credit default swaps.

"Innovation" in the financial industry usually refers to the development of new financial instruments designed to facilitate new types of
investments. Derivatives (CDOs, credit default swaps, derivatives based
on energy futures, and others) are generally developed as financial instruments that shift risk from one party to another—supposedly from a party
that wants to reduce exposure to risk to another party willing to take on
more risk. At times, however, shifting risk can involve spreading risk—
and the consequences of risk—more widely.

Then there was the geographic reorganization of banking. Within states,
where banks had been restricted to operating only a single branch or multiple branches in a single county, increasingly they were allowed to operate
statewide. Then interstate banking came into practice. By the early 1990s,
bank holding companies were allowed to operate large interstate networks
of banks. (A "holding company" is simply a company that owns, either in
total or through controlling interests, other companies.) In 1994, the Riegle-
Neal Interstate Banking and Branching Efficiency Act authorized nationwide
branch banking.

Thus in the last three decades of the twentieth century the financial industry was dramatically transformed. Before the early 1970s, banking had been a profitable but stable—some would say "boring"—sector of the economy. Savings and loan banks (S&Ls) were characterized by the joke that their executives were in a "3–6–3 business"—they took in deposits at an interest rate of 3 percent, made mortgage loans at 6 percent, and were on the golf course by 3:00 in the afternoon. The deregulation of S&Ls, however, made them anything but boring, and the late 1980s saw their general collapse. The S&L crisis of the 1980s placed great costs on the federal government (i.e., on the public) and was a clear though largely ignored warning of the implications of financial deregulation. (See Box 5.2 for more on the S&L crisis.)

The elimination of various regulations, specifying which firms could do what and where, generated a much greater degree of competition. This competition, along with the economic instability of the 1980s, had dramatic impacts on commercial banking as well as on S&Ls. The decline of housing prices after 1979 and then after 1989, which had been at the center of the S&L crisis, contributed to the failure of 1,500 commercial banks in 1983–1992; banks had failed at a rate of about fifty per decade in the late 1960s and early 1970s. (These failures of commercial banks resulted largely in the failing banks being taken over by larger banks, and thus a debacle like that of the S&L industry was avoided.)

The other side of the competition story was the consolidation of the financial industry, as the winners in the new competitive conditions consolidated themselves into fewer and larger firms. In 2007, Loretta J. Mester, senior vice president and director of research at the Federal Reserve Bank of Philadelphia, summarized the consolidation in banking with the following comments:

> A striking amount of consolidation has occurred in the banking industry over the past twenty years, and it has led to some very large banks. In the United States about 11,500 bank mergers took place from 1980 through 2005, which is an average of about 440 mergers per year. And the size of mergers has risen over time. For example, in January 2004 J.P. Morgan Chase agreed to buy Bank One, creating a $1.1 trillion bank holding company. In October 2003 Bank of America agreed to buy FleetBoston, creating a $900 billion bank holding company and making Bank of America the second largest U.S. bank holding company, with $1.4 trillion in assets. (Citigroup is the largest, with $1.6 trillion in assets.)
>
> [. . .] The average asset size of U.S. banks (in real terms) has more than tripled since 1985 and is more than $1.1 billion. Assets are being redistributed from smaller banks to larger banks—now over 75 percent

Box 5.2

The Savings and Loan Crisis:
The Deregulation Disaster of the 1980s

The savings and loan (S&L) crisis of the 1980s provided fair warning of the consequences of financial deregulation. At the time, the failure of many S&L firms was the greatest collapse of U.S. financial institutions since the Great Depression of the 1930s. From 1986 to 1995, 1,043 S&Ls, holding $519 billion in assets, failed. When the assets of the failed S&Ls were sold, the receipts were of course not sufficient to pay off depositors. The funds of the Federal Savings and Loan Insurance Corporation (FSLIC), which insured S&L deposits, were insufficient, and the U.S. Treasury stepped in with $153 billion—$124 billion of which came from taxpayers (and the remainder was charged to the thrift industry).

What happened? S&Ls were among the most stable U.S. financial institutions in the decades following World War II, carrying out the crucial role of providing affordable mortgages to home buyers. The FSLIC insured their deposits up to $100,000. In return for deposit insurance protection, S&Ls accepted close supervision by federal regulators and limited their activities to making long-term home mortgage loans at relatively low interest rates.

That system unraveled beginning in the late 1970s. Inflation and the resulting rise in interest rates made the traditional practices by the S&Ls unviable (see text). It became increasingly difficult for thrifts to fulfill their assigned role: recycling the deposits of small savers into long-term, low-cost home mortgages. Rather than trying to find a way for thrifts to continue in that role, Washington policy makers claimed to solve the problems of the S&Ls by deregulating them. Beginning in the last year of the Carter administration and continuing under the Reagan administration, Congress removed interest rate ceilings on deposits and permitted thrifts to invest in a wider range of assets—commercial real estate, financial futures contracts, junk bonds, and other high-risk projects. On top of that, federal regulators allowed thrifts to use questionable accounting procedures to increase reported capital levels. At the same time, government spending cuts reduced the staff and resources of the examiners charged with overseeing the newly deregulated industry.

By the late 1980s the results were coming in, and the problems of the S&Ls were far worse, not far better, after deregulation. As housing prices fell in the early 1980s and then again at the end of the decade, and as economic instability of the period continued, the troubles of the S&Ls became increasingly apparent. Regulators, in a futile effort to stem the

Box 5.2 *(continued)*

problems, made matters worse by allowing a large number of insolvent S&Ls to remain in operation. But the failures came in droves.

The fundamental problem lay in the deregulation of the S&L industry and the firms' inability to handle the related instability. Yet, there was also outright fraud. In June, 1990, *The New York Times* reported: "L. William Seidman, who is in charge of the day-to-day management of the [S&L] cleanup, said that fraud had been found in 60 percent of the failed savings institutions and that in half of those, it had been the main element in the institution's demise. Phony appraisals, self-dealing, loans to family and associates, kickbacks and payoffs were rife."

In the most notorious case, Charles Keating, the chairman of Lincoln Savings and Loan, was sent to jail for securities fraud. Five U.S. senators (including John McCain, the 2008 Republican candidate for president) tried to derail regulators' attempt to close Keating's firm; the firm's failure had cost U.S. taxpayers $3 billion. The Keating Five, as they were called at the time, had received $1.3 million in political contributions from Keating. In total more than 1,000 senior S&L insiders were convicted of felonies during the S&L crisis, in sharp contrast to the zero arrests (as of mid-2010) in the financial crisis of recent years.

By 1987 the FSLIC fund was insolvent, and U.S. taxpayers picked up the tab for the FSLIC honoring its commitment to insured depositors of the failed S&Ls. By 1995 nearly half of the federally charted S&Ls open in 1986 had closed their doors.[2]

of industry assets are in banks with more then $10 billion in assets (measured in 2005 dollars), compared with 40 percent in 1985 . . . The top ten banks in terms of asset size are holding over 50 percent of industry assets, compared with about 25 percent in 1985.[3]

The financial deregulation that facilitated this concentration had expanded from the 1980s onward, in both ideology and practice, and it reached its symbolic high point (or low point, depending on one's perspective) with enactment of the Financial Services Modernization Act of 1999 (the Gramm-Leach-Bliley Act), which repealed much of the Glass-Steagall Act of 1933. While Glass-Steagall had required the separation of different kinds of financial institutions, Gramm-Leach-Bliley allowed their combination and thus made it possible for firms to operate as financial holding companies, including commercial banks, investment banks, and insurance companies, under one overarching enterprise. While the original sponsors of the bill (Phil Gramm of Texas, Jim Leach of Iowa, and Thomas J. Bliley, Jr., of Virginia) were Republicans, the bill obtained extensive support from congressional Democrats, was pushed by the Democratic administration, and signed into law by Democratic president Bill Clinton. A thoroughly bipartisan effort.

To a large degree, the passage of Gramm-Leach-Bliley and its repeal of Glass-Steagall were symbolic because consolidation of different parts of the financial industry was already underway. In particular, in 1998, Citibank had merged with Travelers Insurance (which had the investment firm Smith Barney among its subsidiaries) to form the Citigroup holding company. This combination would have violated existing law but was allowed under a temporary waiver process, based on the assumption that the law would soon be changed. The enactment of Gramm-Leach-Bliley—a process in which Citigroup was not a disinterested bystander—made the waiver, in effect, permanent and opened the financial conglomeration process to other firms as well. The new law symbolized, in its advocates' eyes, that the era of government regulation of financial services was at an end, that the "big government" controls implemented in the wake of the Great Depression were gone, and that in the new era The Market would drive financial activity.

The impact of Gramm-Leach-Bliley, however, was more than symbolic. In two ways it helped set the stage for the economic debacle that became apparent in 2007 and 2008. First, by allowing the conglomeration of different kinds of financial institutions, the law facilitated the spread of financial collapse; when problems developed with home mortgages the entire financial industry was brought to its knees. Second, with the conglomeration of firms in the industry, very large financial firms were transformed into huge financial firms. These huge firms were "too big to fail" in the sense that failure of any one of them would have far reaching—perhaps disastrous—negative impacts, not only in the financial sector but in the entire economy. Gramm-Leach-Bliley was probably not essential to the development of the crisis. Some very large commercial banks, banks that were probably already "too big to fail," existed before its enactment; also, substantial commercial banking was not part of the operations of some of the largest investment banks that got into trouble (e.g., Lehman Brothers). Nonetheless, this legislation helped set up the financial conditions that would generate disaster.

Gramm-Leach-Bliley was not the only important piece of legislation deregulating financial activity at the turn of millennium. Especially important was the Commodity Futures Modernization Act (CFMA) of 2000, which provided for the trading and valuation of financial derivatives with very limited government oversight. The act placed a whole area of finance outside the realm of regulation. Among the derivatives excluded from regulation by the CFMA were the energy derivatives that lay at the basis of the 2001 Enron scandal (in which Enron had overstated its earnings by accounting practices that manipulated the values of derivatives) and the now infamous credit default swaps that became so important in the financial collapse in 2008. As with Gramm-Leach-Bliley, the CMFA transformed ad hoc agreements into law. The arrangements allowed nonregulation of financial activity—in the CMFA case the trading of derivatives—which was integral to the crisis that followed a few years later. Also, like Gramm-Leach-Bliley, the CMFA represented a bipartisan effort. (Credit default swaps will be explained Chapter 6.)

The association between the process of deregulation and the gains that accrued to the financial industry is apparent in the figures on corporate profits (Figure 5.1). In the 1970s and 1980s, the financial sector had on average accounted for 20 percent of all corporate profits. In the 1990s, this figure rose to 30 percent and then jumped up to 35 percent in the 2000–2008 period (with a peak of 44 percent in 2002). Also, the financial sector's gains are reflected in the huge bonuses that were awarded to individuals in the industry and that have been the source of popular outrage in the wake of the financial implosion.[4]

Ideology, Policy, and Bubbles

The explicit legislative steps to deregulate financial activity were quite important, contributing a great deal to the industry's profit surge and, as we will discuss shortly, to the emergence of economic crisis. These explicit steps, moreover, were bound up with the increasing dominance of free-market ideology. This ideology provided the rationale for the legislation: things could be "left to the market," and all would be well. The role of ideology was also evident in providing the rationale for specific actions, such as the granting of the temporary waiver that allowed the consolidation of Citigroup (though here it is difficult to distinguish between the roles of ideology and the raw power of a huge firm).

Perhaps more important than deregulation (the elimination of existing regulations) was the failure to establish new regulations as new financial activities emerged, and the lax enforcement (or no enforcement at all) of regulations that did continued to exist.

Independent mortgage companies, hedge funds (see Box 6.1), and the trading of credit default swaps were never effectively regulated. In the realm of lax enforcement, there was the inaction of the Securities and Exchange Commission (SEC), failing to exercise its authority in overseeing a range of financial activity. Probably the most publicized lack of SEC enforcement

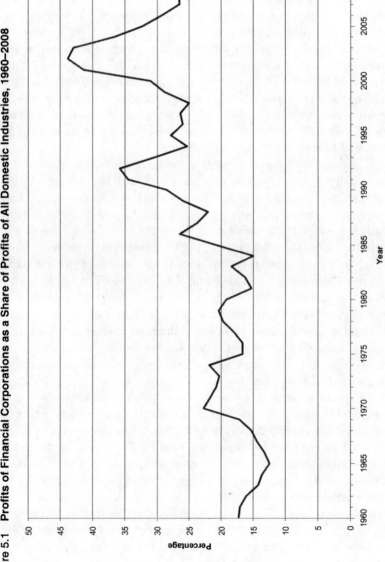

Figure 5.1   Profits of Financial Corporations as a Share of Profits of All Domestic Industries, 1960–2008

Source: Economic Report of the President 2010, Table B-91.

was its failure to heed warnings about the fraudulent activities of Bernard Madoff, who we now know was running the largest Ponzi scheme in history. (See Box 5.3 on Ponzi schemes and the housing bubble.) A more widespread impact, however, resulted from the regulatory authorities turning a blind eye to the fraudulent activity that took place with home mortgages as the housing bubble inflated during the early years of the new millennium. As we will see, this nonenforcement of regulations in housing was a crucial link in the emergence of the economic crisis. Ideology provided the framework, the rationale, for the regulators simply not doing their jobs, as well as for the narrowing of their jobs through deregulation. (The development of the housing bubble, however, should not be attributed simply to fraud and the lack of regulation that would have prevented that fraud. Also of importance, probably greater importance, was the widespread expectation—sometimes termed "irrational exuberance"—that housing prices would continue to go up and up. More on this in the next chapter.)

Ideology also provided a foundation for the actions of the Federal Reserve, which played a major role in creating the conditions for crisis. While control of Congress and the White House shifts between Republicans and Democrats, for more than thirty years the Federal Reserve has been well-controlled by Republican appointees. Alan Greenspan, appointed Chairman of the Fed by Ronald Reagan in 1987, continued in office through the Clinton administration and both Bush administrations, until retiring in 2006. Greenspan's successor, Benjamin Bernanke, was appointed by George W. Bush and reappointed in 2010 by Barack Obama. Greenspan, an acolyte of the novelist and free-market fanatic Ayn Rand, more than any other individual held sway over economic policy in the years leading up to the crisis. He was a thorough opponent of regulation—in finance and elsewhere in the economy—and maintained that economic policy should cede more and more ground to The Market.

Aside from his role as an advocate of deregulation, Greenspan's principal practical contribution to the emergence of crisis was in his handling of monetary policy. Both in the 1990s and 2000s, Greenspan's policies at the Fed contributed to speculative bubbles, the first time in the stock market (the dot-com bubble) and the second time in the housing market. In both periods, the Fed maintained a low interest rate policy, though more so in the latter period than in the former.

A ready availability of money (the relatively low interest rates) is almost always a strong spur to the rise of the stock market. Low interest rates allow purchasers of equity to do so with substantial leverage (i.e., by borrowing, using other people's money). In addition, low interest rates (the rate of return on bonds) tend to make bonds a less attractive investment than stocks. The

Box 5.3
What is a Ponzi Scheme? Was the Banks' Creation of the Housing Bubble a Ponzi Scheme?

As badly as the banks have operated, the housing bubble was not a Ponzi scheme. In some respects, however, it was even worse! A Ponzi scheme is based directly on fraud. The scheme's operators deceive the participants, telling them that their money is being used to make investments that have a high return. In fact, no such investments are made and the operators are simply paying high returns to the early participants with the funds put in by the later participants. To stay viable, a Ponzi scheme has to grow—and grow rapidly. When its growth slows, the early participants can no longer be paid high returns. At this point, the operators disappear with what's left of the participants' funds—unless the authorities step in and arrest them, which is what happened with Charles Ponzi in 1920 and Bernard Madoff in 2009.

Fraud certainly was important in the recent housing bubble. Mortgage companies and banks used deceit to get people to take on mortgages when there was no possibility that the borrowers would ever be able to repay the loans. Not only was this fraud, but this fraud depended on government authorities ignoring their regulatory responsibilities. However, the inflation of the housing bubble—like bubbles generally—did not depend on fraud. Most of the bubble's development was there for everyone to see. With the principal problems out in the open and with the authorities not only ignoring those problems but contributing to their development, one might say that the situation with the housing bubble was worse than a Ponzi scheme. Madoff bilked his marks out of $50 billion, but trillions were lost in the housing bubble.

Bubbles involve actual investments in real or financial assets—housing in the years since 2000, high tech stocks in the 1990s, and Dutch tulips in the seventeenth century. People invest believing that the price of the assets will continue to rise; and as long as people keep investing, the price does rise. While some early speculators can make out very well, this speculation will not last indefinitely. Once prices start to fall, panic sets in and the later investors lose.

So a bubble and a Ponzi scheme are different, but they have elements in common. Usually, however, the losers in a Ponzi scheme are simply the direct investors, the schemer's marks. A bubble like the housing bubble can wreak havoc on all of us.

stock market bubble of the 1990s, however, was given its major impetus not by low interest rates but by what came to be called an "irrational exuberance" over the potential of innovations arising from developments with information technology.

The term "irrational exuberance" obtained wide notice when it was used in a speech by Alan Greenspan on December 5, 1996.[5] Perhaps because they were worrying about the build up of the stock market bubble and hoping Greenspan would restrain that build up, many observers took Greenspan's use of this term to indicate that the Fed would act to restrain the expansion of stock prices. However, it soon became clear that the Fed was not going to rein in the stock market, and the upward spiral continued apace in 1997. Indeed, in retrospect, Greenspan's speech can be read as a signal that the Fed would not act to restrain the market. Certainly, the Fed's lack of action made this clear,

The Fed's encouragement of the 1990s stock market bubble lay not only in policy, but also in Greenspan's statements about the underlying real strength of the economy. Seeing the force of information technology as the foundation for that strength, and thus for the strength of the stock market, Greenspan apparently did not believe in the existence of a bubble. His views were most evident in a March 6, 2000, speech in which he praised the force of the new technology, explaining the "spectacular performance" of the economy during the 1990s as having its "source [in] the revolution in information technology."[6] Four days later the NASDAQ index peaked, and then began its fall; a year later it had lost two-thirds of its value. (The NASDAQ is the stock exchange with a high concentration of information technology and other "high-tech" firms.)

Greenspan's belief that the stock market bubble of the late 1990s was not a bubble but a surge based on the real performance of the economy was a reflection of his strongly held ideological faith in the operation of markets. His views, moreover, were given credence by the "efficient market hypothesis," which had become so widely accepted among economists. This hypothesis avowed that financial asset prices reflect all available information and that financial markets, in effect, operate rationally. Irrational exuberance was not possible within the framework of this theory or within Greenspan's ideological framework.

To a large extent, Greenspan's handling of monetary policy in the 2000s was similar to that of the 1990s, facilitating the emergence of a speculative bubble, denying the bubble's existence, and failing to take actions that might have averted the subsequent crash. The Federal Reserve policies of the 2000s are part of the immediate causes of the crisis, a story that we will take up shortly.

Here let us simply point out that the crisis that hit so hard in 2007 and 2008, however much it was a consequence of the way our economy is organized, had real people and real policies behind it. Alan Greenspan was one of those people, and the Fed's policies were major factors at the foundation of the crisis. Also, Robert Rubin, Secretary of the Treasury under Bill Clinton, and his successor Lawrence Summers, bear a large share of responsibility for the damaging deregulation policies, along with their Republican collaborators in the Congress, most notably Senator Phil Gramm. (Maintaining continuity with his Democratic and Republic predecessors, President Obama appointed Summers to the top economic position early on in his administration.) The presidents themselves—from Reagan through George W. Bush—were of course not idle bystanders in this process. And there have been the numerous nabobs of finance who carried out high-risk practices, which, when they failed, led to economic collapse with all its incumbent hardships for millions of people in the United States and elsewhere. These high-level figures in financial firms also used their money and influence to assure that their friends in Washington established the policies that were so immediately profitable for them and so ultimately damaging for nearly everyone else. The list could be extended, for there were few corporate executives or policy makers in either party since Reagan's presidency who challenged the ideas and practices that brought us to where we are today.

The Run-up to 2007–2008

When the U.S. economy emerged from the relatively mild recession following the bursting of the dot-com stock market bubble, there were no policy changes that altered the trend of previous decades. The infamous tax cuts during the presidency of George W. Bush, which significantly lowered tax rates for the very rich, reversed the policies of the early Clinton years. It was, however, the Clinton tax increases that were out of line with the trend. The Bush tax cuts were fully in line with the conservative ideology that had held sway since Reagan's ascendancy to the White House, and they clearly reflected the power of the very rich in bringing about economic policies that served to make them even richer. One more step down the road of rising inequality, Bush's tax policy helped set the stage for 2007–2008.

As with earlier tax cuts—for example, those put in effect by Reagan at the beginning of the 1980s—the tax cuts legislated in 2001 were rationalized as providing a spur to economic growth. Indeed, the title of the legislation was the Economic Growth and Tax Relief Reconciliation Act of 2001. However, consistent with the general record of trickle-down economics (or, to again use the sobriquet applied by Galbraith, "horse and sparrow" economics), the years following 2001 exhibited relatively anemic growth. The economy expanded at only 2.7 percent per year between 2001 and 2007, the slowest postrecession recovery on record. This slow economic growth was one more important factor contributing to the implosion of 2007–2008.

The catalyst of the implosion, as is well known, was the so-called subprime debacle and the associated collapse of the housing market. The housing bubble began to inflate in 1997, and housing prices (again, adjusted for inflation) rose by 85 percent (7.1 percent annually) in the period from 1997 to 2006. No other similar stretch of time in the years since 1890, the years for which we have data, experienced a rise this great[7] (see Figure 5.2). To anyone who cared to look and think, this escalation of housing prices was a classic speculative bubble, with buyers willing to pay higher and higher prices because they thought prices would rise still higher. Moreover, homebuyers were willing to take on increasing amounts of debt in order to finance their purchases, and financial institutions were willing to provide more and more loans.

Many of these loans were made to people who were in a poor position to repay the loans, and they were thus charged high interest rates. They were less than "prime" borrowers, and were referred to as "subprime borrowers." Therefore the loans made to these people were called "subprime loans." However, subprime loans—that is, loans with high interest rates—were issued to many other homebuyers, to people who were not in a poor position to repay. These were people who—given their incomes, the stability of their employment, and other factors normally considered in issuing loans—were qualified for standard (prime) mortgage rates, but who were issued loans at higher, subprime, rates. There is, then, an important distinction between "subprime borrowers" and "subprime loans," and many people who were not "subprime borrowers" ended up with "subprime loans."

Financial institutions were able to charge high rates to borrowers who were qualified for lower rates because the institutions had information and experience that the borrowers did not have. Most people take out mortgages to buy homes only a very few times in their lives, but financial institutions make mortgage loans every day. (This is what economists place under the rubric of "asymmetric information," and is one of the broad reasons why markets don't work as well as their advocates generally claim.) Thus the institutions have a great advantage over most borrowers, and, unless they are effectively regulated, can, and will, often use this advantage to issue mortgages at high rates. This is known as predatory lending. (Predatory lending not only led to excessively high interest rates for borrowers who were not subprime, but surely also led to rates for subprime borrowers that

Figure 5.2 Index of Housing Prices, Inflation Adjusted, 1890–2009 (1890 = 100)

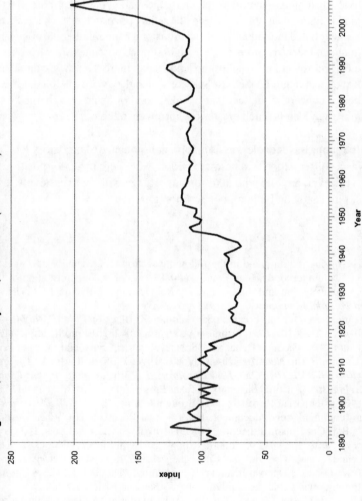

Source: Robert Shiller, *Irrational Exuberance.* Princeton: Princeton University Press, 2000 (Broadway Books 2001, 2d ed., 2005). The data are updated quarterly, and are available online at http://www.econ.yale.edu/~shiller/data.htm.

were even higher than might be justified by the actual risk in lending to them.) Economist and housing market analyst Jim Campen has described the situation in these terms:

> Whereas the prime mortgage market resembles the market for major appliances—where retailers sell refrigerators at the same advertised price to all customers—the subprime mortgage market has been more like the market for used automobiles. Here the selling price and other charges often are negotiated individually with each customer and salespeople often have financial incentives to obtain the highest price possible. Many (probably most) borrowers from subprime lenders pay more than they would have if they had obtained the best loan for which they were qualified. Of particular concern is the fact that the likelihood of being overcharged for a mortgage loan is much greater for borrowers of color.[8]

So the subprime debacle was as much a consequence of predatory lending as it was a consequence of lending to people who were in a poor position to repay. However, anyone who takes on a mortgage with an excessively high interest rate can soon be in a poor position to repay.

Notes

1. The discussion here and in the following section relies heavily on James T. Campen, "Neighborhoods, Banks, and Capital Flows: The Transformation of the U.S. Financial System and the Community Reinvestment Movement," *Review of Radical Political Economy* 30 (4), 1998, pp. 29–59.

2. Sources used for this box include: "William K. Black on Fraud," *Bill Moyers Journal,* April 23, 2010, www.pbs.org/moyers/journal/04232010/profile.html; David Rosenbaum, "The Savings Debacle: A Special Report: A Financial Disaster With Many Culprits," *The New York Times,* June 6, 1990; William K. Black, *The Best Way to Rob a Bank is Own One: How Corporate Executives and Politicians Looted the S&L Industry* (Austin: University of Texas Press, 2005); Alan Blinder and Mark Zandi, "How the Great Recession Was Brought to an End," July 27, 2010, www. economy.com/mark-zandi/documents/End-of-Great-Recession.pdf; Vince Valvano, "Bush's Bail-Out Bonanza: Fending Off Crisis in the Savings and Loan Industry," *Dollars & Sense,* May 1989; Timothy Curry and Lynn Shibut, "The Cost of the Savings and Loan Crisis: Truth and Consequences," *FDIC Banking Review,* January 1, 2000; and Federal Deposit Insurance Corporation, "The S&L Crisis: A Chrono-Bibliography," www.fdic.gov/bank/historical/s percent261/index.html.

3. Loretta J. Mester, "Some Thoughts on the Evolution of the Banking System and the Process of Financial Intermediation," *Economic Review,* First and Second Quarters, 2007, Federal Reserve Bank of Atlanta, www.frbatlanta.org/filelegacydocs/erq107_Mester.pdf.

4. The data on corporate profits are from the *Economic Report of the President 2010,* Table B-91.

5. "Remarks by Chairman Alan Greenspan at the Annual Dinner and Francis Boyer Lecture of The American Enterprise Institute for Public Policy Research," Washington, D.C., December 5, 1996, www.federalreserve.gov/boarddocs/speeches/1996/19961205.htm.

6. Remarks by Chairman Alan Greenspan, "The revolution in information technology," speech before the Boston College Conference on the New Economy, Boston, Massachusetts, March 6, 2000, www.federalreserve.gov/boarddocs/speeches/2000/20000306.htm.

7. The housing price data appear in Robert Shiller, *Irrational Exuberance* (Princeton: Princeton University Press, 2000; 2d edition, 2005), are updated quarterly, and are online at www.econ.yale.edu/~shiller/data.htm.

8. Jim Campen, "Changing Patterns XV, Mortgage Lending to Traditionally Underserved Borrowers and Neighborhoods in Boston, Greater Boston and Massachusetts," 2007, Mauricio Gastón Institute for Latino Community Development and Public Policy, University of Massachusetts/Boston, January 2009, p. 2, www.mcbc.info/files/CP15-Jan09 percent20Report-web.pdf.

6

Tracking the Evolution of the Crisis

The immediate causes of the general economic debacle that began to become apparent in 2007 run from:

- the buildup of debt, to
- the inflation of the housing bubble, to
- the collapse of the bubble, to
- the impact of the collapse on the financial industry, to
- the implosion of the overall economy

Yet behind this immediate causal chain lies the inequality-power-ideology nexus to which we have given so much emphasis. This nexus and its impacts are not the whole story; other factors are involved, including the international factors that we deal with in later chapters. However, the inequality-power-ideology nexus is the essential part of the story. So let us explain the connections, starting with the links between inequality and the buildup of debt. These connections are described in diagram of Figure 6.1, and we will refer to this diagram as we go along.

The Buildup of Debt

During the 1990s, mortgage debt outstanding on one- to four-family houses rose from 61 percent to 69 percent of after-tax personal income, and then ballooned to 107 percent by 2007. All mortgage debt—including debt on multifamily dwellings and commercial properties—rose from 89 percent to 91 percent of after-tax personal income in the 1990s, and then to 140 percent in 2007 (see Figure 6.2). Mortgage debt rose most rapidly in this period, but other forms of household debt also increased.[1] The overall burden of households debt payments in 2007 stood at 13.9 percent of disposable personal income, the highest level on record since 1980 (the first year for which data are available).[2] While the expansion of people's reliance on debt to pay for their housing and other purchases had been sliding upward for several decades, the escalation was especially rapid leading into the crisis.

Figure 6.1   **From the Inequality-Power-Ideology Nexus to the Implosion of the Economy**

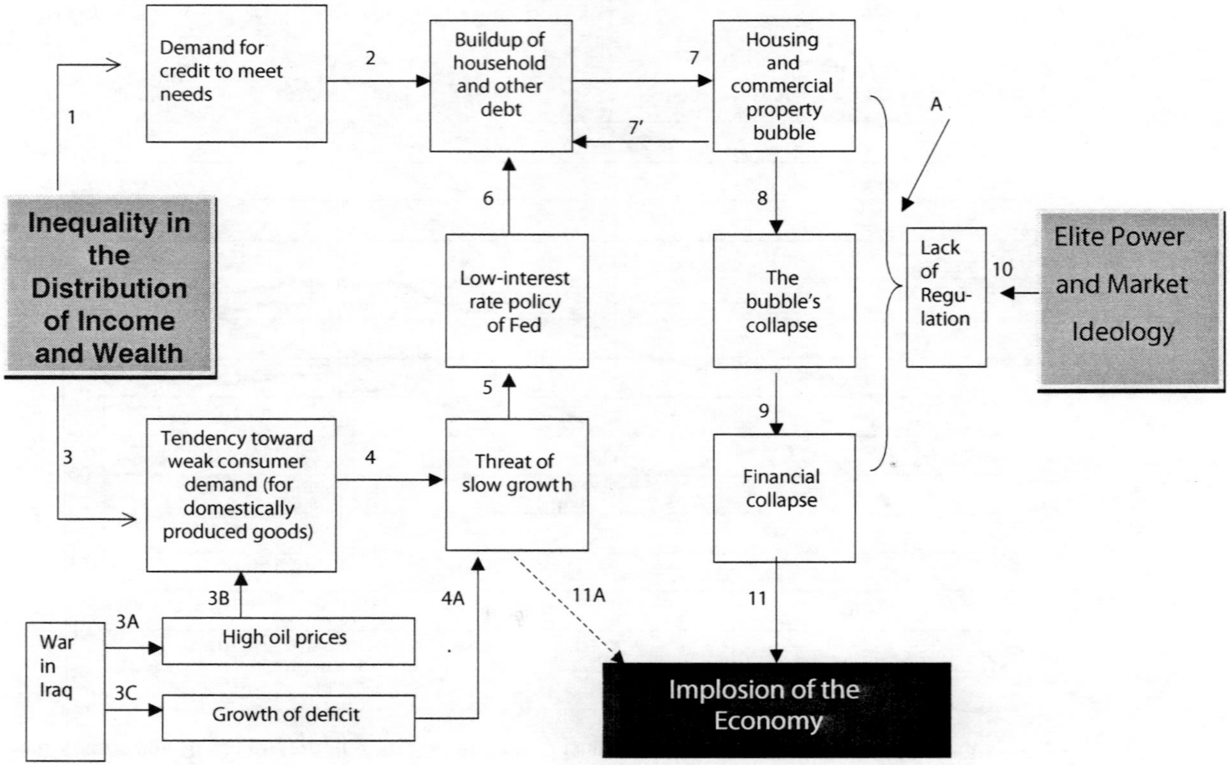

Figure 6.2 **Mortgage Debt Outstanding as Percentage of Disposable Personal Income, 1960–2008**

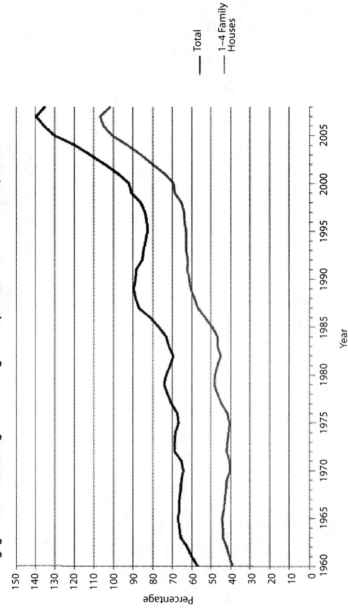

Sources: Economic Report of the President 2010, Tables B-31 and B-75.
Note: The difference between "Total" and "1–4 Family Houses" includes mortgages on multifamily properties (more than four units), commercial properties, and farm properties.

Inequality contributed to this escalation of debt in two ways, affecting both the demand for and supply of credit. On the demand side, rising inequality translated into a growing gap between the incomes of most members of society and their needs. Needs, beyond basic biological needs, are socially determined; that is, they depend upon the standards of society. Some of these socially determined needs are tangible. For example, as society's income rises more and more production of goods and services takes place away from the home. In recent decades, this has been evident in the rising role of women in the paid labor force. Thus there is a need for more transportation, more childcare services, and more food preparation services. Some socially determined needs are less tangible but no less real. For example, standards of transportation safety, communication (cell phones), living space, and entertainment all rise along with average income; with the rise of these standards come greater needs.

The incomes of most people, however, did not increase along with the rise in needs. For the 2000 to 2007 period, average weekly earnings in the private sector were 12 percent below their average for the 1970s (in inflation-adjusted terms). Family incomes were partly maintained by more people working in the paid labor force, as the labor force participation rate (the percentage of people age 16 and over in the labor force) rose form 60 percent in the early 1970s to 66 percent in the early 2000s.[3] Nonetheless, from 1980 to 2005 the share of income going to the bottom 60 percent of families fell from 35 percent to 29 percent.[4] While the spread between those at the top and most of the people was growing, the average income rose substantially—the average being pulled up by the income increases of those at the top; inflation-adjusted average disposable personal income more than doubled between 1970 and 2007.[5] Under these circumstances of the average income being pulled up by the gains of those at the top while most people experienced virtual stagnations of their incomes, more and more families relied more and more heavily on credit to meet their needs—everything from food to fuel, from education to entertainment, and especially housing (arrows 1 and 2 in Figure 6.1).

Inequality brought about an increase in the supply of credit by leading the Federal Reserve to lower interest rates, thus making credit more readily available. Inequality meant weak growth of income for the majority of the population, which in turn resulted in a tendency for the weak growth of aggregate consumer demand (arrow 3). Weak consumer demand would, in turn, tend to slow economic growth (arrow 4), as consumer demand is the main driver of economic expansion. The Fed's policy to increase the supply of credit by lowering interest rates (arrow 5) was intended to counter this tendency toward weak consumer demand and slow economic growth.

Consumer demand accounted for two-thirds of aggregate demand in the 1990s and slightly more in 2000–2007.[6] That is, in spite of the weak growth of income for the majority and the tendency of this weak growth to under-mine consumer demand, consumer spending grew apace. This was possible because of the buildup of debt brought about by the combination of people's demand for credit to meet their needs and the policies of the Fed to increase the supply of credit. (In addition, consumption could grow more rapidly than incomes as peoples saved a smaller portion of their incomes.)

The Fed's efforts to bolster consumer demand by making credit readily available and thus to maintain at least a modicum of economic growth were especially evident in the early 2000s. During the 1990s, the federal funds interest rate averaged 5.1 percent, but fell to an average of 3.4 percent in the 2000 to 2007 period—and averaged only 1.4 percent in the 2002 to 2004 period.[7] (The federal funds interest rate is the rate that banks charge one another for overnight loans and is a rate directly affected by the Fed-eral Reserve.) It is worth emphasizing that the interest rate on adjustable rate mortgages (ARMs) tends to be based on short-term interest rates (e.g., 6-month or 1-year U.S. Treasury bonds). Thus, in keeping short-term inter-est rates low, the Fed had a direct impact on mortgage rates for ARMs, and it was the issuance of these types of mortgages that greatly increased in the years of the housing bubble's inflation. (In addition, the large inflow of funds to the United States from abroad contributed to the low interest rates. This is an issue we will examine in Chapter 8.)

This loose monetary policy pursued by the Fed was partly a response to the tendency toward weak consumer demand created by income inequality, but it was also a response to the impact of the Iraq War on aggregate de-mand. The U.S. invasion of Iraq reduced the world supply of oil by cutting off Iraqi production and, by creating uncertainty surrounding the whole Middle East, threatened future supplies. Thus the invasion was the major factor leading to a 115 percent increase in the inflation-adjusted price of oil between 2003 and 2007 (arrow 3A). This higher price of oil meant that in 2007 U.S. consumers had about $270 billion less to spend on other items, weakening consumer demand for domestically produced goods (arrow 3B) and thereby threatening to undermine domestic production.[8] The U.S. invasion of Iraq, by its effect on the government's need for credit, played a further role in bringing about the Fed's loose monetary policy. The war (along with the Bush's tax cuts) significantly contributed to the reemergence of the government's budget deficit (arrow 3C). By maintaining low interest rates, the Fed was following the classic monetary policy of "accommodation," increasing the money supply to meet the government's growing need for credit. Otherwise, the heavy government borrowing to finance the (partly) war-created deficit could have pushed up interest rates, generating a threat to economic growth (arrow 4A).

With a low price for credit—low interest rates—people and businesses responded by taking on more credit, especially for the purposes of purchasing homes and commercial property (arrow 6). The result was the very large and rapid buildup of debt. The increasing reliance of U.S. consumers on credit has often been presented as a moral weakness, as an infatuation with consumerism, and as a failure to look beyond the present. Whatever moral judgments one may make, however, the expansion of the credit economy has been a response to real economic forces—inequality and consequent government policies, in particular.

Businesses, too, had experienced a long-term increase in reliance on debt to finance their operations, and this reliance rose substantially in the early 2000s. In 1980, total debt of nonfinancial businesses was 53 percent as large as GDP, and the figure had risen to 58 percent in 1997. Then, over the decade leading to the crisis, business debt shot up: in 2007 it was 75 percent as large as GDP.[9] The escalation of business debt indicates the high degree to which the nonfinancial sector of the economy was dependent on credit, making it especially vulnerable to the problems that arose in the financial sector and helps to explain why the financial collapse led so quickly and thoroughly to the implosion of the economy (arrow 11). Also, the dependence of the nonfinancial sector on credit reflected the shift in power and profits toward the financial sector.

It was the buildup of household debt, however, that was intimately bound up with the development of the housing bubble (arrows 7 and 7'). Indeed, to a large degree the buildup of household debt *was* the housing bubble, as households took on large amounts of debt to buy homes. Part of the reason that people were willing to pay high prices for homes was that once the housing bubble began to inflate they expected that the value of their homes would continue to rise. This assumption involved the same sort of "irrational exuberance" that had driven the stock market bubble ten years earlier. As with the stock market bubble, government authorities—especially Alan Greenspan and his successor Benjamin Bernanke—denied that the housing bubble was a bubble. While the bubble's inflation continued, many people did do very well buying and selling houses. Even excessive mortgage payments appeared not to be a problem when prices were rising because the homeowners could take out new loans on the higher value of their homes, thus obtaining the cash to meet the excessive mortgage payments. It was a practice that worked as long—or only as long—as the bubble kept inflating. The expectations of ever-rising prices may have been "irrational," but they were nonetheless a powerful force.

Yet, while expectations were important, a large factor affecting people's willingness to pay higher and higher prices for homes was, as we have noted, a result of the low price of credit. For most homebuyers, monthly payments are of greater concern than the price of the house. For any given house price, lower interest rates mean lower monthly payments. Thus, with a lower interest rate, homebuyers are willing to buy higher priced homes. For example, the monthly payments on a thirty-year $250,000 mortgage at 5 percent are exactly the same as the monthly payments on a thirty-year $201,720 mortgage at 7 percent. Presumably, then, buyers would be willing to pay almost $50,000 more for a house at the lower rate than at the higher rate. But, while the monthly payments would be the same, the amount of debt would be greater.

Furthermore, the housing bubble was the basis for an additional expansion of debt, as many home owners took out home equity loans to use the value of their houses as the basis for other spending—everything from college tuitions to vacation expenses. The pushing of these loans by lenders is illustrated by the slogan Citibank used in its home equity loan ad campaign: "Live Richly." This was supplemented in one ad by: "There's got to be at least $25,000 hidden in your house. We can help you find it."[10] In 1991, outstanding home equity loans amounted to $222 billion, rose to $407 billion in 2000, and then skyrocketed along with the housing bubble to over $1 trillion by 2006. Thus, from an amount that was 5 percent as large as disposable personal income in 1991 and 5.5 percent in 2000, home equity loans outstanding had become 10 percent as large as disposable personal income by 2006.[11]

The Inflation and Collapse of the Housing Bubble

The housing bubble, however, did not inflate simply as a result of low interest rates and a speculative craze (i.e., the belief that prices would go on rising indefinitely). Deregulation and lack of regulation, which had been the product of the elite power and market ideology evolving over previous decades (arrow 10), provided the context (bracket A in Figure 6.1) in which the low rates and the speculation had their damaging impact.

Subprime lending is often seen as the central factor in the inflation and the collapse of the housing bubble. Yet, while subprime lending was important, its role is best understood as one part of a web of factors. Its role, taken by itself, was relatively straightforward. By making loans to people who would not ordinarily qualify for prime loans, financial institutions were pushing up the demand for housing; they were thus pushing up the price of housing (i.e., blowing up the bubble). As noted in Chapter 5, however, subprime lending was not confined to the loans made to people who would not ordinarily qualify for prime loans (the subprime borrowers). It also included mortgages issued to well-qualified borrowers who were taken advantage of by mortgage issuers—and we can assume that many of the loans to subprime borrowers were also at excessively inflated rates.

The subprime borrowers were, by definition, people who would be less likely to be able to meet the payments on their loans, and therefore the financial institutions charged them high interest rates. The high interest rates then made it more difficult for the borrowers to meet their payments. As it came to pass, many subprime borrowers were not able to make the payments on their loans, and the resulting defaults on subprime mortgages started the deflation of the bubble. In 2006, the annual number of foreclosures began to move upward, increasing to about 940,000 from the 2005 level of about 810,000. In 2007 there were over 1.5 million foreclosures, and the number kept on climbing—2.3 million in 2008 and 2.8 million in 2009.[12]

In a sense, high interest rates charged to subprime borrowers were self-justifying. Because the financial institutions charged high interest rates, the borrowers were less likely to make their payments. Because they were less likely to make their payments, the institutions charged higher interest rates to cover their losses. Moreover, the prime borrowers who were issued subprime loans (i.e., loans with higher-than-prime interest rates) were caught in a similar sort of conundrum. They had loans which, because of the higher-than-justified interest rates, they would likely not be able to service. If not set up for failure, they were set up to make their failure more likely.

Yet it was more than high interest rates that led to the problems with the subprime mortgage market. Loans were often structured in ways that resulted in initial payments that were relatively low, only to be followed by sharp increases in payments after the first few years. These were adjustable rate mortgages (ARMs) with low "teaser rates" at the outset. Thus borrowers, focusing on and basing their judgments on the initial payments, believed they could make the payments. When the increases came, however, they could not. So the problem was more than the existence of subprime loans, but also the terms on which these loans were issued—and here the lack of regulatory oversight was important (to which we will return shortly).

The adjustable rate mortgages with initial "teaser rates" were simply one example of the problematic loan practices that were followed in the lead-up to the housing crisis—and they were practices that took place well beyond the subprime market. Other such practices included so-called NINA loans, "no income no asset" loans made to people who provided no verification of their financial status. One step beyond the NINA loans were the NINJA loans—"no income no job [and no] assets." With many of the loans in these categories, very small or no down payments were required. Within the mortgage industry, this whole set of loans was dubbed "liar loans" because they were based on borrowers and lenders lying about borrowers' ability to repay—indeed, the lenders often encouraged such lying. One example is provided by a December 28, 2008, *The New York Times* story on the failed Washington Mutual Bank:

> As a supervisor at a Washington Mutual mortgage processing center, John D. Parsons was accustomed to seeing baby sitters claiming salaries worthy of college presidents, and schoolteachers with incomes rivaling stockbrokers'. He rarely questioned them. A real estate frenzy was under way and WaMu, as his bank was known, was all about saying yes.
>
> Yet even by WaMu's relaxed standards, one mortgage four years ago raised eyebrows. The borrower was claiming a six-figure income and an unusual profession: mariachi singer.
>
> Mr. Parsons could not verify the singer's income, so he had him photographed in front of his home dressed in his mariachi outfit. The photo went into a WaMu file. Approved.[13]

Of course there are only limited data on these fraudulent liar loans. However, the data that do exist provide a good picture of the overall phenomenon of "alternative" and subprime mortgages—the categories of loans that would catalyze the crisis and which included the fraudulent loans. In 2004, $385 billion of alternative mortgages were issued, constituting 12.5 percent of all mortgages. Then both the amount and share in the mortgage market of the alternative mortgages shot upward: $824 billion in 2005, 26.4 percent of mortgages; $958 billion and 32.1 percent in 2006; $958 billion and 28.8 percent in 2007. Subprime mortgages that were packaged as mortgage-backed securities had been only 1.4 percent of all mortgages in 1994 and were still only 5 percent of the total as late as 2003—but then rose to 13.7 percent of the total in 2004, to 16.3 percent in 2005, and 16.2 percent in 2006. In 2009, with the crisis well developed, alternative mortgages had fallen to 0.5 percent of all mortgages and subprime mortgages to 0.05 percent. (The "alternative" category includes interest-only mortgages, option adjustable rate mortgages, forty-year balloon mortgages, and other alternative mortgages made at near subprime conditions. It is not clear from the data the extent to which the "alternative" category and the subprime category overlap.)[14]

Why Make Unsafe Loans?

With the rapid expansion of subprime and alternative mortgages, it was clear that many of these loans would not be repaid and that widespread foreclosures would occur sooner or later. But if it was so clear that these loans would fail, why were the financial institutions making these unsafe loans? And how did such a wide spectrum of financial institutions get involved, taking on excessive risk (driving too fast) that would ultimately affect the whole economy—and wreak such devastation on the rest of us?

One answer to these questions—an incorrect answer—places the origin of the mess in the Community Reinvestment Act (CRA), which was originally established in 1977 with the goal of encouraging financial institutions to provide credit in the communities where they operated, including low-income communities. Political conservatives have sometimes argued that the CRA pressured banks to make unsafe loans to low-income groups—African Americans and Hispanics, in particular; this pressure, they have then claimed, generated an excessive amount of loans that would fail. They therefore have placed blame for the crisis on the political liberals who championed the CRA (and on the "irresponsible" minority borrowers). However, the CRA specifies that credit should be provided in a manner "consistent with safe and sound operations . . . the law [does not] require institutions to make high-risk loans that jeopardize their safety."[15] In any case, the CRA only applies to federally regulated banks and thrift institutions where deposits are insured by the FDIC. Mortgage companies and mortgage brokers are not federally regulated and operate outside the purview of the CRA.

Most important, the Federal Reserve responded to the claim that the CRA helped to generate the subprime crisis by examining the data. The Fed found that "only 6 percent of all higher-priced loans [i.e., subprime loans] were extended by CRA-covered lenders to lower-income borrowers or neighborhoods in their CRA assessment areas, the local geographies that are the primary focus for CRA evaluation purposes." Further, the studies found that "CRA-related loans appear to perform comparably to other types of subprime loans." The Fed's studies have thoroughly discredited the political conservatives' blame-the-CRA claim—a claim that lacked evidence in the first place and was hardly plausible in an era when conservatives, not liberals and certainly not poor people, controlled the federal government.[16]

So why, then, did financial institutions make unsafe loans that they must have known would often fail? A large part of the answer lies in the fact that the institutions were not being regulated. In some cases, the institutions were not covered by existing regulations; mortgage companies, for example, had great leeway in the ways that they structured their loans. In other cases, where the institutions were covered by existing regulations—the example of Washington Mutual mentioned earlier—the regulators failed to do their job. This failure was in large part a reflection of the ideology of deregulation, an ideology that said that the market would take care of itself. If the market took care of itself, then lenders would not make unsafe loans, at least not generally, and there was thus no need for regulators to act.

Limits on regulation, however, were not simply left to the force of ideology. In early 2004, the Bush administration, through action by the Office of the Comptroller of the Currency (OCC), officially asserted the authority of the federal government in overseeing the mortgage industry, protecting the industry from most state laws regulating mortgage credit, including state antipredatory lending laws. The OCC's action, which was widely opposed by state attorneys general, effectively replaced the more stringent state regulations with weaker (and poorly enforced) federal regulations. There was some precedent for the OCC's assertion of federal authority. In 1996, during the Clinton administration, the Office of Thrift Supervision (OTS) had similarly preempted federally chartered savings and loan institutions from numerous state mortgage regulation laws. Yet the 2004 OCC action went much further and, coming in the midst of the housing bubble's inflation and during the expansion of subprime lending, appears to have had substantial consequences. While ideology may have provided a rationale, the power of the industry itself was the foundation for ensuring that the OCC (and the OTS) would put more energy into protecting the banks than in protecting the consumers.[17]

Nonetheless, whether or not a particular financial institution is covered by regulation, any commercial transaction is legally proscribed if it is fraudulent. Undoubtedly, many of the mortgage transactions in the period of the developing housing bubble were fraudulent. There is no law against "liar loans" per se, but they involved fraud (lies) and are therefore illegal whether or not the institution making the loan falls under existing banking regulations. The general lack of prosecution of these frauds is one more manifestation of the lack of government oversight of market activity, one more manifestation of the application of elite power and market ideology. William Black, a former federal regulator, in office during the S&L scandal of the 1980s, sees this mortgage fraud as having been an "epidemic." Interviewed on *Bill Moyers Journal* on April 3, 2009, Black offered the following explanation of the failure of the government to prosecute this fraud:

> The FBI publicly warned, in September 2004, that there was an epidemic of mortgage fraud, that if it was allowed to continue it would produce a crisis at least as large as the Savings and Loan debacle. And that they were going to make sure that they didn't let that happen. So what goes wrong? After 9/11, the attacks, the Justice Department transfers 500 white-collar specialists in the FBI to national terrorism. Well, we can all understand that. But then, the Bush administration refused to replace the

missing 500 agents. So even today, again, as you say, this crisis is 1,000 times worse, perhaps, certainly 100 times worse, than the Savings and Loan crisis. There are one-fifth as many FBI agents as worked the Savings and Loan crisis.

The government's working together with the industry to destroy regulation. Well, we now know what happens when you destroy regulation. You get the biggest financial calamity of anybody under the age of 80.[18]

Still, the lack of regulation and the lack of prosecution for fraud only explain why the financial institutions *could* make these unsafe loans. But why *would* they make these loans? Why was it in their interest to do so? Why would anyone make a loan that they could be pretty sure would not be repaid?

Here the issue of securitization, the bundling of mortgages into mortgage-backed securities (MBSs), comes into play. As pointed out earlier, MBSs were not a new innovation of the 2000s, but had been developed decades earlier by the government-sponsored enterprises and then by private financial institutions. They were seen as relatively safe investments because each MBS embodied diversification. In buying an MBS or shares in an MBS, an investor was buying a stream of payments from a large number of homeowners. If some homeowners failed to meet their payments, the investor would be insulated from loss because the vast majority of other homeowners would still be making their payments. Therefore the MBSs were seen as a safe investment—as long as there were no general, systemic problems in the housing market.

Even with the general, systemic problems that began to emerge in 2006 and 2007, the MBSs did protect the *makers of the mortgage loans* from the risk created by their own reckless (often fraudulent) loan making. But the MBSs did not protect the *holders of the MBSs* containing the mortgage loans. The mortgage makers who were issuing the subprime and other bad mortgages "unloaded" those mortgages in MBSs and therefore were not at risk when the borrowers failed to make their payments. This transfer of risk from the makers of the loans to the holders of the loans (through the MBSs) explains why financial institutions were so willing to make loans when they knew the borrowers would, in all likelihood, default on those loans. The makers of the mortgages were able to collect fees for issuing the loans and then avoid the risk associated with their actions.

The risks involved in the mortgages were spread further by the creation of Collateralized Debt Obligations (CDOs). Here things get a bit complicated. To create MBSs, mortgage lenders (e.g., mortgage companies or commercial banks) place mortgages into a legal entity, a trust, and the trust then issues the MBSs, backed by the mortgages it holds. The MBSs themselves can be placed in trusts, and these trusts can then issue securities, CDOs, backed by the MBSs. So CDOs are securities backed by MBSs backed by mortgages. There are still further complications. First, both MBSs and CDOs can be set up in ways that different purchasers accept different degrees of risk and receive different claims on the income generated by the underlying securities. These different shares of risks and claims embodied in a particular MBS or CDO are called "tranches." (Tranche is simply a French word meaning portion, slice, or section.) Second, a second level of CDOs can be created, issued by a trust holding CDOs; that is, just as a CDO is backed by an MBS, a second-level CDO is backed by a CDO that is backed by an MBS. Then there are "synthetic CDOs," the value of which is not directly backed by other CDOs (or MBSs) but is simply based on the movement in value of other CDOs. The rationalization offered by advocates of the development of these complex securities has been that they reduce risk through diversification. Experience in the crisis that appeared in 2007 and 2008, however, demonstrated that CDOs and MBSs served to spread risk in a way that negatively affected the whole financial system—and then the whole economy. (It is of some interest that the first CDO was issued in 1987 through the financial firm Drexel Burnham Lambert. Three years later, Drexel Burnham Lambert was bankrupt as a result of its engagement with illegal activities in the junk bond market.)

As we have said, many of the bad mortgages that lay behind the MBSs and CDOs undoubtedly involved fraud, and this fraud was possible because, as William Black said, the government was "working together with the industry to destroy regulation." The issue, however, was not simply fraud in the formal, legal sense. In making loans financial institutions are not simply proscribed from committing legal fraud; they are also required by regulations to follow prudent practices. The regulators were simply not doing their jobs. While the crisis appeared under George W. Bush's administration and therefore it was on the Republicans' watch that the regulation failure became apparent, the foundation for this failure had been laid over the preceding decades, and Democrats as well as Republicans were thoroughly involved. (Perhaps had a Democratic administration been in office after 2000, things would have worked out differently. Certainly the Bush administration exacerbated problems by undercutting regulation and by its almost fanatical advocacy of the leave-it-to-the-market ideology. Yet the foundation for trouble was well in place before 2001, and it is most probable that some sorts of difficulties, likely severe difficulties, would have emerged in any event.)

The question remains: Why were the holders of the CDOs (and, for that matter, MBSs) willing to hold them? After all, a substantial number of the CDOs were held by large financial firms, most of the very largest financial firms, where decision makers supposedly know about and understand risk. The large firms first entered the process as underwriters, taking the CDOs from the original makers of the mortgages and then handling the selling of them on financial markets—or holding the CDOs themselves. Then they further traded in these derivatives, speculating on the variations in their value (just as they similarly trade in alls sorts of financial instruments). Even while the decision makers in the large financial firms were probably aware that the mortgage-backed CDOs were very risky, they were willing to hold them and trade them because they were focused on the short-term profits that could thus be obtained.

Which begs the question: why focus on short-term profits? The answer lies in the competition in the financial industry and in the way that financial firms, when they are not adequately regulated, can expand their operations. The focus on the short term is also a result of the way salaries and bonuses are determined for high-level decision makers and traders.

As the housing bubble inflated, financial firms were making strong returns on CDOs (and on related derivatives, about which more shortly). If one firm failed to take part in these risky operations, they were in jeopardy of losing their wealthy clients to other firms that did take part in the blowing up the bubble. John Cassidy, a columnist for *The New Yorker* magazine, effectively set out the situation.

> If Merrill Lynch sets up a hedge fund to invest in collateralized debt obligations, or some other shiny new kind of security, Morgan Stanley will feel obliged to launch a similar fund to keep its wealthy clients from defecting. A hedge fund that eschews an overinflated sector can lag behind its rivals, and lose its clients. So you can go bust by avoiding a bubble . . . [T]here's no good way out of this dilemma. Attempts to act responsibly and achieve a cooperative solution cannot be sustained, because they leave you vulnerable to exploitation by others. If Citigroup had sat out the credit boom while its rivals made huge profits, [its CEO] would probably have been out of a job. . . . The same goes for individual traders at Wall Street firms. If a trader has one bad quarter, perhaps because he refused to participate in a bubble, the result can be career-threatening.[19] [For the definition of a hedge fund, see Box 6.1.]

Any firm, financial or nonfinancial, must respond to the actions of its competitors. Because they can create credit, however, financial firms are in a special position with regard to their ability to extend their operations. On the basis of a limited amount of capital, they can extend more and more credit—for example, taking on more and more CDOs. In traditional banking operations, the regulatory authorities both limit the extent to which firms can create credit on a given amount of capital and require that the extension of credit be undertaken with due prudence. Derivative markets, however, have been largely unregulated, greatly reducing, if not entirely removing, the limits on the firms' creation of credit—that is, the limits on their purchases of CDOs and other derivatives. Ultimately, of course, the financial institutions were limited by the confidence that investors had in their operations, but confidence would be maintained as long as the bubble was inflating.

And then there were (and still are) the incentives built into the way salaries and bonuses have been awarded to the decision makers in financial firms—the high-level executives and the traders who buy and sell derivatives. Regarding this system, we can do no better than to quote at length from a July 2009 article in the *Cambridge Journal of Economics* by the economist James Crotty:

> The current financial system is riddled with perverse incentives that induce key personnel in virtually all important financial institutions— including commercial and investment banks, hedge and private equity funds, insurance companies and mutual and pension funds—to take excessive risk when financial markets are buoyant. For example, the growth of mortgage securitisation generated fee income—to banks and mortgage brokers who sold the loans, investment bankers who packaged the loans into securities, banks and specialist institutions who serviced the securities and ratings agencies who gave them their seal of approval. Since fees do not have to be returned if the securities later suffer large losses, everyone involved had strong incentives to maximise the flow of loans through the system whether or not they were sound. Total fees from home sales and mortgage securitization from 2003 to 2008 have been estimated at $2 trillion. . . .
>
> Top investment bank traders and executives receive giant bonuses in years in which risk taking generates high revenue and profits. Of course, profits and bonuses are maximised in the boom by maximising leverage, which in turn maximises risk. In 2006, Goldman Sachs' bonus pool totaled $16 billion—an average bonus of $650,000 very unequally distributed across Goldman's 25,000 employees. Wall Street's top traders received bonuses of up to $50 million that year. In spite of the investment bank disasters of the second half of 2007, which saw Wall Street investment banks lose over $11 billion, the average bonus fell only 4.7 percent. In 2008 losses skyrocketed causing the five largest independent investment banks to lose their independence: two failed, one was taken over by a conglomerate, and two became bank holding companies to qualify them

Box 6.1

What Is a Hedge Fund?

A hedge fund is a type of mutual fund. In all mutual funds, the money of multiple investors is pooled and invested according to the decisions of the funds' managers. Regular mutual funds are subject to various government regulations, as are some other financial institutions, such as commercial banks. The rationale for these regulations is that they protect the individual investors.

Hedge funds, however, avoid most regulations by limiting participation to a small number of "qualified" individuals and institutions (e.g., pension funds or college endowment funds) with large sums of money. To be "qualified," an investor must have a net worth of at least $5 million, excluding her or his home. Because they have large sums of money, these wealthy investors supposedly do not need the protection that regulation is assumed to provide.

Largely unregulated, hedge funds can engage in activities that would be off limits to regular mutual funds. In particular, they can undertake more risky investments, which sometimes means that they can obtain very high returns associated with risky investments. They can also operate with a good deal of secrecy, exempt from the reporting requirements of regular mutual funds.

The term "hedge" in finance means off-setting the risk of one investment by undertaking another investment. For example, if a farmer invests to grow corn, he may make an agreement to sell that corn at harvest time for a fixed price. He thus "hedges" and protects himself from the risk that the price will fall. Hedges can be accomplished in financial markets in various ways, including the use of derivatives, insurance policies, and complex off-setting investments. Hedge funds got their name from this system of handling risk, but a central role for hedging is not essential to their activities.

What is central to their activities is the way they calculate their fees. As is the case with other investment funds, hedge funds charge a fee to the individuals and institutions that provide the funds with money. But hedge funds have been able to charge relatively high fees, including performance fees on top of the basic management fees. The basic fees run 1.5 percent to 2 percent of the total investment, and the performance fees typically run 20 percent of positive returns—sometimes higher. In some cases, management fees run to 5 percent combined with performance fees of over 40 percent. Furthermore, while hedge fund managers get their hefty performance fees when their funds achieve positive returns, they do not lose anything when their funds have negative returns. In effect, they are saying to their investors: If I perform well, we both win; but if I perform poorly, you lose. So it is not difficult to see why the managers of hedge funds do so well.

Box 6.1 *(continued)*

It is difficult, however, to see why so many investors put their money into hedge funds. Part of the explanation lies in the fact that rich individuals are often not smart investors, and they are drawn in by the popular image, the billions made by some funds, and the aura of success surrounding the stories of hedge fund managers who take home billions. Also, the institutional investors in hedge funds—local pension funds or college endowment funds, for example—are not especially "smart." It may also be that investors with large sums of money are willing to put at least a portion of their money into hedge funds, looking for the higher returns that the funds do sometimes obtain.

However, whatever returns are obtained "sometimes," overall hedge funds do not do significantly better than other types of investment funds. While the secrecy of hedge funds makes it difficult to determine their over-all returns, one 2006 study concludes: "overall performance of hedge funds . . . is about the same as that of U.S. equities [as measured by the Standard and Poor's Index of 500 equities] . . . [H]edge funds underperformed the stock market . . . during the six year, 'bull market' run-up to 1999, while on average they outperformed the stock market during the six year 'bear market' (or lull period) through 2005." According to another report, in the period from January 2007 to May of 2008, hedge funds returned on average 3.1 percent and were out-performed by corporate bonds issued by firms in high-income countries. One might conclude that hedge funds are an undistinguished group of investments.

Yet, because of the heads-I-win-tails-you-lose character of the fees that hedge funds charge, hedge fund managers are a distinguished group. In 2009, the top 25 hedge fund managers received payments totaling $25.3 billion, with the highest paid receiving a record $4 billion and the manager at the bottom of the group obtaining "only" $350 million. It is, we may assume, the stories of these individuals that generate the aura of success surrounding hedge funds.

What's more, these hedge fund managers pay minimal federal income taxes because they are allowed to classify their payments as capital gains rather than as salaries, and thereby they pay a low tax rate on their incomes—typically only 15 percent, compared to the top income tax rate of 35 percent. There is no good reason for this favorable treatment of hedge fund managers' incomes—other than the apparent power they are able to wield. The result is that the rest of us either pay more in taxes or get by with fewer public services.[20]

for bailout money. Yet Wall Street bonuses were over $18 billion—about what they were in the boom year of 2004 . . . Bonuses at Goldman are expected to average $570,000 in 2009 in the midst of the crisis. . . .

About 700 employees of Merrill Lynch received bonuses in excess of $1 million in 2008 from a total bonus pool of $3.6 billion, in spite of the fact that the firm lost $27 billion. The top four recipients alone received a total of $121 million while the top 14 got $249 million . . . Losses reported by Merrill totaled $35.8 billion in 2007 and 2008, enough to wipe out 11 years of earnings previously reported by the company. Yet for the 11-year period from 1997 to 2008, Merrill's board gave its chief executives alone more than $240 million in performance-based compensation. . . .

One of the most egregious examples of perverse incentives can be found in insurance giant AIG's Financial Products unit. This division, which gambled on credit default swaps (CDSs), contributed substantially to AIG's rising profits in the boom. In 2008 the unit lost $40.5 billion. Though the US government owns 80 percent of AIG's shares and invested $180 billion in the corporation, AIG nevertheless paid the 377 members of the division a total of $220 million in bonuses for 2008, an average of over $500,000 per employee. Seven employees received more than $3 million each. . . .

These examples show that it is rational for top financial firm operatives to take excessive risk in the bubble even if they understand that their decisions are likely to cause a crash in the intermediate future. Since they do not have to return their bubble-year bonuses when the inevitable crisis occurs and since they continue to receive substantial bonuses even in the crisis, they have a powerful incentive to pursue high-risk, high-leverage strategies.[21]

There was, in addition, the role of the credit rating agencies, private firms that examine the risk involved in financial instruments and rate the instruments on various scales. For example, Moody's, one of the "big three" rating firms, designates a rating of Aaa for "obligations [debts] . . . judged to be of the highest quality, with minimal credit risk." Moody's uses several levels of ratings, going down to obligations with a C rating, "the lowest rated class of bonds . . . typically in default, with little prospect for recovery of principal or interest." Bonds rated Ba1 or lower by Moody's are often referred to as "junk" bonds, with "questionable" or worse "credit quality."[22] Eighty-five percent of the credit rating market is in the hands of three firms, Moody's, Standard and Poor's, and Fitch.[23] Throughout the early 2000s, all three were giving high ratings to mortgage-based CDOs, indicating that they were low-risk investments.

As it turned out, of course, the rating agencies were wrong. When the housing market imploded, CDOs that had been given high ratings were revealed to be "junk." The problem was not only that the rating agencies were wrong; nor was it only that all of "the big three" were systematically wrong. As bad as the impact of their mis-ratings was, the problem lay deeper. The rating agencies are paid by the underwriters of the debts, the banks and others financial firms that manage the issuing of debts (CDOs and various other forms of debt). This arrangement is similar to a food critic being paid by the restaurant whose food is under review; paying for the review, the restaurant expects a good rating, and the critic knows that a bad rating will mean no future contracts with the restaurant. So it was with the rating agencies. They were (and continue to be, though see the discussion of new regulatory legislation in Chapter 9) involved in an inherent conflict of interest. On the one hand, they presented their ratings as objective and independent. On the other hand, they were being paid by the underwriters to provide high ratings. The need to provide high ratings trumped objectivity and independence.

The excessively high ratings given to mortgage-based CDOs contributed to excessive investment in these financial instruments, and thus exacerbated the financial debacle that appeared in 2007–2008. Indeed, it would be reasonable to see excessively high, even unjustifiably high, ratings as an essential link in the chain of events that generated the crisis.

The Bubble Bursts

Even though the mortgage-based CDOs were generally rated as relatively safe investments, investors wanted protection against the possibility that something would go wrong, that the seemingly good investments might turn bad. So they bought insurance, just as a healthy person buys life insurance, or a good driver buys auto insurance, or the owner of a brick house with smoke detectors buys fire insurance. Firms that sell life insurance or auto insurance or fire insurance are required by regulators to maintain a certain amount of capital in reserve. A fire insurance company need not keep sufficient capital in reserve to pay off if all the houses it insures burn down the same night. That doesn't happen. The company is, however, required to maintain sufficient capital pay off in a reasonable worst-case scenario. So one would think that such capital reserve requirements would be similar for firms selling insurance on debts.

One would be wrong. The firms selling insurance on debts did not want to be constrained by capital reserve requirement regulation. So instead of calling their insurance policies "insurance" they called them "credit default swaps." By this slight of hand—or slight of verbiage—the firms avoided the capital reserve requirements. The regulators looked the other way.

Moreover, credit default swaps were effectively exempted from extensive government regulation by the Commodity Futures Modernization Act of 2000. Consequently, credit default swaps could be widely traded among investors without significant regulations. Specifically, there was no requirement for the seller of a credit default swap—like the seller of other forms of insurance policies—to hold sufficient capital to cover the insurance policy if the insured CDO failed.

Together the CDOs and credit default swaps made up a huge volume of financial activity. Derivatives are first created with connections to actual assets. But then derivatives are created on other derivatives—as the swaps are derivatives based on CDOs, which are derivatives based on MBSs, which are derivatives based on mortgages. And then there are the synthetic CDOs noted earlier, which are not actually backed by income-generating assets, but basically involve bets on how the values of other CDOs will change. Thus the volume of existing derivatives can become huge. Estimates place the amount of the essentially unregulated trading in these derivative financial instruments at several tens of trillions of dollars. Moreover, the market in these financial instruments has spread far beyond United States, involving financial institutions in many other parts of the world. (Precisely because the derivatives are generally unregulated and therefore often not reported, the estimates of their volume and where they are held are rather rough.)

A combination of legislation and lax enforcement (or no enforcement) of existing regulations had provided the financial institutions with great leeway in their operations. The resulting situation exhibited both the concentration of power in the hands of the very wealthy—especially the very wealthy in finance—and the dominance of the promarket ideology that denied the need for government intervention in economic affairs. The very limited regulation of financial activity and reliance on the "rational" actions of market participants to ensure a smoothly functioning economy contributed to the development of the housing bubble and would exacerbate the impacts when the bubble burst.

All bubbles—the run-up of the prices of a particular asset or set of assets through exorbitant speculation based on debt financing—eventually burst (arrow 8). Still, the bursting of the housing bubble of the early 2000s can be traced to identifiable causes. Most generally, during the inflation of the bubble, housing prices were rising much faster than incomes—especially much faster than the incomes of the great majority of the population; so, even with low interest rates, the escalation could not continue indefinitely. As it is with someone walking out toward the end of a large tree branch, it is not easy to tell exactly when the branch will break, but it surely will break. Yet with the housing bubble, it should have been possible to determine with a reasonable degree of accuracy when the branch would break. From the outset of the bubble's inflation in the late 1990s and early 2000s, it was to a large extent based on adjustable rate mortgages with initial low "teaser" rates, and then, after a few years, much higher interest rates. It was foreseeable that when these higher rates came into effect in significant numbers, many home owners would not be able to make their payments, their mortgages would go into default, foreclosures would follow, and housing prices would begin to fall.

Irrational exuberance may have prevented many investors—homebuyers and financial operators—from seeing what was coming, but not all. For example, according to an April 16, 2008, story in the *Bloomberg News,* "Paulson & Co. [a hedge fund], which oversees about $28 billion, made money betting on the collapse of subprime mortgages in 2007. The Paulson Credit Opportunities Fund soared almost sixfold, helped by bets on slumping housing and subprime mortgage prices, according to investor letters obtained by Bloomberg."[24] And John Paulson, the manager of the hedge fund, obtained for himself $3.7 billion from these operations in 2007. However, in early 2010, it appeared that Paulson may not have been as prescient as he seemed to have been when he raked in his billions. According to the civil fraud case brought against Goldman Sachs by the government in April 2010, Paulson appears to have been involved with Goldman Sachs in creating the CDOs that he bet would fail. (See Box 6.3.)

Now back to the CDOs and credit default swaps. When many homeowners were unable to pay their mortgages, the loans went into default and the value of the CDOs—the derivatives backed by MBSs backed by mortgages—fell. But the value of CDOs did not simply fall; the values of these derivatives became effectively unknown, as no one could determine which ones would actually fail and which would not. The complicated connection between the CDOs and the underlying mortgages and the uncertainty about the mortgages made it all but impossible to determine the value of the CDOs. Likewise, the values of the credit default swaps—derivatives, the value of which was based on CDOs—became virtually impossible to determine. What, after all, is the value of an asset (a CDO or a swap) that is derived from the value of another asset (housing), when the value of that other asset is in freefall? So, as the decline of housing prices and the prospect of spreading defaults became increasingly apparent, the markets for CDOs and credit default swaps largely disappeared. These derivatives were linked to the value of mortgage payments, and mortgage payments were in serious trouble and thus highly uncertain.

The virtual disappearance of a market for CDOs and swaps created severe problems for financial institutions that held large amounts of these instruments. AIG for example (as noted earlier in the quotation from James

Crotty), held a large volume of swaps. As its holdings were promises to pay the value of CDOs if those CDOs failed (i.e., they were insurance policies on CDOs) the value of its swaps fell drastically. Indeed, for all practical purposes, these swaps were not sellable. Who would purchase the obligation to pay off homeowner's insurance policies if massive urban fires were threatening the country's major cities?

The market for these derivatives had been, to a substantial extent, the large financial institutions. Lehman Brothers, Bear Stearns, Citibank, and others all held large amounts of these assets on their books. So, as the housing bubble burst, as many home owners failed to meet their mortgage payments, and as the value of CDOs and credit default swaps fell, many banks (including some of the largest banks) saw a sharp decline in the overall value of their assets. Not only were many—very many—banks losing large amounts of the value of their assets, but no one knew how much value was being lost or how much value remained with the banks.

The operation of the financial industry is to a large extent dependent on the rapid movement of money among the financial firms. The firms continually borrow from one another on a short-term basis to meet their obligations and take advantage of opportunities. Yet when a firm is in trouble—that is, when the value of its assets is falling and indeterminate—other firms will not make loans to it. No one knew better about the trouble in the financial industry than the financial firms themselves, and therefore increasingly in 2008 they became reluctant to make loans to one another. Not only did it become difficult, if not impossible, for financial institutions to obtain loans from one another; but also, and for the same reasons, it became increasingly difficult for the financial institutions to raise capital.

So activity in the financial industry slowed. The CDOs and swaps held by the firms had in effect poisoned the system, and thus, these assets came to be called "toxic" assets. In the early fall of 2008, there was the threat that the financial system would to a large extent stop operating, that it would "freeze up" or "melt down"—ironically, two opposite metaphors for the same thing (arrow 9). Although the bursting of the bubble began to appear in 2006 and its deflation continued through 2007, the impact on the financial sector became fully clear only in 2008 as major financial firms began to crumble.

Bear Stearns was the first big one to fall.

Failing Banks, Bailouts, and Implosion

Bear Stearns was a large investment bank, the seventh largest in the country in 2006 in terms of total capital. The firm had been an early developer of mortgage-backed CDOs and credit default swaps. It had purchased these derivatives and sold them to its own hedge funds. As the housing bubble expanded, the overall value of these financial instruments increased, and Bear Stearns's hedge funds used them as collateral to take out loans from other financial institutions. Thus the firm's operations became highly leveraged (i.e., based on a high ratio of debt to capital). While housing prices rose and the value of the CDOs also rose, Bear Stearns did very well. Using other people's money (the loans), the firm obtained a high rate of profit on its own capital—up until the housing market began to collapse in 2006.

The problems for Bear Stearns were evident by the summer of 2007. According to a June 12, 2007, *Business Week* report, "Investors in a 10-month-old Bear Stearns hedge fund are learning the hard way the danger of investing in risky bonds with borrowed money. The investment firm's High-Grade Structured Credit Strategies Enhanced Leverage Fund, as of Apr. 30, was down a whopping 23 percent for the year."[25] But things would only get worse. Heavily invested in derivatives connected to the housing market, Bear Stearns could not maintain confidence among investors and creditors as the housing market continued to fall. By March 2008, its requests to borrow in order to finance its daily operations were being denied by lending institutions, and investors were pulling out their capital. Once confidence in a financial institution starts to fail, it is difficult to halt the decline. On March 10, Bear Stearns issued a press release, claiming, "There is absolutely no truth to rumors of liquidity problems [i.e., insufficient funds to pay off creditors] that circulated in the market."[26] As one might expect, such a denial only gave strength to the rumors.

Fearing that a collapse of such a large investment bank, with debts outstanding to numerous other financial institutions, would cause a more general crisis in the financial system, on Friday, March 14, at 9:00 A.M. the Federal Reserve announced that, with its guarantee, the J. P. Morgan Chase bank was providing a $30 billion loan to Bear Stearns. It didn't work, perhaps because it underscored the degree of the firm's problems. In the first half hour of trading after the announcement, Bear Stearns's stock dropped by 40 percent. In the subsequent days, J. P. Morgan Chase bought Bear Stearns, completing the acquisition by the end of the month at $10 per share. A year earlier, the firm's stock had been at $170 per share. Stockholders, in the vernacular of the market, took a bath. But the creditors were saved, and the demise of Bear Stearns did not appear to bring disarray to the entire financial market.

In this acquisition, the Federal Reserve insured J. P. Morgan Chase against loses of up to $29 billion on the "ill-liquid" assets it was obtaining in its purchase of Bear Stearns (that is, on the derivatives that had lost their value and were, it appeared, unsellable). This was the first step in the federal government's bailout of the financial sector that would reach an unprecedented level by the end of 2008. The chairman of the Federal Reserve, Ben Bernanke, justified this step to Congress, arguing that had Bear Stearns been allowed simply to fail the result could have been "a chaotic unwinding" of investment throughout the economy. He added: "The adverse effects would not have been confined to the financial system but would have been felt broadly in the real economy through its effects on asset values and credit availability."[27] Regardless of whether Bernanke was correct about the extent of the damage that would have resulted had Bear Stearns's creditors lost out, the Fed's actions created a clear precedent—namely that the federal authorities would step in to protect creditors if a large financial institution was on the verge of failure; such firms would be treated as "too big to fail." (There is the important question of whether there were alternative ways to protect the financial system that might have been better for the rest of us. This is an issue we will discuss in Chapter 9.)

The willingness of the federal authorities to protect the financial system was further established in early September when the government in effect took over Fannie Mae and Freddie Mac. These two institutions had been operating as government sponsored enterprises, owned by private investors but created by and at least implicitly backed by the federal government. As Fannie Mae and Freddie Mac were holding some $5 trillion in mortgage-backed securities, they, like Bear Stearns and other fully private institutions, had made themselves especially vulnerable to the collapse of the housing bubble. With the value of their holdings falling, the two institutions were in danger of being unable to raise sufficient capital to maintain solvency, let alone continue to play their role in the housing market where they had provided 70 percent of mortgage funds in the earlier part of 2008.[28] On September 7, federal authorities announced that Fannie Mae and Freddie Mac were being placed in "conservatorship," which meant they were effectively controlled by the government. As part of the takeover, the U.S. Treasury would purchase up to $200 billion in preferred stock in the two institutions and would also provide them extensive credit.

Reporting on this takeover, *The Washington Post* called it "one of the most sweeping government interventions in private financial markets in decades."[29] Following on the Fed's action in preventing Bear Stearns's bankruptcy and the continuing statements of both Fed Chairman Bernanke and Treasury Secretary Henry Paulson that such actions were needed to protect the viability of the financial system and the rest of the economy, the Fannie Mae and Freddie Mac effective takeovers seemed to ensure that the government would not shy away from stepping in to protect the viability of financial markets. The strong free market ideological precepts of Paulson, Bernanke and, indeed, of the entire Bush administration were apparently being put aside in the face of reality. The precedent for preventing the failure of a large financial institution, initiated with Bear Stearns, now appeared to be reinforced by the Fannie Mae and Freddie Mac actions. Yet, while the precedent seemed very clear on September 7, the federal authorities failed to follow it a few days later when Lehman Brothers, the nation's fourth largest investment bank, moved toward collapse.

Lehman Brothers' difficulties had developed in a similar manner to those of Bear Stearns. Heavily engaged in housing market–related investments, the firm did very well as the housing bubble expanded. Lehman Brothers was not only engaged in derivative trading but had also acquired five mortgage companies, including BNC Mortgage, which specialized in the subprime market, and Aurora Loan Services, which specialized in so-called Alt-A loans (i.e., loans to borrowers between prime and subprime that required limited documentation by the borrowers). By early 2008, as was the case with with Bear Stearns, Lehman Brothers was fighting rumors of its impending demise and searching for capital infusions. By September, with the value of its stock falling precipitously, the firm's executives were attempting to negotiate its sale to another large financial institution. Briefly, it seemed as though Barclays or Bank of America might step in. But the deals all fell through. On September 15, Lehman Brothers, in existence since 1850, declared bankruptcy. It was the largest bankruptcy in U.S. history.[30]

As Fed Chair Bernanke had warned in justifying the bailout of Bear Stearns, the failure of such a large financial institution would have far–reaching, near-disastrous impacts. In the six weeks following September 15, the Dow Jones stock market index dropped by 25 percent. Financial institutions virtually stopped lending, spreading the difficulties of the financial sector to the "real economy" (arrow 11), which was already in trouble (arrow 11A). In the third quarter of 2008, real GDP had fallen at a 4 percent annual rate; in the final three months of the year, GDP fell at a 6.8 percent rate, and then at a 4.9 percent rate in the first quarter of 2009.[31] At the beginning of 2009, it was officially recognized that the U.S. economy was in recession and had been for a full year. The bankruptcy of Lehman Brothers was by no means the lone factor causing this general economic implosion—which, after all, was thoroughly underway well before Lehman's collapse and was pushed along by other events (including the almost simultaneous bailout of AIG, see page 111). This collapse of Lehman Brothers, however, was an important event, exacerbating an already bad situation.

In spite of its importance, there has been no reasonable explanation as to why the government authorities, the Fed and the U.S. Department of Treasury, allowed Lehman Brothers to go under. Why, when they had moved in to rescue Bear Stearns and taken over Fannie Mae and Freddie Mac, did they sit on their hands while Lehman Brothers collapsed? One answer is simply incompetence. A better explanation is probably incompetence driven by free-market ideology. While Fed Chairman Bernanke and Treasury Secretary Paulson and others in the federal government had been pushed by reality to intervene in the financial market in those earlier cases, they had clearly been loath to do so. The action ran up against their deeply held prejudices, their ideological precepts, about the proper role for government in economic affairs. Bernanke, for example, had demonstrated his position in a 2002 event honoring Milton Friedman, the leading free-market economist of the late twentieth century. Bernanke had both joined the general peons to Friedman and had praised directly Friedman's analysis of the Great Depression.[32] In addition, in his academic work prior to joining the Fed, Bernanke had argued that the Fed should in effect ignore financial bubbles, a view that apparently garnered the support of his predecessor Alan Greenspan.[33] Treasury Secretary Paulson was also well known for his conservative economic outlook, and seemed to view his earlier success at Goldman Sachs as a demonstration of the wonders of the free market. So, faced with Lehman Brothers' impending collapse, they seem to have done what they wanted to do instead of what they needed to do. Incompetence perhaps, but incompetence that can only be explained in the context of their ideology.

As much as the lack of action to save Lehman Brothers made an important contribution to the growing economic debacle, ironically the government's actions to save financial institutions probably did at least as much in late 2008 to push along the general economic crisis. By intervening to prevent the bankruptcy of Bear Stearns and by moving Fannie Mae and Freddie Mac into conservatorship, the federal authorities had signaled loudly and clearly that they viewed the economic situation as extremely dire. When the government sends such a signal, instead of providing reassurance to firms and citizens, it can add to the obvious signs of severe economic distress—so things get worse.

And then there was AIG.

On the day after Lehman Brothers entered bankruptcy, on Tuesday, September 16, the Paulson-Bernanke duo announced that the government, via the Federal Reserve, would provide $85 billion to bail out the insurance giant American International Group (AIG). This action gave the government formal ownership-control of the firm. AIG was the originator of many of the credit default swaps that had become "toxic" when the housing market imploded. With the failure of the CDOs based on housing mortgages, AIG stood to lose billions in paying off the credit default swaps that were insurance policies on these CDOs. To do so would have bankrupted the company. The infusion of cash from the government staved off this outcome. *The New*

Box 6.2
AIG: False Advertising

On the back cover of *The New Yorker* magazine of August 25, 2008, there appeared an ad with the picture of a smiling, relaxed-looking young man. Above his head is a large "+15." The text of the ad reads:

One less thing to worry about and it's a beauty.

Deciding where to invest your retirement savings can be pretty stressful. Put your mind at ease. With the AIG companies, you're tapping into more than 85 years of wisdom and expertise that can help make your retirement savings last.

Not worrying can reduce stress and add 15 years to your life

We've helped over 5 million people retire stronger. Getting started is simple. Ask your financial advisor about AIG or visit retire stronger.com.

live longer retire stronger never outlive your money

And at the bottom of the page:

AIG The Strength to Be There

Three weeks after the date of the ad, on September 17, 2008, *The New York Times* wrote: "Fearing a financial crisis worldwide, the Federal Reserve reversed course on Tuesday and agreed to an $85 billion bailout that would give the government control of the troubled insurance giant American International Group (AIG)."

York Times called the AIG action by the Federal Reserve "the most radical intervention in private business in the central bank's history."[34]

In 2008, AIG was the eighteenth-largest public corporation in the world according to the *Forbes* magazine listing of the top two thousand firms.[35] It owned hundreds of companies around the globe, and the operations of these subsidiaries included a wide variety of ventures—everything from life insurance and auto insurance to credit default swaps, airplane leasing, crop insurance, and home mortgages. Had AIG failed and not met its obligations to its customers or its creditors, the impacts would have been severe and extensive. Federal authorities feared an unraveling of credit markets—a "meltdown" or a "freeze up," depending on your choice of metaphors.

The provision of government support for AIG only began with the $85 billion of September 2008. By early 2009, the government had pumped in a total of $173 billion to shore up the company. As was the case with the other financial institutions that received federal largesse, AIG paid out substantial bonuses in 2009—specifying some $165 million for its employees (though this was not a large amount by the standards of the industry). The real scandal in the AIG arrangements, however, was not the bonuses. Instead it was that more than half of the government funds, $93 billion, went directly from AIG to Goldman Sachs and other large financial institutions: Goldman Sachs ($12.9 billion), Societe General ($11.9 billion), Deutsch Bank ($11.8 billion), Barclays ($8.5 billion), and several others with lesser billions. These payments were due because AIG had issued the credit default swaps, the insurance policies, on the CDOs held by these banks. As the CDOs went bust, the insurance was owed. The banks to which AIG had issued the swaps were paid in full, 100 percent on the dollar. The government authorities, who were in legal control of AIG, justified these payments as honoring contracts. There was, nonetheless, plenty of room for negotiation, in part because many of these banks were also receiving support from the government. Furthermore, when the banks made their arrangements with AIG they took into account—or should have taken into account—the possibility of AIG's inability to pay in full. In the end, the government's support of AIG was one more payment to the politically well-connected Goldman Sachs and other large firms.[36]

There is no good explanation for why the federal authorities let Lehman Brothers fall but propped up AIG. Perhaps, however, it is sufficient to point out, as we have previously, that the federal authorities—Bernanke and Paulson, in particular—were caught between their ideology and reality. Under these circumstances, one should not be surprised by contradictory and, indeed, incompetent actions.

As we have also suggested, the bailout of AIG may well have contributed as much to the increasing disarray and decline in financial markets as did the failure of Lehman Brothers. Most important, the bailout, as much as the failure, underscored (if it needed underscoring) the fact that many major financial institutions were in deep trouble. Confidence in the financial system was lower than it had been since the Great Depression. Financial institutions would not loan money to one another, and they were making few loans to even their best customers in the rest of the economy. They were hoarding their cash for better times, or the big firms were using their cash to buy up

---

Box 6.3

**A Nice Scam for Goldman Sachs: Selling Assets to Clients
and Betting They Would Fail**

Here's how it worked. Goldman Sachs created mortgaged-backed collateralized debt obligations (CDOs) that it sold to its clients—pension funds, insurance companies, and various other investors. Believing these CDOs were good investments, presumably because Goldman Sachs was urging their purchase, the clients spent billions buying them. For a while the clients made money off these investments.

Then, according to *The New York Times*, "Worried about a housing bubble, top Goldman executives decided in December 2006 to change the firm's overall stance on the mortgage market, from positive to negative, though it did not disclose that publicly"[37]—that is, the firm did not tell its clients. So Goldman Sachs started making CDO investments that would pay off only if the housing bubble deflated. The firm was betting the CDOs would fail, or at least drop in value.

When the housing market started to go bust and the CDOs did fall in value, Goldman Sachs made billions, and its clients lost billions. Goldman Sachs was not the only financial institution to profit from this sort of duplicitous practice. Others, according to *The New York Times*, included Deutsche Bank and Morgan Stanley, as well as some smaller firms.

On January 13, 2010, at hearings of the Financial Crisis Inquiry Commission, established by Congress to investigate the crisis, the commission's chair, Phil Angelides, confronted the head of Goldman Sachs, Lloyd Blankfein, on this issue: "I'm just going to be blunt with you. It sounds to me a little bit like selling a car with faulty brakes and then buying an insurance policy on the buyer of those cars . . . It doesn't seem to me that that's a practice that inspires confidence in the market."[38]

But it seems the story falls into the always-worse-than-you-think-it-is category. As noted in the text, the April 2010 fraud case brought by the government against Goldman Sachs revealed that the company along with hedge fund manager John Paulson had created the CDOs that they were betting against. Should the Angelides metaphor have included that they sabotaged the brakes in the car they were selling?

---

the smaller failing firms. With the heavy dependence of nonfinancial firms on credit—their debt was 75 percent as large as GDP—the withholding of credit was devastating. Already weakened by the slow growth of the economy over the entire decade and suffering further from the weakening consumer demand as unemployment grew and from fear (well founded) that things would get worse, economic activity plummeted. GDP declined at an annual rate of 4.0 percent in the third quarter of 2008, then at a 6.8 percent rate in the final quarter of the year, and at a 4.9 percent rate in the first three months of 2009. Official unemployment soared to over 10 percent of the workforce by late 2009; counting workers who had given up looking for jobs and those who could only obtain part-time work, the unemployment figure hovered around 17 percent. Widespread economic distress dominated people's lives (arrows 11 and 11A).

At the beginning of 2009, the U.S. economy—pulling the global economy along with it—was in the worst downturn since the Great Depression of the 1930s.

Notes

1. *Economic Report of the President, 2010,* Tables B-30, B-75, and B-77.

2. The Federal Reserve Board, "Household Debt Service and Financial Obligations Ratios," www.federalreserve.gov/releases/housedebt/default.htm.

3. See Box II.1 regarding the sources of income distribution data.

4. Earnings and labor force participation data are from the *Economic Report of the President, 2010,* Tables B-47 and B-39, respectively.

5. *Economic Report of the President, 2010,* Table B-31.

6. *Economic Report of the President, 2010,* Table B-1.

7. *Economic Report of the President, 2010,* Table B-73.

8. Authors' calculation based on data from U.S. Department of Energy, U.S. Energy Administration, Independent Statistical Analysis, www.eia.doe.gov/energyexplained/index.cfm?page=oil_home#tab2.

9. Federal Reserve Board, Federal Reserve Statistical Release, Flow of Funds Accounts, "Debt Outstanding by Sector," www.federalreserve.gov/releases/z1/current/accessible/d3.htm and *Economic Report of the President 2010,* Table B-1.

10. See Louise Story, "Home Equity Frenzy Was a Bank Ad Come True," *The New York Times,* August 14, 2008, www.nytimes.com/2008/08/15/business/15sell.html.

11. The home equity loan figures are from the Federal Reserve Board, Finance and Economics Discussion Series, "Sources and Uses of Equity Extracted from Homes," www.federalreserve.gov/pubs/feds/2007/200720/feds200720.html. Disposable personal income from *Economic Report of the President 2010,* Table B-30.

12. Cynthia Angell and Robert M. Miller, "Measuring Progress in U.S. Housing and Mortgage Markets," *FDIC Quarterly* 2010 *4* (1), pp. 29–35. These numbers are estimated from Chart 9 on page 33.

13. Peter S. Goodmand and Gretchen Morgenson, "Saying Yes, WaMu Built Empire on Shaky Loans," *The New York Times,* December 28, 2008, www.nytimes.com/2008/12/28/business/28wamu.html.

14. Inside Mortgage Finance, "The 2010 Mortgage Market Statistical Annual" (Bethesda, MD: Inside Mortgage Finance Publications, Inc.), pp. 3 and 6.

15. The Federal Reserve Board, "Community Reinvestment Act," www.federalreserve.gov/dcca/cra/.

16. The studies are summarized in a December 3, 2008, speech by Federal Reserve Board of Governors member Randall S. Kroszner. The quotations are from that speech, which is available online at federalreserve.gov/newsevents/speech/kroszner20081203a.htm. Also, see NeighborWorks America, "Don't Blame Subprime Mortgage Crisis or Financial Meltdown on CRA," www.stablecommunities.org/library/dont-blame-subprime-mortgage-crisis-or-financial-meltdown-cra.

17. For discussion of the impact of OCC actions, see Lei Ding, Robert G Quercia, and Alan White, *State Anti-Predatory Lending Laws: Impact and Federal Preemption Phase I Descriptive Analysis,* Research Report, Center for Community Capital, University of North Carolina, October 5, 2009, www.ccc.unc.edu/documents/Phase_I_report_Final_Oct5,2009_Clean.pdf.

18. *Bill Moyers Journal,* www.pbs.org/moyers/journal/04032009/transcript1.html.

19. John Cassidy, "Annals of Economics, Rational Irrationality, Why Markets Fail," *The New Yorker,* October 5, 2009.

20. Sources for this box include: Andy Baker, "Better than beta? Managers' Superior Skills Are Becoming Harder to Prove," *The Economist,* February 28, 2008; Arindam Bandopadhyaya and James L. Grant, *A Survey of Demographics and Performance In the Hedge Fund Industry,* Working Paper 1011, Financial Services Forum, College of Management, University of Massachusetts Boston, July, 2006; "Hedge-Fund Performance," *The Economist,* May 15, 2008; Nelson D. Schwartz and Louise Story, "Pay of Hedge Fund Managers Roared Back Last Year," *The New York Times,* March 31, 2010.

21. James Crotty, "Structural Causes of the Global Financial Crisis: A Critical Assessment of the 'New Financial Architecture,' " *Cambridge Journal of Economics* 33 (4), 2009, p. 565. This passage is reprinted by permission of Oxford University Press.

22. Moody's Investors Service, *Rating Symbols and Definitions,* July 2010, http://v3.moodys.com/researchdocumentcontentpage.aspx?docid=PBC_79004.

23. David Segal, "Debt Raters Avoid Overhaul After Crisis," *The New York Times,* December 7, 2009, www.nytimes.com/2009/12/08/business/08ratings.html.

24. Tom Cahill and Poppy Trowbridge, "Paulson's $3.7 Billion Top Hedge Fund Pay, Alpha Says," Bloomberg.com, April 16, 2008, www.bloomberg.com/apps/news?pid=20601087&sid=a00fuYxe7n7g&refer=home.

25. Matthew Goldstein, "Bear Stearns' Subprime Bath," *Business Week,* June 12, 2007, www.businessweek.com/bwdaily/dnflash/content/jun2007/db20070612_748264.htm.

26. Roddy Boyd, "The Last Days of Bear Stearns," *Fortune,* March 31, 2008, http://money.cnn.com/2008/03/28/m,agazines/fortune/boyd_bear.fortune/.

27. *Bloomberg News,* April 2, 2008: www.bloomberg.com/apps/news?pid=20601087&refer=worldwide&sid=a7coicThgaEE.

28. Zachary A. Goldfarb, "Fannie, Freddie Unlikely to Return Aid," *The Washington Post,* July 31, 2009, www.washingtonpost.com/wp-dyn/content/article/2009/07/30/AR2009073003937.html and Zachary A. Goldfarb, David Cho, and Binyamin Appelbaum, "Treasury to Rescue Fannie and Freddie," *The Washington Post,* September 7, 2008, www.washingtonpost.com/wp-dyn/content/article/2008/09/06/AR2008090602540.html.

29. "Treasury to Rescue Fannie and Freddie," as cited in the previous endnote.

30. Investopedia, "Case Study: The Collapse of Lehman Brothers," www.investopedia.com/articles/economics/09/lehman-brothers-collapse.asp?viewed=1.

31. Bureau of Economic Analysis, National Economic Accounts, "Percent change from preceding period," www.bea.gov/national/index.htm#gdp.

32. "On Milton Friedman's Ninetieth Birthday," Remarks by Governor Ben S. Bernanke at the Conference to Honor Milton Friedman, University of Chicago, Chicago, Illinois November 8, 2002, www.federalreserve.gov/BOARDDOCS/SPEECHES/2002/20021108/default.htm.

33. See Ben Bernanke and Mark Gertler, "Monetary Policy and Asset Price Volatility," *Economic Review,* Federal Reserve Bank of Kansas City, Fourth Quarter 1999, p. 43, where the authors conclude, "it is neither necessary nor desirable for monetary policy to respond to changes in asset prices [i.e., bubbles]." Regarding Greenspan's reaction to Bernanke and Gertler's work, see John Cassidy, "Anatomy of a Meltdown," *The New Yorker,* December 1, 2008, p. 51.

34. Edmund L. Andrews, Michael J. de la Merced, and Mary Williams Walsh, "Fed's $85 Billion Loan Rescues Insurer," *The New York Times,* September 16, 2008, www.nytimes.com/2008/09/17/business/17insure.html.

35. Forbes.com, "The Global 2000," April 2, 2008, www.forbes.com/lists/2008/18/biz_2000globa108_The-Global-2000_Rank.html.

36. For details on this aspect of the AIG matter, see the Reuters report of March 16, 2009, www.reuters.com/article/idUSN1548789520090316.

37. Gretchen Morgenson and Louise Story, "Banks Bundled Bad Debt, Bet Against It and Won," *The New York Times,* December 23, 2009, www.nytimes.com/2009/12/24/business/24trading.html?_r=1&pagewanted=1.

38. Caitlin Kenny, "Financial Crisis Inquiry Commission Day One," *NPR,* January 13, 2010, www.npr.org/blogs/money/2010/01/financial_crisis_inquiry_commi.html.

Part IV
Globalization and Instability

In the early years of the new millennium, just as the housing bubble in the United States was rapidly inflating, factories in China's coastal city of Datang were turning out nine billion pairs of socks a year. That's a pair socks for every person in the world, and then another pair for about half. Lots of socks. Datang is known, not surprisingly, as Socks City. Each year, according to *The New York Times,* "its annual socks festival attracts 100,000 buyers from around the world."[1]

In supplying a huge share of the worldwide supply of a particular garment, Datang is not alone. According to the *Times:* "Southeast from [Datang] is Shenzhou, which is the world's necktie capital. To the west is Sweater City and Kid's Clothing City. To the south . . . is Underwear City." These cities, and others like them, have been focal points of industrial activity in China's remarkable economic expansion over the last thirty years. It has been not only a remarkable economic expansion; it has also been a remarkable export expansion, as the socks, the neckties, and the other garments have been sold to consumers around the world, especially in the United States. China's remarkable industrial and export expansion has been fuelled by a seemingly endless supply of low-wage labor drawn from the countryside; by investors from Taiwan, Japan, and South Korea lining up to get in on the action; and by consumers in the United States and elsewhere who have been happy to purchase low-priced goods.

As U.S. consumers bought the Chinese garments and other goods in Walmart, Target, Saks Fifth Avenue, Nordstrom, or Macy's, they of course paid in dollars. The U.S. importers, in turn, used the dollars to purchase yuan, the Chinese currency, with which they then paid the Chinese suppliers of the goods. These purchases of yuan by U.S. importers tended to push up the price of the yuan (i.e., more dollars per yuan). However, the Chinese government through the Chinese central bank has long followed a policy of controlling the value of the yuan relative to the dollar, that is, "pegging" the value of the yuan. It has done this by creating more yuan and using this growing supply of yuan to buy dollars. This has kept the value of the yuan in terms of dollars relatively stable, and it also has led to the accumulation of very large dollar holdings by the Chinese central bank. These dollar holdings have been used to buy U.S. government bonds and some private bonds and stocks.

The Chinese central bank's strategy of using dollars earned from Chinese exports to buy U.S. financial instruments contributed to a huge supply of funds, a "giant pool of money," which was available for people, firms, and the U.S. government to borrow. This huge supply of funds coming into U.S. credit markets kept interest rates low, at least low relative to what they would have been otherwise. The Chinese central bank was not alone in creating this giant pool of money. Other countries' central banks—Japan's, for example—were following a similar strategy. Also, with the high price of oil following the U.S. invasion of Iraq, governments and wealthy individuals in oil-exporting countries were shoveling money into U.S. financial instruments. Then there were the very rich within the United States, who, as they obtained a larger and larger share of all income, continued to seek ways to make more. And finally there were the policies by the Federal Reserve, which, as we have pointed out, was providing funds in an effort to stimulate aggregate demand and thus economic growth.

Yet among the international factors, the role of the Chinese stands out. By the time the crisis had become full blown, the Chinese government was the largest purchaser of the U.S. government's debt. Indeed, one might say that the U.S. and Chinese governments had developed a symbiotic relationship, each doing well by serving the other's needs. While this symbiotic relationship appeared to work, however, it had problems. It was—and is— an unstable relationship; changes in one government's policies or problems in the world economy could upset it and cause disruptions far and wide. Closely related to the instability, there was—and is—no established means of cooperation by which the governments could regulate and control their intertwined financial relationship.

It is one of the paradoxes of the global system that, while economic activity has become increasingly international, political activity—including the political activity that regulates economic activity—has continued to be thoroughly national. Like any national economy, the international economy needs systems of regulation, including regulation of finance, to function stably and effectively. However, whether it is trade in socks, the movement of funds around the world, or the interconnected movement of socks and money, such a system of regulation is absent.

A relatively unregulated global economy is not a "natural" phenomenon. The current global economy was created, created to a substantial degree by the U.S. government and U.S. business. The same underlying factors— inequality, power, and ideology—that shaped the domestic U.S. economy also shaped the global economy.

Note

1. David Barboza, "In Roaring China, Sweaters Are West of Socks City," *The New York Times,* December 24, 2004, www.nytimes.com/2004/12/24/business/worldbusiness/24china.html.

7

Shaping the Global Economy

Ever since Adam and Eve left the garden, people have been expanding the geographic realm of their economic, political, social, and cultural contacts. In this sense of extending connections to other peoples around the world, globalization, is nothing new. Also, as a process of major change and instability that can embody both great opportunities for wealth and progress and great trauma and suffering, globalization at the beginning of the twenty-first century is following a well-established historical path.[1]

"Greatest Events," "Dreadful Misfortunes," Instability and Change

We are fond of viewing our own period, the period of the newest phase of globalization, as one in which great transformations are taking place, and it is easy to recite a list of technological and social changes that have dramatically altered the way we live and the way we connect to peoples elsewhere in the world. Yet, other surges of globalization in the modern era have been similarly disruptive to established practices. The surge that marked the beginning of modern globalization came with the invasion of the Western Hemisphere by European powers and with their extension of ocean trade around Africa to Asia. Adam Smith, writing *The Wealth of Nations* in 1776, did not miss the significance of these developments:

> The discovery of America, and that of a passage to the East Indies by the Cape of Good Hope, are the two greatest and most important events recorded in the history of mankind . . . By uniting, in some measure, the most distant parts of the world, by enabling them to relieve one another's wants, to increase one another's enjoyments, and to encourage one another's industry, their general tendency would seem to be beneficial.[2]

Alongside of what Adam Smith saw as the great gains of globalization (not his term!) were the slaughter by battle and disease of millions of Native Americans, the enslavement and associated deaths of millions of Africans, and the subjugation of peoples in Asia. Smith did recognize the "dreadful misfortunes" that fell upon the peoples of the East and West Indies as a result of these "greatest and most important events"—though he does not mention Africans in his expression of concern. He saw these misfortunes, however, as arising "rather from accident than from any thing in the nature of the events themselves"—a very strange view, given the depredations of colonial rule and the enslavements of millions as the basis for economic organization in the newly connected lands.

This first stage of modern globalization illustrates not only the combined great gains and "dreadful misfortunes" that have characterized globalization, but also the vast scope of the process and the momentous changes that it engendered. This huge surge of commerce that followed from the European conquest of the Americas and forays into Asia disrupted economic relations around the world, and, in particular, in Europe it set in motion the emergence of modern capitalism. Part of the disruption was the great inflation of the six-teenth century, brought about by the huge expansion of the supply of precious metals (money) from the Western Hemisphere. The consequent political and economic changes are relatively well known. Equally momentous were the huge cultural transformations that were tied to the great expansion of eco-nomic contacts among the continents. Peoples moved, or they were moved by force. As they came to new locations and in contact with other peoples, almost every aspect of their lives was altered—from what they ate ("Italian" spaghetti with tomato sauce comes from Asia, the spaghetti, and America, the tomatoes) to their music (jazz is now the best known example, blending the backgrounds of different continents to emerge in America) to religion (the cross accompanied the sword in the era of colonial conquest).

The second great surge of modern globalization came in the nineteenth century, both as product and cause of the Industrial Revolution. On the one hand, the expansion of industry generated large reductions in transport costs that brought huge increases in international commerce. On the other hand, for the emerging commercial centers of Europe and North America, the opening of foreign markets and access to foreign sources of raw materials fueled (sometimes literally) the expansion of industry. Great Britain, as the "workshop of the world," was at the center of these changes and over the course of the century saw its foreign trade triple in relation to national income.[3]

Britain during the nineteenth century provided a foreshadowing of current-day globalization as it officially touted "free trade" as the proper mode of organization for commerce—not just for itself, but for the entire world. The gospel of free trade was then carried around the globe by the British Royal Navy; and heroic ideological gymnastics allowed a growing colonial empire to be included under this same rubric. However, as the British historian E.J. Hobsbawm has commented, "British industry could grow up, by and large, in a protected home market until strong enough to demand free entry into other people's markets, that is 'Free Trade.'"[4] In today's globalization it is the United States, a country that also attained its economic power with substantial protection, that preaches the gospel of free trade to the rest of the world.

Current-day globalization is, by and large, a continuation of the process that began in the nineteenth century, which in turn had its roots in the great transformation that began along with the sixteenth century. Two world wars, the Great Depression, and the removal of sizable parts of the world from capitalist commerce (most important, the Soviet Union and China) disrupted the progress of globalization for some sixty years and shifted its center from Great Britain to the United States, but it is now back on track. By the 1980s, the extent of economic connections (measured in terms of the amount of international trade and investment compared to total output) that had been established among the world's national economies by 1913 had been re-attained, and in subsequent years international trade and investment have continued to expand their roles in the economies of most nations.

At every stage of globalization, while the movement of people, commodities, raw materials, and precious metals has been the visible representation of the changes, finance has also been well involved. In their *A History of Corporate Finance,* Jonathan Baskin and Paul Miranti, Jr., comment that, "The influences that perennial problems of information and risk have exerted on finance have been evident since the dawn of civilization. Beginning in Mesopotamia nearly five thousand years ago, the Sumerians and their Babylonian successors perfected rudimentary contracts of rationalizing commerce, finance, and private ownership. . . . Later during the Greco-Roman era new financial institutions *facilitated the expansion of economic activity.* Coinage, bills of exchange and new modes of pubic finance were broadly *transmitted through the expansion of the empires* of Alexander and Caesars" (p. 29; emphasis added). Financial institutions, however, were not always separate from trading institutions, and Baskin and Miranti describe the joint stock companies (the precursors of modern corporations) as providing the financial foundations for globalization during the era of Europe's expansion into the Western Hemisphere and around Africa to Asia. The extensive time and substantial risks involved in the long-distance trade of these earlier phases of globalization induced the development of financial arrangements and institutions to handle these aspects of commerce.[5]

These brief comments on the history of international commerce remind us that we should not confuse globalization, in the sense of the extension of economic and other connections across international boundaries, with free trade or unregulated commerce. The great surge of modern globalization that began at the end of the fifteenth century took place largely through colonialism and the creation of empires. In the great expansion of international trade associated with the Industrial Revolution in the nineteenth century, each major power, including the United States, cultivated its own foreign markets and sources of raw materials while practicing protection of its domestic markets. Only Great Britain, with its industry already well established through protection, proclaimed the desirability of free trade (and, as we just noted, Britain maintained its empire and used it naval power to ensure market access in various countries). During the second half of the twentieth century, the grand entrance of East Asian countries—Japan, then South Korea and Taiwan, China, and several others—into international commerce took place in virtually every case with government playing a large, decisive role directing and supporting the process.

Moreover, there is really no such thing as free trade, if by this term we mean the absence of government influence on international commerce. Virtually everything that governments do—from supporting public schools to providing the roads and ports (air and sea) through which commerce takes place, from establishing labor laws to protecting patents—has impacts on a country's international commerce. A lack of import tariffs and export subsidies does not remove government influence from that commerce. The pretense that we can have a world of free trade is no more realistic than to believe we can somehow revert to a mythical "state of nature." So the issue is not free trade versus regulation, but which sorts of regulations we will have. (Nonetheless, many economists continue to present analyses touting free-trade globalization as the key to increasing the rate of economic growth in low-income countries. For the explanation of what's wrong with important representative analyses of this sort, see Appendix B.)

The United States at Center Stage

At the middle of the twentieth century, with the United States at the center of world commerce and holding extreme military and political power, the newest phase of globalization was about to begin. But it did not "just happen." Current globalization, like earlier eras of globalization, has not been simply a consequence of technological changes in transportation and communications that have made the world effectively smaller, facilitating the spread of commerce. Nor has current globalization been the "natural" result of the ever-present drive for profits, where firms continually seek new markets, natural resources, and labor. Technological changes and the endemic drive for profits have certainly been important, as they were important in earlier phases of globalization. Yet globalization is always a political process as well, involving conscious planning and actions by governments and firms. The global spread of economic activity may in some sense have a "natural" component, but the speed and the character of globalization are determined by political decisions.

The U.S. government and U.S. business began planning for the post–World War II era even before the United States entered the war. Much of this planning was carried out in a collaboration between the government and the Council on Foreign Relations (CFR), a private organization made up of high-level business executives, government officials (former and current), and prominent academics. A central focus of this planning concerned the organization of the global economy after hostilities ended, and the planning was based on the question: What did the U.S. "national interest" require in terms of U.S. access to world markets and resources?

According to Laurence Shoup and William Minter in *Imperial Brain Trust: The Council on Foreign Relations and U.S. Foreign Policy*, planning during the early phase of World War II led to the conclusion that "as a minimum, the American 'national interest' involved free access to markets and raw materials in the British Empire, the Far East, and the entire Western hemisphere."[6] As the planning progressed, the area of U.S. interests was referred to as the "Grand Area." As the war progressed and as allied victory became increasingly likely, the Grand Area became increasingly large as did the anticipated dominant position of the United States in the Grand Area. As early as May 1942, the chairman of the Department of State's security sub-committee of the Advisory Committee on Postwar Foreign Policy, Norman Davis (who was at the time also CFR president), stated that it was probable that "the British Empire as it existed in the past will never reappear and that the United States may have to take its place."[7]

The U.S. planners of the post-World War II world order, however, did not envision a U.S. empire on the model of the British Empire. They did focus a great deal on the economic issues of access to raw materials and markets around the globe. But the planners saw the mechanism for promoting U.S. economic interests through international commerce as very different from the British colonial system. With the extremely dominant economic position that the U.S. government and U.S. business would clearly have in world affairs after the war, the controls of a formal colonial system were neither necessary nor desirable. U.S. economic interests could be accomplished by an "open door" policy, a policy that gave all players unrestricted access to markets and resources. The dominant position of U.S. firms would ensure that with equal access they would obtain what was needed in terms of resources and markets—and, not incidentally, in terms of the expansion of their own profits.

An open door was not a new concept in U.S. foreign policy. As a formal doctrine, it had been articulated at the end of the nineteenth century by Secretary of State John Hay. With expansion into East Asia after the Spanish-American War and colonial possession of the Philippines, the U.S. government was concerned with the possibility that other imperial powers already ensconced in China would prevent U.S. access to Chinese resources and markets. To forestall such action, in the fall of 1899 Hay asserted to the other major powers involved in China that all should agree to unrestricted access and refrain from using their control of ports to limit commerce by other powers. Hay's action had mixed success, but it marked an important step toward U.S. entrance into world economic affairs as an increasingly powerful player.

The situation after World War II was very different. In 1899, the United States was simply one of many contending powers—one of several major players—in world commerce. As many other nations already held colonial territories—Britain especially, but also several others, including France, Germany, Italy, and Japan—the United States was attempting to break into the "game." At the end of World War II, the United States had risen to a position of unchallenged economic and political dominance among capitalist countries. In large part this was the result of the war's devastation of other countries while the United States was spared conflict on its own soil. In addition, it was a result of the increasing power of the U.S. economy. The United States was already ahead of other nations before the Depression and the war—and was given a further leg up by the war itself, as war production was a powerful stimulus to the U.S. economy while the economies of other nations had been quite literally flattened. Under these circumstances, an "open door" or "free trade" meant that U.S. firms would have a great advantage in world commerce. They would dominate the game.

Things were not, however, to work out quite as the wartime planners had envisioned. While U.S. power in relation to other capitalist countries was very substantial, it was not absolute. In neither Europe nor Latin America, areas where the United States had its most extensive economic relations, were governments willing to accept the U.S. dictum of free trade. Europeans were concerned with rebuilding their economies after the war, with reestablishing key industries that had been and would be the foundation of economic expansion. In Latin America, as a result of the constraints on world trade created by the Great Depression and then the war, several countries had experienced a burgeoning of industrial production; governments and businesses saw continued industrial expansion as a foundation for future development. In both regions government and business authorities recognized the implications that free trade would have for their own national firms. In a free-trade regime, many of the nationally based firms in Europe would not have been able to recover in the face of competition from the U.S. firms, and similarly in Latin America the firms that had arisen in the 1930s and early 1940s would have been outdone by U.S. competition. In both regions, industrial activity within the countries was seen as the foundation for postwar economic growth.

Postwar economic growth, however, required capital, and, in addition to all their other advantages, U.S. firms had plenty of capital (partly due to the role of the dollar in world commerce; see below). So, while trade barriers would be maintained (or established) to ensure that industrial activity in both Europe and Latin America would take place within the countries, U.S. firms were allowed—indeed, they were welcomed—to invest in these regions. Thus the U.S. firms did get access to markets and resources in the years following World War II, but they did so more by foreign investment rather than by foreign trade. The arrangement was a de facto compromise. The Europeans and Latin Americans got industrial production and the U.S. firms got access. It was an arrangement of "free enterprise," but not of "free trade."

Thus the era spawned a resurgence of U.S.–based multinational firms and also an expansion of international financial investments from the United States. U.S. foreign direct investment (FDI) rose much more rapidly than GDP in the 1950s, and continued to expand substantially in the 1960s— slowing, however, with the economic instability of the 1970s and 1980s. In 1950, the value of U.S. FDI was $11.8 billion, about 4.1 percent as large as U.S. GDP; by 1980, the figure had almost doubled, to 7.7 percent as large as GDP.[8] (FDI is investment in assets where the investor has controlling interest and generally refers to investment in foreign affiliates or subsidiaries of a firm, i.e., the operations of multinational or transnational firms.) By contrast, U.S. foreign trade grew only along with output from 1950 to the late 1960s, the average of imports and exports fluctuating around 5 percent of GNP in those years; not until 1970 did the figure surpass 6 percent of GNP.[9] (See the following pages regarding the changes of the early 1970s and subsequent years.)

An Institutional Framework

An institutional framework for the international expansion of U.S. economic activity and power in the post–World War II era was established as the war approached its conclusion. During the first weeks of July 1944, an international conference involving forty-four nations allied with the United States in the war was held at Bretton Woods, New Hampshire. While ostensibly a conference among partners, the arrangements that came out of the Bretton Woods conference were virtually dictated by the United States. This outcome provided a degree of stability that would facilitate a general economic expansion in the postwar years and would reinforce the dominant position that the United States would hold in the international economy.

At the center of the Bretton Woods arrangements was the establishment of the U.S. dollar as the central international currency. The U.S. government would institute a fixed exchange rate between the dollar and gold at $35 an ounce and would provide gold in exchange for dollars at this rate to foreign holders of dollars. It was the responsibility of other governments, then, to maintain a fixed exchange rate between their currencies and the dollar. If the value of a country's currency fell relative to the dollar, its government would have to use its reserves of dollars (or borrowed dollars) to buy its currency and raise its value; if the value of its currency rose, the government would have to sell its currency to lower its value. In extreme cases, it would have to accept the rise or fall of the value of its currency and set a new value in relation to the dollar—a step that could be very disruptive. For its part, the U.S. government in this system was committed to maintaining a relatively stable value of the dollar.

This fixed exchange-rate system centered on the dollar provided a stability that facilitated the rapid expansion of international commerce in the years following World War II. Moreover, with the dollar treated "as good as gold," there were sufficient funds (sufficient liquidity) to support the rapid expansion of international trade and investment.

The central role of the dollar was also very good for the United States. With the dollar treated on a par with gold, it was as though the U.S. Mint was an inexhaustible gold mine. In particular, as the U.S. firms paid with dollars for imports and foreign investments and as the U.S. government paid with dollars for the foreign costs of military operations, many of those dollars were never cashed for U.S. goods or U.S. assets. The dollars were used as gold had been used in an earlier era—among other countries to pay for their transactions and to hold as reserves. In effect, when dollars were held abroad, either for transactions or as reserves, the holders were providing interest-free loans to the United States. (The position of the United States was analogous to that of an individual who could write checks knowing that many of those checks would never be cashed.) While nice for the United States, the system also provided a stability that also benefited other countries.

The Bretton Woods arrangements, in addition, created the World Bank and the International Monetary Fund (IMF). The Bank would play the role of providing long-term credit for the reconstruction of war-devastated economies and, in later years, for economic development in low-income countries. The IMF was designed to provide credit to governments when they needed funds to maintain the exchange rates of their currencies (e.g., by using the loans from the IMF to buy their own currencies and thus maintain their value). In subsequent years, after the gold-dollar arrangements of Bretton Woods had been abandoned, the IMF became a general provider of credit to governments with international financial difficulties (e.g., as in the 1980s, when a general debt crisis developed—see page 132).

The roles of the World Bank and the IMF as providers of a large amount of credit in the international economy, often credit to governments under severe financial stress, gave these institutions a great deal of power in shaping the economic policies of the recipient governments. Because both institutions were formally dominated by the United States and its closest allies, they operated to a great extent to implement U.S. international economic policy. As conditions for receiving loans, the IMF and the Bank have required governments to open their economies more thoroughly for international trade and investment (including financial investment), reduce government fiscal deficits (mainly by reducing spending), pursue a tight monetary policy, privatize government enterprises, and make their debt payments to private (often U.S.) banks. These two institutions, therefore, were important instruments for shaping the structure of the world economy, for shaping globalization, in a manner consistent with the U.S. government's desire for both free enterprise and free trade.

Yet Bretton Woods did not fully yield the outcomes that the U.S. government desired. U.S. plans for greatly reducing direct barriers to international trade—the creation of a "free trade" system—were not achieved. The establishment of the World Trade Organization (WTO) would have to wait half a century, and even after the WTO's inception on January 1, 1995, many formal, direct barriers to unrestricted trade have continued in place. Bretton Woods, however, did create the General Agreement on Tariffs and Trade (GATT), which provided the organizational framework for moving in the direction of reducing trade restrictions. Under GATT, several "rounds" of trade negotiations were carried out, directed toward establishing consistent rules for international trade and reducing tariffs and other trade restrictions. For example, the "Uruguay Round," which began in 1986 and lasted for over seven years, led to major reductions of tariffs and agricultural subsidies, provided for greater market access for textiles and clothing produced in developing countries, and extended regulations on intellectual property (e.g., patents). The Uruguay Round also led to the creation of the WTO. (The "rounds" of trade negotiations are referred to by the country or city where the negotiations began—as in the *Uruguay* Round and more recently the *Doha* Round.)

The GATT and the WTO—as well as the World Bank and the IMF—have been central instruments by which the U.S. government and its allies shaped globalization. They have not been able to structure the world economy exactly as they desired, but they have been able to do a great deal to reduce direct regulation of the international system and open the economies of other countries to penetration by U.S. firms and large firms based elsewhere.

In spite of the continuing limitations on global commerce in the years after World War II, international trade grew substantially more rapidly than output. In 1950 the ratio of world exports to world GDP was 5.5 percent, well below the 9.0 percent figure of 1929. By the early 1970s, the 1929 figure had been surpassed, as in 1973 it stood at 10.5 percent. In subsequent decades, as the newest era of globalization picked up steam, the trend continued. By the mid-1990s, when the WTO came into being, the ratio of world exports to world GDP stood around 17 percent, and by 2005 the figure had climbed to 20.5 percent. Although the role of international trade in the U.S. economy had not grown rapidly in the decades following World War II, from the 1970s onward things changed. These figures on world trade and the post-1970 participation of the United States in the global expansion of trade illustrate the advance of globalization, at least in the narrow sense of rising commerce among nations.[10]

Moving Beyond the Post–World War II Era

One of the events that marked the end of the post-World War II era and a shift toward different economic conditions and different economic policies in the United States was the formal termination of the central provision of the Bretton Woods agreements. On August 15, 1971, President Richard Nixon announced the closing of the gold window—that is, Nixon announced that the U.S. government would no longer buy gold at $35 and ounce. On the one hand, more and more dollars were being held abroad because during the late 1960s U.S. exports (dollars coming in) declined relative to imports (dollars going out) as firms in other countries began to catch up and compete more effectively with U.S. firms. This outflow of dollars was aggravated by the Vietnam War and other foreign military operations that required spending abroad. On the other hand, rising inflation in the United States (also, as noted in Chapter 3, connected to the Vietnam War) gave the dollar less worth, making foreign governments, firms, and individuals less willing to hold dollars. Under these circumstances, which reflected the declining relative position of the U.S. economy in the international arena, the system based on tying the dollar to gold had become unsustainable. With the continuing shift in the position of the dollar, the United States would not have had enough gold to meet the terms of the Bretton Woods arrangements. Nixon simply acted to end those arrangements before they self-destructed.

In subsequent years, there have been various agreements by which the leading economic powers have attempted to manage the international financial system and the mechanisms of exchange rates among currencies. Moreover, the dollar has continued to be the world's principal reserve currency, and many transactions are based on dollars—international commerce in oil being the most significant. This continuing role of the dollar, however, has not been based on a gold-dollar connection, but on the relative importance of the U.S. economy in international commerce and on a general confidence in the stability of the dollar (that is, a confidence that U.S. authorities would limit inflation).

For our purposes here (and in the following chapter), this termination of the core element in the Bretton Woods arrangements can be seen as a major reduction of direct regulation of the global economy. After August 1971, market forces would play a larger role in determining exchange rates and governments' direct interventions in that market (e.g., through tariffs or by exchange rate controls) would play a smaller role—with some significant exceptions, as we will see. Increasingly important among these market forces were the roles of international investments and financial transactions; the termination of the dollar-gold relationship was one step toward the deregulation of international finance. Whatever the immediate forces that brought about this step, it was a movement along the well-established U.S. trajectory of reducing direct regulation of international commerce.

Speculation, in which currencies are bought and sold with the expectation that their relative values will change advantageously, has been an important element of the "market forces" affecting exchange rates among the currencies of different countries. By the late 1980s, the *daily* volume of these foreign exchange transactions amounted to $500 billion. While some of these transactions were for trade in real goods and services, total world exports in the late 1980s were less than $3 trillion *a year.* In April 2007 these *daily* foreign exchange trades were averaging $3.1 trillion, while in all of 2007 world exports were "only" $14.2 trillion. Thus it would appear that almost all of these foreign exchange transactions, responding to the deregulation of the global economy, were financial speculation.[11]

While advances along this trajectory of integration and deregulation of the global economy were most rapid in the last decades of the twentieth century and the first decade of the twenty-first century, the trajectory itself had long been in place. The major changes of domestic economic policy in the United States and of the organization of the U.S. economy that began in the 1970s (changes we have emphasized in Part II) were not accompanied by a parallel change in the U.S. international economic policy. Indeed, the international economic policy of the immediate post–World War II period, with its focus on the elimination of governments' trade and investment restrictions—a focus, that is, on deregulation—was fully consistent with the domestic policies that were increasingly implemented in the final decades of the twentieth century. While there was, perhaps, a greater political will to intensify this deregulation approach to international commerce, there was no change in the goals of that policy. The vision of globalization did not change.

The opportunities for implementing that vision, however, did change. During the 1960s and 1970s, many low-income and middle-income countries had taken on heavy amounts of debt, largely from banks based in the United States, Europe, and Japan. The loans that constituted these debts had been pushed by the banks in a manner not unlike the way housing loans were pushed in more recent years. Also, many governments in low-income and middle-income countries were eager to take the loans in order to keep their economies growing. With great income inequality and a corresponding elite control of political power, growth was essential to avoid social disruption. However, at the beginning of the 1980s, as the global economy slowed and many countries went into severe recession—recession largely engineered by the U.S. Federal Reserve—the export earnings of many indebted countries plummeted while interest rates rose sharply, and many governments could not meet their obligations to creditors. This was the debt crisis of the 1980s. (Interest rates on countries' foreign debts were generally set in relation to some base interest rate; the base rose with the high inflation of the late 1970s and early 1980s, and then was pushed up dramatically by the Federal Reserve in its efforts to induce a recession, which was presented by the Fed as the means to curtail the inflation.)

Governments in Mexico, Brazil, Argentina, and several other countries in Latin America, as well as several in Central and Eastern Europe and in Africa, were all unable to meet payments on their debts. In general, they were forced to turn to the IMF and the World Bank and directly to the governments of high-income countries to provide them with funds to make the payments. As we have pointed out, however, when the IMF and the Bank provide funds, they also provide conditions, and the U.S. government and others did the same. This "conditionality" has been imposed with the explanation that there is no point in making loans to governments unless those governments take actions to eliminate the problems that led to their inability to meet their loan payments—actions that would supposedly get their economies in proper order.

Yet the policy changes demanded by conditionality have been driven by a particular ideology, the perverse leave-it-to-the-market ideology that had been the driving force in U.S. international economic policy for decades and that had become increasingly dominant within the United States since the mid-1970s. Because some elite groups in the indebted countries saw their own interests served by these policy changes and thus supported them, the changes were not simply "imposed from outside" as some critics have stated. Nonetheless, these changes would not have come, or certainly would not have come so swiftly, without the conditionality that accompanied the outside provision of funds.

These policies did achieve the immediate goals of ensuring that the private lenders (the banks) generally got repaid. They were, however, a poor prescription for what ailed the countries where conditionality was implemented. Mexico provides a good example. The Mexican government's announcement in 1982 that it would not be able to meet its debt payments had heralded the onset of the debt crisis (though, as was the case with the bursting of the U.S. housing bubble in 2006 and 2007, the underlying problems with the debts of many governments were evident earlier to anyone who cared to pay attention). Then, with Mexico's government embracing the new set of policies, the country experienced a lost decade in terms of economic growth. Tight fiscal and monetary policies, exactly the opposite of the policies generally followed in the rich countries during recessions, ensured that the country remained in the economic doldrums throughout the 1980s. The high rates of growth that had been attained in Mexico during the era from World War II through the 1970s have not yet been matched. The privatization of government enterprises was riddled with corruption, enriching private individuals at the expense of society in general. Greatly reducing regulations on foreign trade and foreign investment meant that efforts to modernize Mexico's economy—e.g., by encouraging the development of more high-tech industry—came to a halt, and innumerable small businesses were wiped out as large U.S.–based firms moved in (e.g., by 2003 Walmart had become the largest private employer in Mexico). By and large, the opening to foreign investment simply meant that foreign investment replaced domestic investment, rather than adding to the total. And the opening to international finance brought about severe financial crisis and renewed recession in 1994. (One consequence of these changes was the rising migration to the United States from Mexico.)[12]

Yet the policies of conditionality adopted in Mexico and elsewhere did achieve a major step in the U.S. government's long-pursued goal of deregulating international commerce and creating increasing opportunities for U.S. firms. This success growing out of the debt crisis of the 1980s gave greater vigor to similar U.S. government efforts in the 1990s. Perhaps the most publicized result of these efforts was the creation of the North American

Free Trade Agreement (NAFTA), which came into effect on January 1, 1994, and greatly reduced trade and investment barriers among the United States, Canada, and Mexico. The U.S. government then tried to extend NAFTA to the rest of the Western Hemisphere (not including Cuba) by establishing a Free Trade Area of the Americas, but was unable to do so because of resistance from the governments of several countries. (There was also considerable opposition in the United States from people who saw the trade agreements as threatening environmental protections and from labor groups that saw the trade agreements as undermining wages, employment, and workers' protections.) As a fallback action, in the 1990s and early 2000s the United States established bilateral and sometimes multilateral trade and investment agreements with several other countries, both in the Americas and elsewhere. The Office of the U.S. Trade Representative now lists seventeen countries with which the United States has free-trade agreements, including, among others: Chile, Jordon, Korea, Peru, the Dominican Republic and several Central American countries, Singapore, Morocco, and, of course, (under NAFTA) Canada and Mexico.[13]

In terms of furthering U.S. goals of a deregulated global economy, however, the most significant event was the establishment of the WTO in 1995. The WTO presents itself as having the general purpose of "dealing with the rules of trade between nations." (It is worth noting that the WTO concept of trade includes trade in "services," which encompasses financial services and involves the protection of patents and copyrights.) This "dealing" is guided by a set of principles including, among others, that "the trading system be":

- without discrimination—a country should not discriminate between its trading partners . . . ; and it should not discriminate between its own and foreign products, services or nationals (giving them "national treatment")
- freer—barriers coming down through negotiation
- more competitive—discouraging "unfair" practices such as export subsidies and dumping products at below cost to gain market share.[14]

Establishing such principles has been the goal of U.S. international economic policy at least since World War II. Their statement as guiding principles of the WTO does not mean that they are a description of the reality of global trade and investment, but the advent of the WTO certainly represents a major movement forward for U.S. policy. (Although the WTO includes as one of its principles that the trading system should be "more beneficial for less developed countries," none of the high-income countries— not the United States, Britain, Japan, Germany, or any others—rose to their positions through a "free trade" system in which they did not discriminate in favor of their nationals with numerous policies. Clearly, the application of the WTO's principles greatly reduces the policy options—the "policy space"—for low-income countries.)

Expanding Operations

The set of changes in the organization of the global economy have been reflected in various indicators of international commerce, several of which we mentioned earlier. They have also had profound impacts on the U.S. economy. Most obvious has been the rising volume of imports. The traditional U.S. imports include such items as Brazilian coffee, Central American bananas, German machinery and pharmaceuticals, Canadian lumber, and of course oil from various countries. Recent additions to this list include automobile wiring systems from Mexico (produced in a GM or Ford subsidiary); toys from China, Pakistan, and elsewhere in Asia; clothing from Honduras, Bangladesh, and, again, China; shoes from Indonesia and, still again, China; electronic devices—from Blackberries to iPods—from China, Mexico, Hungary, and Canada; and those socks from Datang. The changes are perhaps most noticeable with regard to clothing. In the mid-1960s, less than 5 percent of the clothing bought and sold in the United States came from abroad.[15] Today, most of us would be hard pressed to find in our closets any garments with a "Made in the USA" label—though high-fashion, custom-made clothes are still produced here.

The data show us what anyone who has been watching for the last several decades already knows. Between 1960 and 1970, imports rose slightly in relation to GNP, from 4.3 percent to 5.4 percent—a change that drew limited attention at the time. Then during the 1970s the figure jumped upward, and imports were 10.5 percent as large as GDP by 1980. In significant part, this change was accounted for by the rise in oil prices during the decade. As oil prices came back down and as the global economy was relatively unstable in the 1980s, by 1990 the figure was essentially the same: 10.8 percent. Then a steady upward trend was established, as the figure rose to 14.8 percent in 2000 and then peaked at 17.6 percent in 2008 (before falling off to 13.7 percent as consumer demand faltered in 2009). Exports have also risen more rapidly than GDP, but not to the same extent as imports. Up through the 1960s, exports exceeded imports by a slight margin—i.e., the United States was a trade surplus country. Then in the 1970s, the United States became a trade deficit country, with imports of goods and services exceeding exports in every year after 1975. Since the mid-1990s, imports have grown much more substantially than exports. The trade deficit rose from 1.2 percent of GDP in 1995 to 3.8 percent in 2000 and above 5 percent in every year from 2004 to 2007. (The deficit fell off to 4.9 percent of GDP as the crisis developed in 2008 and then dropped to 2.7 percent as demand in the U.S. economy fell more substantially than demand in the economies of U.S. trading partners.)[16]

These figures on U.S. imports and exports are one major indicator of the increasing integration of the U.S. economy with the global economy, and especially of the acceleration of that integration since the early 1990s. The expanding investment activity of U.S–based firms is another indicator. As we have noted earlier in this chapter, while the global operations of U.S. firms had expanded rapidly following World War II (the operations of multinational firms, or FDI), the rate of expansion slowed with the instability of the 1970s. This less rapid growth of the multinationals' activity continued in the 1980s as U.S. and global economic instability continued. The early 1980s brought about a slight decline in FDI relative to GDP, and at the beginning of the 1990s FDI was no greater in relation to GDP than it had been a decade earlier.

Then a new era of rapidly expanding international investment by U.S.–based firms took place. In 1992, FDI was 7.9 percent as large as GDP; the figure rose to 13.2 percent by 2000, and then leaped to 22.3 percent in 2008—this last surge of FDI growth relative to GDP growth reflected the slow expansion of GDP as well as the rapid expansion of FDI. (At the same time, direct investment from abroad into the United States was also expanding— from 6.7 percent as large as U.S. GDP in 1992, the figure almost doubled to 12.4 percent in 2000 and then rose to 14.9 percent in 2008.)[17] The U.S.–based firms engaged most heavily in international operations are ones with familiar names. Among the world's ten largest nonfinancial firms in 2006 were General Electric with 63 percent of its assets abroad, ExxonMobil had 71 percent of its assets abroad, and Ford with 47 percent and Walmart with 73 percent of their assets outside the United States. Likewise, the largest U.S. financial firms are all major international operators—Citibank, Bank of America, J.P. Morgan Chase, Goldman Sachs, and Morgan Stanley, for example.[18]

Up through the 1980s most international operations of U.S-based firms had been directed toward obtaining access to foreign markets or raw materials. Market-motivated operations were partly driven by barriers to trade but also by the advantages gained by locating production close to the market. Raw material–motivated operations were determined by the location of the raw materials (oil, copper, bauxite, other minerals) and conditions suitable for tropical agriculture (bananas, sugar, pineapples). Investment abroad primarily motivated to take advantage of low-wage labor was a relatively minor component of these operations.

In recent decades, the *direct* use of low-wage labor in the operations of multinationals continues to be of secondary importance. However, there has been a burgeoning of the *indirect* use of low-wage labor through subcontracting. Subcontracting has become important as part of a relatively new process in the global economy: the development of global production systems in which low-wage labor in low-income countries has often played a substantial role. Instead of setting up their own production facilities, the multinational firms often rely on local firms to supply the products. This is the case, for example, with those socks in Datang. Indeed, it is the case with garment production generally, in China, Bangladesh, Honduras, and other low-income countries. For the multinational firms, subcontracting arrangements allow them to avoid the problems—both direct and political—of managing a low-wage labor force in low-income countries. Yet the multinationals, virtually always based in high-income countries, maintain control over many aspects of the production process—including design, technology, and related research and development. The output of this subcontracting process then shows up as imports to the United States and has contributed to the rapid growth of the import figures that we have presented.

According to the International Labour Organization (ILO), "Some 65,000 transnational corporations, with around 850,000 foreign affiliates, coordinate global supply chains that link firms across countries, including local sub-contractors who work outside the formal factory system and outsource to home workers . . ."[19] And, as the ILO points out, this global production system has developed without multilateral rules to govern its key elements. Thus these systems are a prime example of the direction in which U.S. policy has pushed globalization—toward a relatively unregulated system of international commerce.

Ending the Twentieth Century with Global Finance

Creating an unregulated system of international commerce has certain similarities to the fable of "The Sorcerer's Apprentice." Conjuring up a system that appears to ease burdens, the U.S. government and its allies may in fact have conjured up a system that will run amok. Clear signs that the increasingly unregulated global economy could readily run amok appeared in the East Asian financial crisis of 1997.

The crisis began in Thailand, where the economy had been growing rapidly for several years. The Thai government had followed a system of holding the value of its currency, the baht, constant in relation to the dollar—i.e., a "pegged" exchange rate. The rapid growth and the stability provided by the pegged exchange rate had attracted a substantial amount of foreign investment, including loans (i.e., financial investment). The heavy reliance on foreign loans was in large part a result of the fact that the baht was pegged at a relatively high value in relation to the dollar, and thus borrowing from abroad was relatively cheap (i.e., lots of dollars could be obtained for relatively few baht). However, in 1996 when export growth and the overall growth of the Thai economy slowed, foreign investors began to pull their funds out of the country. Because much of the foreign funds that had come into Thailand were financial investments and because the Thai government did not restrict the movement of funds in and out of the country, those funds could be moved out quickly. (Money that can be moved quickly is often referred to as "hot money.") This movement of funds out of Thailand meant that the baht was being exchanged for dollars, putting downward pressure on the value of the baht and creating an expectation that the Thai government would drop the "peg" and lower the value of the baht. This expectation led investors to move their funds out of Thailand even more rapidly. As a result, the value of the baht collapsed, and the government was forced to abandon the peg to the dollar. This movement of "hot money" and the consequent fall in the value of the Thai currency led the country into a general economic downturn.

Had the 1997 crisis remained only a Thai crisis, it still would have illustrated the problems associated with a lack of regulation of the international economy. Thailand's difficulties were very much connected to the unregulated (unrestricted) movement of foreign funds in and then rapidly out of the country. While such movement of international funds has been associated with economic disruptions in earlier eras, the problem was especially pronounced in the Thai situation.

As it was, the crisis did not remain only a Thai crisis. It quickly spread to other East Asian countries. Indonesia and the Republic of Korea were severely affected, and Hong Kong, Malaysia, Laos, and the Philippines also felt the impact. While other countries of the region escaped from most of the negative effects, all were affected to some degree by the loss of demand for their products and by the increasing wariness of foreign investors. In part, the spread of the crisis was a result of similarly problematic situations in some of the other countries, as excessive debt had become a common problem. However, it was not only the reliance on debt that led to crisis. In addition, international capital managers were highly sensitive to the possibility of problems and could (and would) move funds in and out—especially out, in this case—very quickly. Thus, the concerns of international investors that the crisis would spread led them to pull their funds out of other countries, as well as Thailand—which ensured that the crisis would spread. This phenomenon can be likened to a run on a bank. Once depositors become concerned that a bank may fail, they rush ("run") to take out their deposits, and they thus ensure that the bank will fail. Governments have regulations in place that prevent bank runs. In the United States, for example, the Federal Deposit Insurance Corporation requires banks to insure deposits, and depositors thus need not fear losing their funds if a bank fails. But, increasingly, insufficient regulations have been in place in the international financial system. In the global economy, however, it is not financial institutions that are subject to failure, but the economies of nations that, if not subject to failure, suffer severe disruption.

The East Asia crisis led several governments of counties in that region to seek loans from the IMF. As usual the IMF made the loans along with "conditionality." And, as often has been the case, the IMF's conditions appear to have made the crisis worse. Demanding that governments reduce their budget deficits, the IMF was in effect demanding that they reduce aggregate demand and thus worsen their recessions. Perhaps of more lasting importance, however, was the IMF's condition that the governments take steps to open their economies further to international commerce, including international investment. This was an especially perverse step for countries such as Korea that had achieved extraordinarily rapid economic growth with policies of direct government regulation of foreign trade and investment. It was also a step that exacerbated the conditions that had contributed so greatly to the emergence and spread of the crisis—the nonregulation of international capital movements.

In addition to laying the groundwork for future crises by weakening the regulation of international finance, the 1997 crisis set in motion policies in many countries that would feed directly into the crisis that emerged a decade later. With China leading the way, many countries pursued policies that led to large trade surpluses—exports greater than imports—allowing them to keep in reserve a substantial portion of the foreign currency they received from selling their exports to the United States and other high-income countries. China's trade surpluses averaged 7.0 percent of its GDP from 2006 to 2008, while the major oil-exporting nations totaled up trade surpluses that averaged a huge 23.4 percent of their GDPs during those years. These reserves would allow the countries to reduce dependence on foreign borrowing that could evaporate at the first signs of economic problems—as had happened in Thailand. Furthermore, as those reserves accumulated, the trade surplus nations went from being international borrowers to international lenders.[20]

To a large extent, these funds were invested in the United States, financing the U.S. government's budget deficit as well as private investment. And, just as the funds flowing from China and elsewhere were generated by trade surpluses, the inflow of funds to the United States were the counterpart of this country's huge trade deficits, which rose to an unprecedented level of over 6 percent of GDP in 2006–2008. Overall, in the decade leading up to the crisis in the United States, these extremely large and unprecedented global imbalances transferred perhaps as much as $5 trillion from the low-income countries to the high-income countries—especially to the United States.[21] As we will discuss in the next chapter, this huge flow of funds contributed to low interest rates in the United States and thus to the buildup of debt and the housing bubble that lead into the crisis.

And so the conditions were established for the new millennium. The East Asian crisis of 1997 illustrated the problems of an unregulated global financial system, led to a further undermining of regulation, and set the stage for a much larger crisis. It would seem that the widely quoted words of John Maynard Keynes, writing in the midst of the Great Depression of the 1930s (and concerned as much with political/military conflicts as with economic issues), had been thoroughly forgotten—or, if not forgotten, ignored:

> There may be some financial calculation which shows it to be advantageous that my savings should be invested in whatever quarter of the habitable globe shows the greatest [return]. But experience is accumulating that remoteness between ownership and operation is an evil in the relations among men, likely or certain in the long run to set up strains and enmities which will bring to nought the financial calculation.
>
> I sympathize, therefore, with those who would minimize, rather than with those who would maximize, economic entanglement among nations. Ideas, knowledge, science, hospitality, travel—these are the things which should of their nature be international. But let goods be homespun whenever it is reasonably and conveniently possible, *and, above all, let finance be primarily national.* Yet, at the same time, those who seek to disembarrass a country of its entanglements should be very slow and wary. It should not be a matter of tearing up roots but of slowly training a plant to grow in a different direction (emphasis added).[22]

Notes

1. These initial paragraphs draw text from Arthur MacEwan, "What Is Globalization?" *Radical Teacher,* Fall 2001 (61), pp. 2–7.

2. Adam Smith, *The Wealth of Nations* (New York: Random House, 1937 [1776]), p. 590.

3. Charles P. Kindleberger, *Foreign Trade and the National Economy* (New Haven: Yale University Press, 1962), Table 11-2, p. 180. In the 1805–1819 period, exports plus imports divided by 2 averaged 8.4 percent of national income, and was 8.5 percent in 1820–1829. In 1900–1909 the figure was 26.6 percent and rose to 29.4 percent in 1910–1913.

4. E.J. Hobsbawm, *Industry and Empire* (Harmondsworth: Penguin Books, 1968), p. 31.

5. Jonathan Barron Baskin and Paul J. Miranti, Jr., *A History of Corporate Finance* (Cambridge: Cambridge University Press, 1997).

6. Laurence Shoup and William Minter, *Imperial Brain Trust: The Council on Foreign Relations and U.S. Foreign Policy* (New York: Monthly Review Press, 1977), p. 128.

7. As quoted by Shoup and Minter, p. 164.

8. FDI figure for 1950 from Table 1 in Obie G. Whichard, "Trends in the U.S. Direct Investment Position Abroad," *Survey of Current Business* 1981 (February), pp. 39–56. FDI figure for 1980 from U.S. Department of Commerce, Bureau of Economic Analysis, "U.S. Direct Investment Position Abroad on a Historical-Cost Basis: Country Detail," www.bea.gov/international/datatables/usdpos/usdpos_77. htm#pos80. GDP figure for 1980 from *Economic Report of the President 2010*, Table B-1. For 1950, GNP is used and is from *Economic Report of the President 1975*, Table C-1.

9. Data from *Economic Report of the President 1975*, Table C-1 for GNP and Table C-8 for imports and exports.

10. World Trade Organization, *World Trade Report 2007* Appendix, Table 3, p. 49, www.wto.org/english/res_e/booksp_e/anrep_e/world_trade_report07_e.pdf.

11. Foreign exchange transactions data from the Bank for International Settlements, *Triennial Central Bank Survey of Foreign Exchange and Derivatives Market Activity in 2007—Final results,* December 2007 and earlier years. World export data from UNCTAD, *Handbook of Statistics, 2009* (New York: United Nations Publications, 2009), www.unctad.org/en/docs/tdstat34_enfr.pdf.

12. This summary of the Mexican experience draws on Arthur MacEwan, "Liberalization, Migration, and Development: The Mexico-U.S. Relationship," *Revista de Economia Mundial* 2006 (14), pp. 57–85, www.sem-wes.org/revista/arca/rem_14/rem14_2I.pdf.

13. The U.S. trade agreements are listed on the website of the Office of the United States Trade Representative, www.ustr.gov/trade-agreements/free-trade-agreements.

14. World Trade Organization, "Principles of the Trading System," www.wto. org/english/thewto_e/whatis_e/tif_e/fact2_e.htm.

15. Robert Ross, *Slaves to Fashion: Poverty and Abuses in the New Sweatshops* (Ann Arbor: University of Michigan Press, 2004), p. 107.

16. Figures calculated from data in the *Economic Report of the President 2010*, Table B-1.

17. The data referred to in the previous paragraph and the figures here on U.S. FDI abroad and foreign FDI in the United States are on a historical-cost basis. The data on U.S. FDI are from the U.S. Department of Commerce, Bureau of Economic Analysis (BEA), "U.S. Direct Investment Abroad: Balance of Payments and Direct Investment Position Data, Industry detail (includes all industries), Position on a historical-cost basis, industry detail by selected country," http://www.bea.gov/international/di1usdbal.htm.

The figures for foreign FDI in the United States are from various BEA tables. The GDP figures used in the calculations are from *Economic Report of the President 2010*, Table B-1.

18. UNCTAD, "The World's Top 100 Non-financial TNCs, Ranked by Foreign Assets, 2006," in UNCTAD, *World Investment Report 2008* (New York and Geneva: UNCTAD, 2008), p. 220, www.unctad.org/en/docs/wir2008_en.pdf.

19. International Labour Organization, "The Nature and Impacts of Globalization," www.ilo.org/legacy/english/fairglobalization/download/toolkit/module4.pdf.

20. The source for the data on China's trade surpluses and the trade surplus of the major oil-exporting nations is the *UNCTAD Handbook of Statistics 2009.* See Table 1.3.1, "Value of trade balances, and as percentage of imports of countries and geographical Regions," and Table 8.1.1, "Nominal gross domestic product: Total and per capita of countries and geographical regions." The major oil-exporting nations are the Middle East minus Egypt plus Russia.

21. See Anton Brender and Florence Pisani, *Globalised Finance and Its Collapse* (Dexia, Belgium: Dexia SA and Dexia Asset Management, 2009), p. 77, www.dexia-am.com/NR/rdonlyres/DC3E445C-427E-4A69-ADC6–4B10374D6FE8/0/Globalisedfinance.pdf.

22. John Maynard Keynes, "National Self-Sufficiency," *The Yale Review,* June 1933 *22* (4), pp. 755–769, www.mtholyoke.edu/acad/intrel/interwar/keynes.htm.

8

China, the United States, and the Crisis

At the beginning of 2006 a flurry of news items reported on a Chinese map of the world purported to be a 1763 copy of a map first made in 1418. It showed the various continents of the world with a reasonable amount of accuracy, suggesting that Chinese navigators were circumventing the globe well before the much-celebrated European "Age of Discovery."

The authenticity of the map—and, by implication, the extent of Chinese early seafaring—is in dispute. However, *The Economist* magazine, in discussing the unveiling of the map and related information wrote that, as compared to the story of Europeans being the first to undertake great sea voyages and circumvent the globe, "It seems more likely that the world and all its continents were discovered by a Chinese admiral named Zheng He, whose fleets roamed the oceans between 1405 and 1435."[1]

Some of the early Chinese sea voyages are well documented. According to the historian David Landes:

> From 1405 to 1431, the Chinese undertook at least seven major naval expeditions to explore the waters of Indonesia and the Indian Ocean . . . These flotillas far surpassed in grandeur the small Portuguese fleets that came later. The ships were probably the largest vessels the world had seen: high multideck junks (but that is a misleading term) acted as floating camps, each carrying hundreds of sailors and soldiers, testimony to the advanced techniques of Chinese shipbuilding, navigation, and naval organization. The biggest were about 400 feet long, 160 feet wide (compare the 85 feet [length] of Columbus's *Santa Maria*), had nine staggered masts and twelve square sails of red silk. These were the so-called treasure ships . . . Other ships met other needs: eight-masted "horse ships" . . . ; seven-masted supply ships . . . ; six-masted troop transports; five-masted warships . . . ; and smaller fast boats to deal with pirates. The fleet included water tankers, to ensure a fresh supply for a month or more . . . The first of these fleets, that of the eunuch admiral Zheng He . . . in 1405 consisted of 317 vessels and carried 28,000 men."[2]

China in the era leading up to the fifteenth century was not only the world's leading seafaring nation. Its central regions were at least on a par with European nations in terms of wealth, and the country was far advanced in terms of the complexity and extent of political organization.

Things changed of course. For reasons that are a continuing matter of dispute among historians, by the middle of the fifteenth century China halted its seafaring expeditions. Whether as cause or consequence of this retreat from global involvement—or perhaps as both cause and consequence—the Chinese economy faltered. As European powers extended their empires and advanced economically, China became part, a large part, of the impoverished world. While the country continued to exist as a single political entity, central authority was greatly weakened. By the end of the nineteenth century, while not a formal colony, the country was thoroughly dominated by European powers and Japan—and with the "open door" assertion in 1899, the United States tried to gain a share of the spoils. For most of the first half of twentieth century, "the starving masses of China" became a common symbol of poverty.

Then things changed again. In 1949 the Communist revolution came to power, establishing a strong central authority, greatly reducing economic inequality, and instituting broad social changes (in health care and education, for example)—but accomplishing relatively limited and erratic progress in terms of economic growth. In 1977, China's GDP per capita (in real purchasing power terms) was $469. This was slightly below the figure for India, and about 60 percent of the average for African countries. China's per capita GDP was only 5 percent of that for the United States, which had a per capita GDP in 1977 of $9,216.

From the late 1970s onward, however, China has experienced a period of extremely rapid economic growth. By 1990 China's per capita GDP was 8 percent of that of the United States; by 2000, 12 percent; and by 2008, 22 percent of the U.S. level. In thirty-one years, one generation, China's per capita GDP had increased by seven-and-half times, an annual growth rate of 6.5 percent.[3] Even while this economic expansion has been accompanied by a marked increase of income inequality and by degradation of social programs in health care and education, the growth of the economy has pulled hundreds of millions of Chinese out of absolute poverty. (All of these figures and comparisons in dollars are in terms of real purchasing power, not in terms of existing exchange rates.)

In large part, the country's economic growth success in recent years has been based upon a set of reforms in the late 1970s and early 1980s that gave much more leeway to private business and market activity. Nonetheless, the Chinese government has maintained a large role in directing the economy, and to some degree the success built on the economic and social changes of earlier years (though those earlier years also generated some economic disasters).

China and Globalization

China's rapid economic resurgence in recent years has been remarkable in itself, going far toward restoring the country to the relative position it held among nations in the fifteenth century. With the expansion of recent decades, its economy has become the world's second largest, exceeded in overall size only by the U.S. economy (though per capita income is only a fraction of that in the United States). This resurgence has also been remarkable in its impact on world commerce, and China is now a major player in the global economy. Its international trade and its involvement in world financial affairs have had far-reaching impacts—including impacts that affected the emergence of the economic crisis that appeared in 2007 and 2008.

Although China's involvement in the international economy has been truly global, its emergence as a major player in world commerce is perhaps best illustrated by the rapid expansion of its trade with the United States. From the less than 1 percent of U.S. imports that came from China in 1984, in 2009 China accounted for more than 18 percent of U.S. imports—a larger share than that of any other country.[4] China's rising role as a supplier of U.S. imports has been most apparent in the vast increase of Chinese-made goods in U.S. stores. During fifteen minutes at a local Target store in early 2010, it was difficult to find an item without a "Made in China" label: vacuum cleaners and rug steamers, knife sets and dinner plates, small refrigerators and microwave ovens, luggage and LCD monitors, bed quilts and three-ring notebooks, picnic tables and glass candle holders—all made in China. And the list of "Made in China" Target items goes on and on, including of course various items of clothing, numerous toys, various electronic devices, and, of course, socks—most likely from Datang. Then there are the dog food additives and wallboard, which both came to notice because of contamination. Lest one assume that U.S. imports from China are simply cheap consumer goods, an April 8, 2010, *The New York Times* story reported that, "The Chinese government has signed cooperation agreements with the State of California and General Electric to help build [high-speed rail] lines." China would be "supplying the technology, equipment and engineers" for the projects.[5]

As China has become the largest single source of imports for the United States, the United States has become China's largest single market. It is not, however, only the U.S. market that has pulled in Chinese goods. China has also penetrated markets around the world; countries in both Asia (Japan,

South Korea, Singapore, and India) and Europe (Germany, The Netherlands, and Britain) are among the top recipients of Chinese exports. On the other side of the trading system, while China has been exporting huge amounts of consumer goods and some other products, the items China imports have been largely industrial raw materials (oil, metallic ores, iron, and steel) and equipment (electrical machinery, power-generation equipment, optics, and medical equipment).

In the same manner as U.S. involvement in the global economy did not "just happen," the Chinese engagement with international commerce emerged as a process well-promoted by the Chinese government. At the center of the Chinese government's promotion of the country's exports has been its regulation of the value of the Chinese currency and its associated actions with regard to international financial investments. By maintaining a low value of the yuan in relation to the dollar, the government has ensured that Chinese goods would be relatively inexpensive for U.S. (and other) buyers—even less expensive than they would be as a result of the low labor costs in China. In maintaining the low value of the yuan, the government has used the dollars obtained from Chinese exports to the United States to purchase financial instruments—bonds primarily, and largely U.S. government bonds.

As we described in the introduction to Part IV, U.S. importers purchase Chinese goods by first using dollars to purchase yuan. They then use these yuan to pay the Chinese suppliers. (These transactions generally take place through agents rather than directly between the U.S. importers and the Chinese producers.) The growing demand for yuan by U.S. importers—a result of the growing demand by the importers for the Chinese products to, in turn, meet the demand by U.S. customers—tends to push up the price of the yuan in terms of dollars. This is just like a growing demand for cars or tomatoes or (to use a relevant example) houses tends to push up the prices of those items. In each of these markets, there are forces that push in the other direction. As the price of cars, tomatoes, or houses gets pushed up, producers will tend to supply more; so, with some time delay perhaps, the prices will tend to remain relatively stable. With yuan, there are two ways in which the supply will rise and counter the upward pressure provided by the demand of U.S. importers. One of these ways is that the Chinese will increase the amount of U.S. goods that they purchase, and will provide more yuan on the international market to buy dollars to pay for those U.S. goods.

There is, however, the other way in which the supply of yuan is increased, countering the upward pressure on the price of the yuan resulting form U.S purchases. The Chinese central bank exercises its authority to create more yuan and uses these yuan to buy dollars. This keeps the price of the yuan low relative

Box 8.1

The Renminbi and the Yuan

Chinese currency is sometimes referred to as the yuan and sometimes as the renminbi. Two names for the same thing? Not quite. The yuan is a particular unit of the Chinese currency; other units are the jiao, which is one-tenth of a yuan, and the fen, which is one-tenth of a jiao. So the yuan, the jiao, and the fen are analogous to the dollar, the dime, and the penny in the U.S. currency. Renminbi means "people's currency." Thus it refers to the currency in general, not to a particular unit. In the United States, there is no equivalent term for the currency, which is simply referred to as "dollars." Thus when people speak of the value of the Chinese currency relative to the U.S. currency, they may speak of the renminbi relative to the dollar or the yuan relative to the dollar. In the text, we use the term yuan, but we could have used the term renminbi.

to the dollar—that is, low relative to what it would be without the Chinese government's intervention in the currency market (through the action of the central bank). Instead of only two players in a U.S.-China exchange—the U.S. importer and the Chinese producers—there is a third party, the Chinese central bank. When the exchange is done the Chinese producers of the goods get the yuan, the U.S. importers get the goods, and the Chinese central bank gets the dollars. At least the Chinese central bank gets the dollars it needs to purchase in order to keep the value of the yuan (in terms of dollars) relatively stable. In recent years, the Chinese central bank has accumulated a lot of dollars (and also currencies of other countries, but mainly dollars). By March 2009, China's foreign exchange reserves had risen to $2 trillion, having grown by a factor of ten since the beginning of the decade.[6]

The Chinese government claims that the policy of maintaining a "pegged" value of the yuan is designed to maintain economic stability and not to promote its exports. However, managing its international currency transactions in this manner and thus keeping the value of the yuan lower than it would otherwise be, the central bank is keeping the cost of Chinese goods low in terms of U.S. dollars (and, generally, in terms of other countries' currencies as well). Estimates vary regarding the extent to which China's currency is thus undervalued (i.e., has less value in relation to other currencies that would be the case without intervention in currency market by the Chinese central bank). Some studies suggest that the yuan is undervalued by as much as 50 percent, while others place the extent of undervaluation as low as 10 or 12 percent.[7]

There is, however, wide agreement that the yuan is in fact undervalued and, as a consequence, the Chinese are able to sell more of their goods in global markets than would otherwise be the case. The success of this export-pushing strategy appears in the large trade surpluses—exports greater than imports—that have characterized the Chinese economy for several years. These trade surpluses have been almost entirely accounted for by China's trade with the United States. During the period 2007 through 2009, China's surplus with the United States averaged $249.8 billion, while its total trade surplus averaged $252.9 billion.[8] It should be emphasized, however, that China's foreign trade success is not simply based on the strategy that keeps its currency undervalued. The large supply of low-wage labor, a highly educated and effectively disciplined labor force (relative to other countries at a similar income level), and a variety of government policies that have promoted economic development and technological progress have also contributed to the country's export success. (Regarding the "discipline" of Chinese workers, which includes the proscription of independent unions, see Box 8.3, p. 155.)

China's Policy Impact in the United States

Beyond its impact on China's own fortunes, the Chinese government's currency and trade strategy has had another important aspect. The Chinese central bank has used a substantial share of its large reserve fund of dollars to purchase U.S. financial instruments, both U.S. government bonds and private securities. In early 2009, more than one-third of China's reserves, $764 billion, was held in U.S. Treasury securities, making China the largest foreign holder of U.S. government debt.[9]

While the Chinese are playing the largest role in supplying funds to the United States and while the Chinese role is especially noteworthy because it is a relatively new phenomenon, funds from abroad are also coming from other countries. In recent years, governments, private firms, and individuals from around the world have invested substantial funds in the United States—as foreign direct investment (which we noted in Chapter 7), as purchases of private U.S. securities, and as purchases of U.S. government bonds. While there has also been a flow of funds in the other direction—as U.S. interests have invested abroad—in recent years the flow of investment funds into the United States has far exceeded the outward flow.[10] A substantial portion of the funds coming to the United States has been purchases of U.S. government bonds by the central banks of other high-income countries; Japan and Britain are the prime examples. Another portion has come from the oil-exporting countries, as they have accumulated a large amount of dollars as

Box 8.2

The Money Flows Uphill

China is the leader. In 2009, the Chinese government and private interests in China held $1.464 trillion in U.S. securities. But other low-income countries are operating in a similar manner, taking their countries' savings and investing the funds in the United States. Brazil held $156 billion in U.S. securities in 2009; Mexico, $81 billion; India, $57 billion; and Thailand and Indonesia, each about $25 billion.

It is supposed to be the other way around, at least according to the advocates of global financial liberalization. Free-market globalization, it is claimed, will bring funds from the high-income countries to the low-income countries, boosting economic growth in the poor parts of the world. But for the last decade or so, the U.S. economy has operated as a giant vacuum cleaner, sucking up the world's savings. Most of the funds come from Japan, Europe, a few other high-income countries, and oil-exporting countries. But about a third comes uphill from the low-income world.

Even with its rapid growth of recent years, China remains a low-income country with a 2008 per capita income of only $6,600 (measured in terms of purchasing power). Brazil had a per capita income of $10,070, and Mexico's was $14,270. For India, Indonesia, and Thailand the figures were $2,960, $3,830 and $5,990, respectively. Yet all of these countries were supplying investment funds, their savings, to the United States, where 2008 per capita income stood at $46,970.

China's extraordinarily high national savings rate imposes considerable costs. Soaring retained earnings (undistributed profits) of Chinese enterprises have done the most in recent years to push up the Chinese national savings rate, which averaged about half of the country's total income from 2005 to 2007. The retained earnings of Chinese enterprises were so high in large part because low wages generated enormous profits. Higher wages, and therefore lower profits and retained earnings, would have benefited Chinese workers.

The savings that flowed out of the Chinese economy into the U.S. economy could have done quite a bit to improve life in China. The Chinese authorities might have devoted those savings to financing a public health care system, tuition-free schools, and old-age security, public programs lost or greatly diminished with China's move to a more market-dependent economy. Instead, China has become one of the most unequal societies in Asia. Likewise, other countries, sending their funds uphill to the United States, have been doing relatively little to relieve the conditions of those at the bottom and to temper their great income inequalities.[11]

a consequence of the high price of oil in recent years. Yet an additional large amount of funds flowing to the United States has come from low-income countries, especially China, but several others as well, including for example, Brazil, Mexico, and India. This phenomenon of funds running "uphill" from low-income to high-income countries is an important and perverse aspect of the increasing reduction of regulation in the global economy. (See Box 8.2 for comments on this feature of globalization.)

In effect, a "giant pool of money" has been pouring into the United States. Since the early 1980s, the country has seen a net inflow of investment funds—more coming in than going out. As early as the mid-1980s, when high interest rates in the United States attracted large amounts of foreign investments, the net inflow of funds rose above 3 percent of GDP, though this figure tapered off as interest rates fell. With the U.S. recession in the early 1990s, the flow of investments went in the other direction—more going out than coming in. Then, from 1992 onward, every year has seen a net inflow, which became quite large in the years leading up to the crisis. From 2000 to 2008, the net inflow of investment funds to the United States averaged 4.9 percent of GDP. In 2006 it peaked at $804 billion, 6 percent of GDP.[12]

With more money available in the United States, interest rates—including mortgage interest rates—were lower than they would have otherwise been. These lower interest rates induced a higher level of borrowing than would otherwise have been the case. Although it is difficult to determine the size of the impact of foreign funds on U.S. interest rates (and the size of the impact differed among different interest rates), a reasonable estimate is that long-term interest rates (which would include mortgage rates) would have been between one-half and one-and-a-half percentage points higher in the midst of the housing boom if not for this inflow of foreign funds.[13] (Recall that in Chapter 6 we pointed out how a lower interest rate makes it possible for a family to pay a higher price for a house, take on a larger mortgage debt, and have the same monthly payments it would have had with a lower priced house and a higher interest rate.)

It was in pushing down U.S. interest rates, then, that the Chinese currency policies contributed to the emergence of the financial crisis in the United States. As we explained in Chapter 6, low interest rates were a key link in the chain of events that led to the crisis. While Federal Reserve policy was the central factor in generating the low interest rates, the "giant pool of money" coming into the country was also important. This does not mean, however, that the Chinese were in some sense to blame for the crisis. First, this pool of money was created by actions of several governments and other entities abroad, not just China. Second, Chinese policies were pushing in the same direction as various other factors; most important, as we have just noted, was the policy of the Federal Reserve.

Of greatest significance for our story, the Chinese policies were part of a complex set of implicit international financial arrangements in which the U.S. government was also a major player. In fact, the Chinese and U.S. governments were involved in a complementary relationship—a relationship that could be characterized as one of co-dependence or symbiosis. So to fill out the story, we need to turn to the relevant U.S. actions.

China-U.S. Symbiosis

Chinese trade and financial policies, undertaken as part of a very effective economic growth program, contributed to the development of the crisis in the United States and have also been a factor in the decline of manufacturing jobs in the United States. Yet those policies also had some significant favorable impacts in the United States, at least in the short-term. Moreover, China was able to pursue its policies so effectively only with complementary U.S. policies and practices. The Chinese purchases of U.S. government securities was the flip side of the large federal budget deficits in the United States, and the purchases of U.S. private securities was the flip side of the rising level of indebtedness by firms and individuals. (Again, we need to emphasize that while the Chinese were the new and largest U.S. partner in this arrangement, several other countries were also involved.)

The short-term gains for the United States in this relationship were substantial. As we have already noted, the funds coming into the United States from China and other countries kept interest rates in the early 2000s significantly lower than otherwise would have been the case—probably 1 percent to 1.5 percent lower. During the early 2000s, the Bush administration was running large budget deficits and borrowing heavily to finance the wars in Iraq and Afghanistan and the tax cuts bestowed on the wealthy. With the giant pool of money coming in, this government borrowing took place at lower interest rates than otherwise would have existed, and it did not excessively push up interest rates for private borrowers. The low interest rates—including low mortgage rates—also meant consumers could expand their purchases even though their incomes were rising slowly (if at all). Thus the weak recovery after the 2001 recession, with the slow growth of jobs and wages but the rapid expansion of profits, did not keep people from increasing their consumption and, equally important, did not create substantial political discontent. Furthermore, the positive impacts of the U.S.-China relationship in the United States were not only a consequence of the funds coming in; goods from China—low-cost goods—were also part of the relationship.

Consumers experienced the benefit of these low-cost goods directly, and the low costs contributed to a relatively low rate of inflation.

So China and the United States had a symbiotic relationship, with their economic connections to each other providing gains on both sides. The government in each country was pursuing policies that depended on the other's complementary policies. The Chinese got massive demand for their exports, which was a major stimulus to that country's economic growth. The U.S. government got to run large fiscal deficits, paying low interest rates for the debt it took on. U.S. consumers got loans at similarly low interest rates. The country as a whole was able to import more than it exported, in effect living beyond its means. Inflation was kept relatively low. All very good.

In the short-term. But the short-term turned out to be fairly short. The rising level of consumer debt, including mortgage debt, was unsustainable. When the housing bubble deflated, things fell apart, hitting especially hard those who had taken on the debt and bringing about the crisis that affected society in general. As to the heavy level of government borrowing, it too generated problems. The emergence of the crisis automatically greatly increased government borrowing, as tax revenues declined sharply and government spending programs were maintained and in some cases—unemployment insurance payments, for example—automatically increased. Furthermore, the crisis required the U.S. government to take on substantial new spending in an effort to pull the economy out of the recession (the "stimulus package"). However, with the buildup of government debt that had taken place in the preceding years, the government's deficits and debts had become quite large. (This is an issue to which we will return in Chapter 9.)

Although the heavy inflow of funds to the United States contributed to the creation of the crisis, as the crisis developed funds started to move in the other direction. In the summer of 2007, the giant pool of money sprang a leak, as foreign investors—and many U.S. investors as well—slashed their holdings of U.S. securities. On net, funds were still flowing into the country, but in the second half of the year the rate of inflow was cut in half. It had become clear that the debacle in the housing market would cause widespread losses for investors, and large numbers of investors sold their U.S. assets, intensifying the crisis and contributing to the collapse of the stock market. While the removal of funds by foreign interests was simply one part of a general phenomenon, it exacerbated the general drying up of the supply of credit for car loans, college loans, and even for corporate loans.

Since 2007, the movement of funds in and out of the United States has been highly volatile. By the end of that year, as the crisis spread to other countries, investors began looking for a safe place to put their money. They rushed to the safest place in the financial world: U.S. Treasury bonds. Then in early 2008, funds again moved out of the United States, and later in the year moved back in. From one quarter of the year to the next, the movement of funds to the United States shifted by hundreds of billions of dollars, and the value of the dollar moved accordingly. From the beginning of 2007 to early 2008, the value of the dollar (measured against currencies of countries with which the United States trades) fell by 12 percent and then rose back up 16 percent by the end of 2008. Under such circumstances it becomes increasingly difficult for firms to anticipate the course of exchange rates and the demand for exports and imports, inhibiting transactions and slowing global economic recovery.[14]

During the years leading up to the emergence of the financial crisis the Chinese and U.S. governments were pursuing their own interests and, for a while, each benefited substantially from these arrangements. China exported the socks from Datang and sent the dollars back to the United States, where they helped make it possible for homebuyers in Las Vegas, Miami, and elsewhere to get low rate mortgages with which they bought increasingly expensive homes. Incomes in China rose very, very rapidly, and consumption, if not income, increased significantly in the United States. The problem was that these operations were taking place in a global economy that was increasingly unregulated. It was globalization created largely by U.S. efforts and in which China was playing an increasing role. The movement of funds and the patterns of trade and investment were mutually beneficial for a while, but the situation was both unstable and unsustainable.

Further Problems in the U.S.-China Economic Relationship?

The instability in the global economy, and in the U.S.-China relation especially, has had far greater negative impacts on the United States than on China. In the United States, global problems combined with domestic problems to generate a severe economic downturn. Factories in China that produced goods for the U.S. market—and for the export market generally—cut back or shut down, and millions of workers became unemployed. Relative to the states and most other countries, however, the economic downturn in China was relatively mild—indeed, it wasn't even a downturn, but only a period of slightly slower expansion. The Chinese government's policies of regulating its economy's connections to global commerce seem to have provided some insulation from the downturn. Also, the government acted relatively quickly to provide a fiscal stimulus as demand for Chinese exports ebbed.

Yet the policies that worked so effectively for China in recent years (China's side of the U.S.-China symbiosis) have some problems that may disrupt or limit the country's economic success in the coming period. To begin with, several factors could combine to generate inflation. These factors include: the Chinese government's policy of increasing the supply of yuan to purchase dollars (and other foreign currencies); the rising prices of imports, associated with the low value of the yuan; and the general pressure on prices resulting from the continuing rapid growth of the economy—due in part to government fiscal stimulus and low interest rates. With GDP growth of 8.6 percent in 2009 and an anticipated growth rate of 10 percent in 2010, Chinese authorities have become concerned with the threat of inflation—even while the official increase of consumer prices remains below 3 percent annually— and may take counter measures, such as raising interest rates.[15]

In spite of an increase in unemployment in China in 2008, over the longer run China will not be able to rely on an "inexhaustible supply of low-wage labor" to keep inflation in check and fuel economic expansion. In early 2010, *The New York Times* reported that, "Just a year after laying off millions of factory workers, China is facing an increasingly acute labor shortage . . . Factory wages have risen as much as 20 percent in recent months . . . Rising wages could . . . lead to greater inflation in China. In the past, inflation has sown social unrest."[16]

It is not only inflation per se that concerns Chinese authorities and threatens continued economic expansion. It is very much the threat of "social unrest" that is already very real in China and would be exacerbated by economic instability. While rapid economic growth in China has raised the absolute incomes of virtually everyone in the country, huge income inequalities have emerged—inequalities among different social classes and between urban and rural regions. These inequalities combined with the rising expectations generated by rapid economic growth have created an atmosphere in which thousands of incidents of violent social unrest have taken place in China each year.[17]

The point here is not to claim that the great economic success of China is about to fall apart. It is simply to stress that the policies that have generated that success have the potential to generate substantial problems within China. Those problems, in turn, would disrupt China's international economic relations—including its symbiotic relationship with the United States. Furthermore, the problems are tied up in part with the manner in which China has engaged with the global economy. On the one hand, the reliance on low-wage labor, partly ensured by the repressive practices of the government toward unions (see Box 8.3), contributes to both to the rapid expansion of exports and the high degree of inequality. On the other hand, the policy of building up huge foreign reserves (largely dollars) and maintaining the low value of the yuan has restrained consumption in China; the policy

Box 8.3

The Real Threat from China: Dismal Labor Conditions

The low prices of Chinese imports into the United States come at the high cost of dismal working conditions and low wages in China, which in turn act as a weight dragging down labor conditions and workers' pay around much of the globe.

In a November 2006 article, "Secrets, Lies and Sweatshops," *Business Week* magazine published this account of working conditions in China: "Occupational safety, wages and hours, and freedom of association (the ability to organize an independent union) are the most common problems in export manufacturing factories. Excess overtime and underpayment for regular hours and overtime are especially frequent. There are no independent trade unions, and attempts to form independent organizations are swiftly repressed. Health and safety violations also are high, and especially serious in industries like construction and mining. In mining, the death rate is around 10 times that of the United States."

In 2008, *The New York Times* reported that worker abuse was still commonplace in many of the Chinese factories that supply Western companies. *The Times* quoted labor activists who reported that factories supplying several U.S. firms—Walmart, Disney, and Dell among them—practiced unfair labor practices, including using child labor, forcing employees to work sixteen-hour days on fast-moving assembly lines, and paying workers less than China's minimum wage. The activists also reported that factories withheld health benefits and exposed their workers to dangerous machinery and harmful chemicals, such as lead, cadmium, and mercury.

Chinese working conditions have improved in recent years, as rapid economic growth has tightened the Chinese labor market, drying up the seemingly bottomless pool of cheap labor. With their improved bargaining position, Chinese workers have had some successes, sometimes through major strikes. Workers in several large export factories have won wage increases in excess of 20 percent. At Honda Lock, which produces vehicle-key systems for Honda cars, workers have even demanded that they be able to elect their own leaders in the government-controlled union.

Yet working conditions in China remain oppressive. In May 2010 a thirteenth worker attempted to commit suicide at Foxconn factory in southern China. The world's largest maker of computer components, Foxconn supplies Apple, Dell, and Hewlett-Packard, among others. While working conditions at this Taiwanese-owned company are far from the worst in China, the hours are long, the assembly line moves too fast, and managers enforce military-style discipline.

Box 8.3 (*continued*)

Chinese workers, attempting to organize and improve their situations, always face the threat that their employer will simply pack up and depart for even lower-cost countries—Bangladesh, Indonesia, or Vietnam, for example. This kind of threat, which helps employers resist improvements in wages and working conditions, has been increasingly effective as modern globalization has greatly reduced limits on the mobility of corporations. Workers in the United States have faced the same threats, increasingly in service sectors as well as in manufacturing. All of these experiences throw into sharp relief the common interests of workers in all countries in improving conditions at the bottom, in robust full-employment programs that raise their incomes and enhance their bargaining power, and in forcing firms to pay the full costs of the disruption that takes place when they abandon a community.[18]

has, in effect, forced a high savings rate on the populace and contributed to the inequality. Thus, whether Chinese economic policies lead to greater social unrest and economic instability or induce the government to alter its policies, the impacts could be substantial in other countries, including the United States. A return to reliance on the mutually beneficial U.S.-China relationship that existed in the early 2000s may not be an option.

Even if maintenance of that relationship were an option, its continuation would present potential problems for the United States. These problems could arise from a reliance on other governments to play a large role in financing the U.S. government's debt in particular and U.S. investment more generally. Emphasis, however, should be on "potential," for, although these issues are widely discussed, the problems are not necessarily as real as they might appear.

One of these problems arises from the fact that having financed the federal deficit in large part by selling U.S. Treasury Bonds to foreign interests, the U.S. government has created a situation in which these foreign interests have a claim on future output in the United States. While these loans from abroad have allowed the United States to "live beyond its means," to consume more than is produced in the country, these claims will require the United States to "live *below* its means" in the future as the loans are repaid.

Whether or not this future obligation to foreign interests—the government of China, the government of Japan, other governments, or foreign private investors—is a "problem," however, depends on how the loans are used. Just as it often makes economic sense for an individual to go into debt, which creates a future obligation to creditors, so too can it be good economic policy for a government or, more broadly, a nation to go into debt to foreign creditors. For an individual, a college loan is an example of a debt that (usually) makes sense. For a country as a whole, loans that increase productive capacity are likely to make sense. In fact, much of the economic progress in the United States during the nineteenth century depended on debt to foreign interests; much of the financing of early railway construction, for example, came from European investors. This nineteenth century investment created productive capacity. When the debts became due, the capacity, the "means," of the United States had been increased. So, when paying back the debts, though the United States was living below its means, people in the United States were still living better than they would have been without the borrowing. Even when debt financing is not directly used to increase productive capacity it can raise the level of economic activity and productive capacity; government spending that simulates economic activity in a recession would provide an example.

The current problem in the United States is that the large buildup of debt—both the government debt and much of the private debt—was not used in ways that increased the country's productive capacity, either directly or indirectly. (Keep in mind, as we will explain in Chapter 9, that the great majority of the government deficit that received attention after it ballooned in 2009 was not primarily a result of the stimulus package of 2009. A large share arose as a consequence of policies adopted in the early 2000s. Another large share was result of the loss of tax revenue and automatic increases in spending, both generated by the recession.) To a great extent, the government debt was used to finance tax reductions for high-income people. While the tax reductions were rationalized with the claim that they would generate higher levels of investment and economic growth, rates of investment in the early 2000s were quite low and growth was slow. Also, the government debt financed expenditures for the wars in Iraq and Afghanistan. Whether one opposes or supports those wars, they did not expand the productive capacity of the U.S. economy. (The deficits of the early 2000s did provide some demand stimulus, raising the level of economic expansion somewhat and thus yielding some expansion of productive capacity. But the experience of the period suggests that this was a very ineffective stimulus.)

The impact of private borrowing on increasing productive capacity of the U.S. economy—the country's "means"—was no better. To a large extent private borrowing was directed toward the expansion of the housing bubble. On top of the original mortgage borrowing, homeowners took out substantial home equity loans to use in a variety of ways, only some of which (e.g., college expenses) raised productive capacity. The problem in all of this, then, is not foreign debt per se, but debt that is not used to expand productive capacity, debt that does not expand the country's ability to pay back the debt.

A second and related potential problem in the U.S.-China relationship is often raised specifically with regard to the large purchases and large holdings of U.S. debt by the Chinese government. What if the Chinese government stopped buying U.S. government debt (or U.S. debt in general)? Or what if the Chinese government started selling off the U.S. Treasury bonds that it holds? In other words, what would happen if the giant pool of money being supplied to the United States dried up? If this were to happen—a very big "if"—the impact on the U.S. economy could be severe. Just as the inflow of the giant pool of funds contributed to low interest rates, which made debt cheap for both the U.S. government and private U.S. interests (individuals and businesses), were China to dry up the pool, interest rates would rise. Indeed, they might rise a great deal. In order to attract funds, the U.S. government would likely have to substantially raise the rate of interest it pays on treasury bonds, and private interests, individuals and firms would have to pay significantly higher interest rates as well. The result could be a cutback in spending that would send the U.S. economy into recession. The scenario becomes especially scary if one posits that China would sell off its U.S. securities rapidly, precipitating a severe economic shock.

The Chinese government, however, would have little (if any) interest in taking this sort of action. If the Chinese central bank were to begin selling off its U.S. securities in large quantity, the value of its remaining dollar investments would start to fall dramatically, yielding billions upon billions of dollars in losses. Moreover, by dumping its dollar assets, the Chinese would be forcing down the value of the dollar relative to yuan, and thus forcing up the cost of China's exports. The negative impact of all this on the Chinese economy would be considerable. Worse yet, another substantial recession in the United States—especially if precipitated by the scary scenario of a rapid Chinese sell-off—would seriously disrupt the entire international economy. With its high degree of integration with the global economy, China would be seriously harmed.

It seems, therefore, that the Chinese government is highly unlikely to engage in a disruptive sell-off of U.S. securities. Nonetheless, the specter of such action illustrates the potential instability that exists in a system of global economic connections that operates with very limited regulation—that is, the potential instability that exists in the current globalized economy. In the same way that a minimally regulated domestic financial sector contributed so greatly to the crisis of recent years, unregulated movement of international funds exacerbated the crisis. With this experience, it is not unreasonable for there to be concern about the difficulties that might arise from the international financial relationships of the United States, including the relationship with China.

The experience of recent years and the various potential problems that we have described here—even while remaining largely as potential problems—demonstrate the sorcerer's apprentice character of the long-running U.S. efforts to structure a deregulated global economy. Those efforts have attained a great deal of success. But, like the sorcerer's apprentice, the U.S. appears to have conjured up something it cannot control, something that may cause a great deal of harm.

Notes

1. *The Economist,* "Chinese Cartography: China Beat Columbus to It, Perhaps," *The Economist,* January 12, 2006, www.economist.com/node/5381851.

2. David Landes, *The Wealth and Poverty of Nations* (New York: W.W. Norton & Company, 1999), pp. 93–94.

3. The basic figures are from Angus Maddison, "Statistics on World Population, GDP and Per Capita GDP, 1–2008 AD," www.ggdc.net/MADDISON/oriindex.htm. The U.S. 1977 figure is from *The Economic Report of the President 2010,* Table B-31. The Maddison figure for 1977 for China is presented here in current dollars by maintaining Maddison's ratio.

4. Calculated from the *The Economic Report of the President 2010,* Table B-105, and the *Survey of Current Business,* September 2010, International Data, Transactions Tables F.

5. Keith Bradsher, "China Is Eager to Bring High-Speed Rail Expertise to the U.S.," *The New York Times,* April 7, 2010, www.nytimes.com/2010/04/08/business/global/08rail.html.

6. Wayne M. Morrison and Marc Labonte, "China's Currency: A Summary of the Economic Issues," Congressional Research Service, June 17, 2009, http://www.fas.org/sgp/crs/row/RS21625.pdf.

7. Various studies are summarized usefully in a *New York Times* article of April 1, 2010: Vikas Bajaj, "Coming Visit May Signal Easing by China on Currency," www.nytimes.com/2010/04/02/business/global/02yuan.html?_r=1&scp=1&sq=renminbi percent20undervalued percent20studies&st=cse.

8. The U.S.-China Business Council, "U.S.-China Trade Statistics and China's World Trade Statistics," Tables 1 and 4, www.uschina.org/statistics/tradetable.html.

9. Morrison and Labonte, "China's Currency."

10. Helen Y. Bai and Mai-Chi Hoang, "Annual Revision of the U.S. International Transactions Accounts," *Survey of Current Business,* July 2010, pp. 36–50, and Christopher L. Bach, "Annual Revision of the U.S. International Accounts, 1991–2004," *Survey of Current Business,* July 2005, pp. 54–67, Table 1.

11. Sources for Box 8.2 include Asian Development Bank, *Asian Development Outlook 2009: Rebalancing Asia's Growth,* Manila, 2009, www.adb.org/documents/books/ado/2009/; Terry McKinley, "Will Pinning the Blame on China Help Correct Global Imbalances?" Centre for Development Policy and Research, Policy Brief No.

2, June 2009, www.gla.ac.uk/media/media_137155_en.pdf; U.S. Department of the Treasury, "Foreign Portfolio Holdings of U.S. Securities" various years, www.treas. gov/tic/fpis.shtml; and World Bank, *World Development Report 2010: Development and Climate Change* (Washington DC: The World Bank, 2010).

12. Bai and Hoang, "Annual Revision of the U.S. International Transactions Accounts," and Bach, "Annual Revision of the U.S. International Accounts, 1991–2004."

13. The higher estimate of one-and-a-half is for 2004 and comes from Stephen Roach, "Global: What Happens if the Dollar Does Not Fall?" Global Economic Forum, Morgan Stanley, November 22, 2004. In "The Impact of Global Capital Flows and Foreign Financing on U.S. Mortgage and Treasury Interest Rates," Ashok Bardhan and Dwight Jaffee write: "The need to maintain a somewhat undervalued Chinese Yuan has caused China to make extensive investments in U.S. Treasury and Agency (bonds and mortgage backed) securities, with the likely result that U.S. mortgage rates have been at least 50 bps lower; indeed a case could be made that U.S. mortgage rates are a full percentage point lower as a result" (Institute for Housing America, June 12, 2007).

14. The data on the movements in the value of the dollar are from the Federal Reserve Bank of St. Louis and are available at research.stlouisfed.org/fred2/series/ TWEXB.

15. See the report in Reuters, "China inflation goal tough but reachable: official," www.reuters.com/article/idUSTRE62J0JQ20100320, and the BBC report, "Chinese inflation hits 16-month high," news.bbc.co.uk/2/hi/8561381.stm.

16. Keith Bradsher, "Defying Global Slump, China Has Labor Shortage," *The New York Times,* February 27, 2010, www.nytimes.com/2010/02/27/business/ global/27yuan.html.

17. Paul Rogers, "China and India: Heartlands of Global Protest," August 8, 2008, *openDemocracy,*
http://www.opendemocracy.net/article/china-and-india-heartlands-of-global-protest.

For an earlier report on such incidents, see Robert Marquand, "In China, Stresses Spill Over into Riots," *Christian Science Monitor,* November 22, 2004, www.csmonitor.com/2004/1122/p01s03-woap.html.

18. Sources for Box 8.3 include Robert Dexter and Aaron Bernstein, "A Life of Fines and Beatings," *Business Week,* October 2, 2000; David Barboza, "In Chinese Factories, Lost Fingers and Low Pay," *The New York Times,* January 5, 2008, www. nytimes.com/2008/01/05/business/worldbusiness/05sweatshop.html; Dexter Roberts and Pete Engardio, "Secrets, Lies, and Sweatshops," *Business Week,* November 27, 2006, www.businessweek.com/magazine/content/06_48/b4011001.htm; William Foreman, "13th FoxconnWorker Reportedly Attempts Suicide," Associated Press, May 27, 2010, abcnews.go.com/Technology/wireStory?id=10755914; Jenn Abelson, "Local Sneaker Firms are Making It in Indonesia," *Boston Globe,* May 29, 2010, www.boston.com/business/articles/2010/05/29/local_sneaker_firms_are_making_it_in_indonesia/; Norihiko Shirouzo, "Chinese Workers Challenge Beijing's Authority," *Wall Street Journal,* June 13, 2010, online.wsj.com/article/SB1000142 4052748704067504575304690307516072.html; Elizabeth Holmes, "U.S. Apparel Retailers Turn Their Gaze beyond China," *Wall Street Journal,* June 15, 2010, online. wsj.com/article/SB10001424052748703627704575298874139834494.html; *The Nikkei Weekly*, "Wage disputes in China put world on notice," June 14, 2010.

Part V
Moving in a Different Direction

Among the various revelations that have emerged about the shenanigans that have gone on in the financial system in recent years, it is difficult to pick one that stands out as the most outrageous. Contenders would include:

- The NINJA loans and the widespread fraud (de facto if not always de jure) in the mortgage industry that these loans represent.
- The implicit (perhaps explicit) arrangement by which the rating agencies gave high ratings to risky CDOs in return for continuing business from the underwriters.
- The huge salaries and bonuses that the financial firms paid out to their top executives and traders when these firms were pulling the economy into disaster and themselves taking government bailouts—and some were failing.
- The payment by AIG, when it had been bailed out and was largely owned by the government, of 100 percent on the dollar to various other financial firms to which it owed payments in connection with failed mortgage-backed securities. Some $93 billion was funneled through AIG to large banks, with Goldman Sachs being the largest recipient at $12.9 billion. The government declined to negotiate lesser payments.

And this is only the short list. It is indeed difficult to pick the most outrageous. But if we had to choose, we would probably select the practice of Goldman Sachs. In 2006 the firm was persuading its clients to purchase CDOs while Goldman Sachs itself was betting against those same CDOs, thus making investments that would pay off only if the CDOs fell in value or failed. Or perhaps we would select none of these actions of private firms and instead focus our outrage on the government officials who collectively pushed the deregulation of finance, facilitated the inflation of the housing bubble, and denied the bubble's existence—Greenspan, Bernanke, Paulson, Summers, Geithner, Rubin, Gramm, and the list goes on. Then there is the outrage of the government's bailout of the bankers. No, there is no shortage of outrages that have been part of the financial and economic crisis.

These outrages, however, are not the root of problem. They are like the boils that can appear on the surface of one's skin—ugly, painful, and in need of direct treatment, but only the symptoms of a deeper malady. Dealing with the boils one at a time and ignoring the systemic infection that has generated them would be of little value; the boils would reappear, perhaps elsewhere on the body, but just as nasty. In fact, things would likely get worse if the underlying infection were not treated. As any decent physician knows, the boils *and* the systemic infection require attention.

With the economic crisis, the U.S. government has taken steps to deal with the manifestations, the symptoms, of the current economic debacle. Some of these steps have been useful, but they have usually been excessively timid and limited in their impact. Some others have been just plain bad. And the legislation that has established new financial regulations, while not useless, has been inadequate to seriously curtail most of the corporate outrages we have just listed—the nasty boils. Nonetheless, the steps at palliative care that have been taken, even though they are only palliative, need to be examined. In doing so (in Chapter 9) we uncover some clues to what needs to be done to deal with the systemic problems. These systemic problems are, as we have emphasized in the preceding chapters, based in the vicious circle of economic inequality, elite power, and perverse ideology that have now come to characterize U.S. society. In the final chapter (Chapter 10) we focus on how this vicious circle can be broken and transformed into a virtuous circle. But, first, the palliative care.

9

Palliative Care

An Appraisal

By the end of 2007, it was widely apparent that things were developing badly for the U.S. economy. The housing bubble was deflating, the troubles of financial firms were mounting, and credit markets had begun to "freeze up." A year later, the National Bureau of Economic Research, the organization that officially declares the existence of recessions, announced that the recession had begun in December 2007. After having ignored problems as they built up over the preceding years, the federal authorities finally took action.

What is interesting and important about the actions that have been taken at the federal level since late 2007 is not simply that, as many analysts have noted, they have been late, limited, insufficient, and sometimes quite harmful. For our purposes, the most significant thing about some of these actions is that they represent very substantial shifts in the direction of government policy that seemed to have been so firmly established in the preceding three decades. The financial regulation legislation that was enacted in the summer of 2010, with all its shortcomings, would have been unthinkable a few years earlier. The large use of deficit spending in order to stimulate economic activity and create jobs, while not large enough and often misdirected, has been a departure in practice and ideology from the experience of recent decades. Even the Troubled Assets Relief Program (TARP), a very negative move as we will argue, tore away the thin façade of the leave-it-to-the-market ideology that had gone largely unchallenged for many years. As has been the case in previous crises, the current economic crisis has opened the door for substantial changes in the organization of the economy.

So far, the door is only slightly ajar, and it could still be slammed shut. Even if opportunities for substantial change remain available, the direction of change is uncertain. Where we go from here will depend in large part on political action. In the next chapter, we offer some suggestions on how political action might be shaped to move things toward greater economic equality, a more democratic distribution of power, and an ideology based on social solidarity and a reduction in simplistic reliance on The Market. First, however, it will be useful to examine the steps that have been taken, both to understand their effects and to see how they have set the door ajar for greater change.

Initial Steps, Late and Limited

As economic conditions worsened in 2007, the first federal response was with monetary policy, an approach fully acceptable within the framework of conservative ideology. The Federal Reserve started pushing down interest rates in the latter half of the year, anticipating that, with this lower cost of credit, firms would borrow, invest, and spur economic growth. Also, and of more immediate importance, the greater availability of money would perhaps make it easier for troubled financial firms to raise the funds they needed. The federal funds rate, the interest rate most directly affected by the Fed, had hovered around 5.25 percent from July 2006 through July 2007, but fell below 4 percent by the beginning of 2008; by the middle of 2008 it was down to 2 percent and was virtually zero by the beginning of 2009—where it remained up until this writing in late 2010.[1]

At the beginning of 2008, the federal government also took steps to counter the economic downturn with fiscal policy and some regulatory adjustment designed to affect housing. The Bush administration's Economic Stimulus Act of 2008, enacted on February 13, included as its main feature tax rebates to low-income and middle-income taxpayers, amounting to $300 per individual in a family, up to a limit of $1,200. The act also contained investment tax incentives for businesses and provisions allowing Fannie Mae and Freddie Mac to increase their purchases of mortgages. The total cost of these measures was about $150 billion.

These initial government responses to the economic crisis came late and had limited impacts. With regard to the monetary adjustments by the Fed, there is little reason to expect interest rate reductions, even ones as large as those that took place in late 2007 and early 2008, to have much impact when businesses and consumers see economic activity dropping off sharply. Even with a low cost of credit, firms are not likely to increase their borrowing to buy new equipment when they expect their sales to be falling. And low interest rates will not induce people to buy new cars to drive to jobs when they fear they may soon have no jobs. Furthermore, in 2008, even if businesses and individuals had wanted to borrow, financial institutions were reluctant to make new loans, fearing that the economic situation would lead to numerous defaults. Credit was "freezing up" because of general uncertainty, not because interest rates were too high.

Similarly, in circumstances of emerging recession and uncertainty, tax rebates will have very limited impact because the recipients, increasingly worried about their jobs and incomes, will save instead of spend a large portion of those rebates. Such saving, which is quite rational from the perspective of the individual, can be counterproductive for society as a whole. Because people see the downturn developing, they save in order to provide for themselves as the downturn worsens. But with people in general behaving this way, demand for products is weak and the downturn does worsen.

A Congressional Budget Office report summarizing the results of various studies of the 2008 tax rebate suggests that recipients spent only about a third, maybe 40 percent of the funds they received.[2] There is no doubt that in a developing recession, tax rebates are generally not a very effective means by which to stimulate economic activity. Yet the powerful conservative ideology, proclaiming that tax cutting is always good, defined the policy. (And, after all, 2008 was an election year, and elections usually trump economic common sense.)

Aside from the extent to which the rebates were spent, the overall amount of spending stimulus contained in the 2008 Economic Stimulus Act was small. In 2007, GDP had been $13.8 trillion. Thus the entire amount provided for by the 2008 act amounted to slightly more than 1 percent of GDP. Even if the rebates had been fully spent and the investment incentives had had their purported impact (instead of simply giving businesses bonuses for investments they would have undertaken in any case), the impact would have done little to stave off a downturn of the severity that was emerging. Constrained by ideological blinders, the Bush administration's responses were misdirected and far too small. Because of their deep faith in the free market, the economic storm that was developing was simply outside the frame of reference of most economic and political officials. Furthermore, their ideology ruled out major government intervention, especially intervention that would require a significant increase in the budgetary deficit. From the perspective of the Bush administration, increases of the deficit were acceptable only to fight wars or reduce the taxes of the rich.

Ideology Gives Way to Reality

But as events of 2008 unfolded, things changed. Ideology began to give way to reality. When the Federal Reserve stepped in to arrange J.P. Morgan Chase's purchase of Bear Stearns, insuring J.P. Morgan against losses on $29 billion of Bear Stearns's "toxic assets," it was clear that the federal government was beginning to take a very active, interventionist role in attempting to prevent the collapse of the financial system and of the economy more generally. In early 2009, after the Bear Stearns intervention was followed by the government's (the Fed's and the Treasury's) AIG takeover and steps to secure the stability of other huge banks, Federal Reserve Chairman Bernanke explained the basis of the Fed's authority for its actions in the following terms:

> Section 13(3) of the Federal Reserve Act authorizes the Federal Reserve Board to make secured loans to individuals, partnerships, or corporations in "unusual and exigent circumstances" and when the borrower is "unable to secure adequate credit accommodations from other banking institutions." This authority, added to the Federal Reserve Act in 1932, was intended to give the Federal Reserve the flexibility to respond to emergency conditions. Prior to 2008, credit had not been extended under this authority since the 1930s. However, responding to the extraordinarily stressed conditions in financial markets, the Board has used this authority on a number of occasions over the past year.[3]

The situation that demanded action, in Bernanke's view, was the trouble faced by the very large financial firms. "Emergency conditions" existed because these firms were "too big to fail," in the sense that their failure would have spread the damage far and wide, both directly because of their extensive links to other financial and nonfinancial firms and indirectly because of the severe undermining of confidence that would have followed. Such damage, especially the damage to confidence, had been clear in the case of Lehman Brothers, when the federal authorities had failed to act. (Of course, even if one accepts the logic of Bernanke's position, one wonders how taking banks' toxic assets as collateral could make the loans "secured.")

TARP, the Bailout, and the Alternatives

After the ad hoc interventions on behalf of Bear Stearns and AIG, the mechanism under which the government bailed out banks was the Troubled Assets Relief Program (TARP), proposed by Secretary of the Treasury Henry Paulson and put in place virtually overnight (but not without considerable controversy) by Congress under the Emergency Economic Stabilization Act of 2008. The law was enacted on October 3 and gave the treasury secretary authority to use up to $700 billion to purchase the banks' assets, especially the toxic housing market assets, and provide capital to distressed banks. TARP funds were quickly provided to many large banks. Later, playing fast and loose under the vague provisions of the act, the Obama administration would use these funds to support businesses outside the financial sector— most notably the automobile firms.

These government interventions, both the ad hoc actions before October 2008 and those that took place under TARP in subsequent months, were extraordinary actions by any standards. For individuals and an administration that professed to define economic policy on the basis of free-market principles, they were ultra-extraordinary. In fact a good deal of the opposition to TARP and the related actions came from conservatives. Their views were perhaps best summed up by Allan Meltzer, a conservative economist and professor at Carnegie Mellon University, who reiterated the comment he had made some time earlier: "Capitalism without failure is like religion without sin. It doesn't work."

The reason that capitalism "doesn't work" when firms are protected from failure is not because such protection is a moral problem, as Meltzer's analogy might be interpreted. Instead, such protection creates a practical problem: the protection maintains poorly run firms (e.g., banks that have taken on too much risk), when the economy would operate better if these firms were allowed to die and to be replaced by better managed firms. Perhaps more important, when firms know they will be saved from their misdeeds by government intervention, they become more willing to take excessively risky actions. If those actions pay off, the firms win big. If the actions do not pay off, the firms will not lose. The losses will be borne by the rest of us, as taxpayers who foot the bill for the bailouts. (Ironically, given Meltzer's analogy, this problem of encouraging risk by providing government protection is called "moral hazard." By implicitly insuring firms against the negative outcomes of their risky behavior, the government is encouraging them not to act in a fully moral manner. The issue, however, is more one of practicality than morality.)

But what about the "too big to fail" issue? It would appear that the government was caught in a dilemma. On the one hand, by bailing out the big banks, it was encouraging the continuation of the very behavior that led the financial system into crisis. If the executives of a big financial institution know that if they get into trouble they will be bailed out, they are likely to return to the practice of making excessively risky investments. More crises are sure to follow. Yet, on the other hand, had the government not acted, had it not bailed out these very large financial institutions, the current crisis would have likely gotten much, much worse. Had AIG been allowed to fail, for example, the impacts would have spanned the globe, with untold—but surely severe—consequences. The authorities—the Fed and the Treasury—came down on the side of bailing out the banks. They apparently figured that it was better to prevent the current crisis from turning into an absolute disaster than to worry about the possibility of future crises. Indeed, these actions have had widespread support in Congress and among economists—if not among the general public—because they appeared to save the financial system from collapse.

This support, however, was based on the false premise that there was only one way to prevent the collapse of the financial system. The Federal Reserve and the Treasury chose to prevent financial collapse not only by bailing out the banks, but by also bailing out the bankers. With the exception of Bear Stearns and Lehman Brothers, both the high-level executives and the owners of stock in the large financial firms were generally protected from losses. Moreover, major creditors who made bad loans, who had bought risky derivatives, were also often protected from losses. A prime example: Goldman Sachs and other firms that were owed billions of dollars by AIG were paid off at 100 percent with government money—taxpayers' money. (Bear Stearns and Lehman Brothers were not trivial exceptions, but they were exceptions—perhaps because they were falling apart before the authorities had fully understood and figured out how to deal with the situation. Perhaps also the authorities were still unable to overcome the limits imposed by their ideology. Furthermore, even as Bear Stearns stockholders "took a bath," they were able to obtain more for their stock in the J.P. Morgan Chase buyout than had been originally negotiated—$10 per share instead of $3 per share—when it was not clear why they got anything at all for their ownership of an essentially bankrupt company.)

The situation could have been handled differently. The most obvious alternative is that the government could have temporarily taken over and controlled the operation of the troubled banks. This is what the government, through the Federal Deposit Insurance Corporation (FDIC), has done various times with small banks that have become insolvent. The FDIC takes over the banks, and then usually finds another bank that will buy the failed bank. The failed banks' stockholders lose their investments and the executives search for other jobs. Similar action could have been taken with the large banks, though the government would have had to run the banks itself (instead of finding other banks to buy up the failed firms). In running the failed banks, the government would have had various means by which to put them back into solvency. One option would have been for the government to move the banks' toxic assets into a "bad bank" that would hold and eventually sell these assets. (See Box 9.1 for an explanation of a "bad bank.") With the toxic assets removed from the banks (now under government control), the government could take steps to reduce the banks' reliance on credit and increase their capital reserves (i.e., reduce their leverage). Then, with the solvency of a taken-over bank restored, the bank could be sold back to the public. If there was a net gain in all of this—that is, if the sale back to the public brought in more than the costs that had been incurred by the government—the former

Box 9.1

What Is a "Bad Bank?"

The concept of creating a "bad bank" was widely discussed when the financial crisis was most severe at the end of 2008 and beginning of 2009. A bad bank is a government-created financial institution that buys the bad assets of existing banks—the CDOs and credit default swaps that had market values far below their face values. Because the market value of these assets had fallen so dramatically, many banks were de facto insolvent (though they may have been avoiding formal insolvency by keeping the assets on their books at their face values). With the bad assets off their hands, the banks could start operating again. The bad bank would hold the bad assets until the market stabilized and then sell them off at whatever price the market would bear.

In a bad bank operation, the crucial issue is: What price does the bad bank pay for these troubled assets? If the banks were temporarily nationalized, then the government would in effect be buying the assets from itself (i.e., the government-run bad bank would be buying from the government-run temporarily nationalized banks). It could then buy the assets at market prices, which would of course be well below their nominal values. The temporarily nationalized banks would then, of course, be insolvent. But the government could inject capital into them, allowing them to function again. Once they were stably operating, these banks could be resold to the public. Through the sale, the government could recoup its capital and other expenses.

The bad bank would over time sell off the troubled assets it had purchased from the banks. Having paid for the assets at market prices, the bad bank should be able to resell them without substantial, if any, loss. A bad bank procedure was employed successfully by Scandinavian authorities in 1991.

stockholders would receive some payment. Otherwise the former stockholders would lose their investment—which is what is supposed to happen when a firm becomes insolvent.

This sort of temporary nationalization of financial institutions is not by any means a radical "anticapitalist" procedure. As noted, the FDIC has taken similar action with small banks. Also, in 2008, the British government followed this sort of procedure with the Northern Rock bank, which, like many U.S. financial institutions, was failing because of its excessively risky investments in mortgage-backed securities. Several prominent, mainstream, politically liberal economists proposed nationalization of the U.S. banks, most notably among them Joseph Stiglitz and Paul Krugman (both winners of the Nobel prize in economics). But most significant, perhaps, is that Alan Greenspan at least urged consideration of the nationalization option. According to the *Financial Times* of February 18, 2009:[4]

> In an interview, Mr Greenspan, who for decades was regarded as the high priest of laissez-faire capitalism, said nationalisation could be the least bad option left for policymakers. "It may be necessary to temporarily nationalise some banks in order to facilitate a swift and orderly restructuring," he said. "I understand that once in a hundred years this is what you do."

The *Financial Times* continued, pointing out that Greenspan was not alone among conservatives:

> "We should be focusing on what works," Lindsey Graham, a Republican senator from South Carolina, told the FT. "We cannot keep pouring good money after bad." He added, "If nationalisation is what works, then we should do it."

What Greenspan, Graham, Stiglitz, Krugman and many others proposed could have worked to prevent the collapse of the financial system as well as TARP. However, temporary nationalization could have avoided bailing out the bankers and the bank stockholders. Then we would not have seen a continuation of either the practices that led the economy into crisis or the obscene salaries and bonuses that provided the incentives for bankers to act as they had.

Looking back on the TARP bailouts from the perspective of 2010, the extent to which they worked in the narrow sense of restoring the operation of the U.S. financial system is not clear. Disaster may well have been prevented. Yet through 2009, as the economy experienced severe recession, there was little to indicate that the banks were using TARP funds to significantly expand credit availability. What cannot be readily determined, however, is the extent to which this was a result of the banks' continued reluctance to offer loans or a result of the nonfinancial sector's reluctance to take on loans in the recessionary circumstances. Ironically, some large banks used the TARP funds to buy other banks, increasing their size and becoming even *more* too big to fail. For example, National City Corporation was taken over by PNC Financial Services in December 2008; PNC had been a recipient of $7.6 billion in TARP funds. Another example, in which one of the largest banks took over another very large bank, is Wells Fargo's purchase of Wachovia Bank at the end of 2008; Wells Fargo had received $25 billion through

TARP.[5] In any case, it is clear that the TARP bailouts were very effective in maintaining the income, position, and power of the financial firms, their executives, and their stockholders.

This power and position of financial firms and their executives and stockholders appears to have had continuing effect, limiting new regulation of finance. If the TARP had been supplemented by the establishment of thorough and effective regulation of the finance industry, it might not have simply reestablished the situation that led into the current crisis. The new legislation enacted in mid-2010 has some positive elements, and the separately enacted regulations of credit and debit cards should provide some significant beneficial changes. But these reforms, which we will discuss later in this chapter, are not thorough and will not be effective in altering important aspects of the operation of financial institutions.

The experience with the bailout of the banks and the lack of sufficient new regulation underscore the fundamental nature of the ideology that has been presented as "free-market ideology." The concept of free markets has wide appeal and has a long history and wide array of economic analyses that provide the rationale for operating an economy in this manner. As it turns out, however, in the practice of the government, whether it is a Republican or a Democratic government, free-market ideology means that the government should do whatever is necessary to protect large firms—these days, especially large financial firms. In normal times, this means allowing large firms to go about their business without government involvement. But when things turn sour, free-market ideology mandates that the government should intervene to take the firms' losses, protect their executives, and maintain their operations. Perhaps this can be rationalized as providing a stability that will allow markets to function effectively once again, but it is hardly what is usually touted as "free markets." It is, however, an approach to economic policy that ensures that firms' gains are private profits while their losses are socialized, falling on society at large. It is also an approach that maintains the highly unequal distribution of income, wealth, and power—perhaps making it even more unequal.

The Stimulus Package of 2009: Yes, But Too Small and Wrongly Constructed

TARP was put in place during the waning months of the Bush administration, but its application was not substantially altered with the arrival of the Obama administration. Where the Obama administration did initiate new practices to counter the economic debacle was with the so-called stimulus package, or, as it was enacted into law on February 17, the American Recovery and Reinvestment Act of 2009 (ARRA). This stimulus package provided $787 billion in tax cuts ($288 billion) and expenditures ($499 billion). The expenditures included $144 billion in state and local relief; $111 billion for infrastructure and science support; $155 billion for programs in education, training, energy, and health care; and $89 billion for "protecting the vulnerable" and other programs.[6] The ARRA was an explicit and large application of Keynesian policy, a major government fiscal policy intervention in the economy of the sort that had been rejected in principle (if not in fact) by U.S. governments for at least three decades. What's more, the spending provisions of the ARRA were not focused on the military, but included a broad range of social expenditures and investments in public programs (e.g., green energy and infrastructure). The legislation thus reflected a major shift in the direction of policy and ideology, the sort of shift that a crisis can generate.

Passage of the ARRA was opposed by virtually all Republicans in Congress. While their arguments against the program had various aspects, including opposition to numerous spending provisions, their main criticism, which has been reiterated in many quarters since the bill was enacted, was that it was too large and would excessively increase the federal budget deficit. They maintained that the large federal budget deficit created by the stimulus package would disrupt rather than promote economic recovery and would place a severe debt burden on future generations. Even conservative critics who recognized that the stimulus would create jobs argued that it would create far fewer jobs than President Obama and other proponents claimed.

The federal budget deficit has become very large. For the fiscal year 2009, which ended September 30, 2009, the deficit was $1.4 trillion, about 9.9 percent of GDP. This was the largest deficit ever in current dollar terms. As a percentage of GDP, the 2009 budget deficit had been exceeded only in wartime. During World War II, the 1943 deficit in relation to GDP peaked at 30.3 percent and was 22.7 percent and 21.5 percent in the two subsequent years. In fiscal year 2010, early estimates indicate that the size of the deficit fell only slightly by comparison with 2009; but with some growth of GDP, the 2010 deficit was about 9.1 percent of GDP (still a higher percentage than any time between World War II and the crisis).[7]

However, this large deficit in 2009 was not created by the stimulus package—or, more precisely, the stimulus package played only a minor role in creating this huge deficit. Even the stimulus package plus the expenditures under TARP do not account for a large part of the huge 2009 deficit. In 2001, when George W. Bush entered the White House as the first president in modern times to begin a term with a budgetary surplus, the CBO established a baseline budget estimate for the next decade. A baseline estimate assumes that there will be no changes in existing law and that the economy will grow at a reasonable rate. Thus, any departure from the baseline can be explained by new laws or a change in the performance of the economy. The CBO baseline estimate of 2001 projected that the 2001 surplus of $281 billion would grow to $710 billion by 2009. So what accounts for the huge gap between a $710 billion surplus and a $1.4 trillion deficit—a difference of over $2.1 trillion?

More than 40 percent (about 42 percent) of the difference is accounted for by the poor performance of the economy—the slow growth from 2001 to 2007 followed by the severe recession. With poor economic performance, particularly with the recession, tax revenues fell off sharply. Also, the recession automatically led to an increase of payments for unemployment insurance and other established social support programs. A similarly large chunk of the difference (again about 42 percent) is explained by pre-2009 legislative changes—and more than half of this was the Bush tax cuts and expenditures for the wars in Iraq and Afghanistan. What's left (about 16 percent) is accounted for in roughly equal amounts by expenditures under TARP and ARRA.[8] (Of course part of the reason that the ARRA stimulus package did not make a larger contribution to the 2009 deficit was that ARRA was enacted roughly halfway through the fiscal year, and it takes time after the passage of an appropriations bill for the money to be spent. In fiscal year 2010, a larger share of the ARRA appropriation was spent and this spending will make a larger contribution to the deficit. At the same time, as the stimulus funds have their impact, they will contribute to economic expansion and a consequent reduction of the deficit—i.e., a reduction relative to what it would have been without the stimulus.)

The real problem with the government's 2009 economic stimulus program was not that it was too large, but that it was too small. A program of $787 billion was insufficient, even by optimistic estimates, to bring the economy back to an "acceptable" level of output and employment. By late 2009, unemployment was at 10 percent. In order to raise the level of economic activity enough to lower the unemployment rate to 5 percent—if not real full employment—it would be necessary for the federal government to provide a stimulus package of over one trillion dollars, almost 40 percent larger than what had been provided through ARRA (The details of this calculation are explained in Box 9.2). The figures in this calculation are, to be sure, very rough but there is every reason to think that they are the right order of magnitude. This is, after all, the worst economic downturn in the United States since World War II, and at that time it was only the much larger deficits (in relation to GDP), the huge war spending, that pulled the economy out of the Great Depression.

Not only was the stimulus package too small; in addition it was poorly

Box 9.2

How Much Stimulus Is Needed? Some Rough Numbers

At $787 billion, the stimulus package created by the American Recovery and Reinvestment Act of 2009 (ARRA) seems like a lot of money. Indeed, it is a lot of money. But it was not enough to bring the economy back to its full potential and to reduce unemployment to a reasonable level.

During 2009, GDP averaged about $14.3 billion. By the end of the year, unemployment was at 10 percent. And there was every indication that, absent strong government action, the rate would continue rising. But for now let's assume that things were stable at 10 percent. So how much would it take to bring unemployment down to an "acceptable" level? Let's call 5 percent unemployment an "acceptable" level, (though in reality 5 percent unemployment is fairly high).

Generally, to reduce unemployment by 1 percentage point requires an increase of GDP by 2 to 3 percent. (This is known among economists as Okun's Law, though it is more a crude approximation than a "law.") To be optimistic, let's use 2 percent. So to reduce unemployment from 10 percent to 5 percent would require an increase of GDP by 10 percent, or by about $1.43 trillion.

It seems reasonable to assume that each dollar of stimulus spending would increase output by $1.50 through the "multiplier" process—that is, through the process by which the dollar gets spent, and then part of that original dollar gets spent, and part of that part gets spent, and so on. However, $288 billion of the total $787 billion of stimulus was not to be spent, but was to be returned to individuals and businesses as tax reductions. As explained in the text, a significant portion of tax cuts is saved and not spent (or, in the case of business cuts, does not stimulate additional activity). So the impact is much less than would be obtained from direct government spending. A reasonable assumption is that, on net, the $288 billion simply increases output by $288 billion—i.e., a multiplier of 1.

Then the total impact of the stimulus package would be $1,036.50 billion (i.e., 1.5 x 499 + 1 x 288). This would increase GDP by 7.25 percent, leaving unemployment at about 6.4 percent. In order to get the unemployment rate to 5 percent, an additional $399 billion of stimulus would have been required (assuming it would be distributed between tax cuts and spending as the actual stimulus was being distributed). That is, the stimulus would have to have been $1.086 trillion or 38 percent greater than the $787 billion.

Box 9.2 *(continued)*

This is a very rough estimate. However, it is based on optimistic assumptions regarding the multiplier, the level of unemployment that would be "acceptable," and the relationship between increases of GDP and reductions of unemployment. It would be hard to argue that the stimulus provided in the ARRA would have been enough to accomplish a sufficient lift of GDP and a sufficient reduction of unemployment.

As it turned out, of course, unemployment continued to be well above 9 percent at least on through 2010—not even close to the 6.4 percent that our numbers predict. Why? First of all, at the end of 2009 the economy was not stable at 10 percent unemployment, and the situation would probably have gotten much worse without the stimulus. Second, our estimate was based on optimistic assumptions; in fact, it would probably take closer to a 3 percent rise in GDP—instead of a 2 percent rise—to reduce unemployment by 1 percent. Third, without a sufficiently large stimulus from the government, the private sector remained skeptical and continued to hold off on investment and employment. Fourth, it takes a long time for the stimulus money to actually be spent. As of August 2010 (18 months after the ARRA was enacted) only about 75 percent of the stimulus money had actually been spent, and the full effect of spending is never seen until well after the money has been paid out. Finally, employment always lags behind output expansion, and in this crisis employment has been especially slow to pick up.[9]

Opponents of the stimulus have cited the continuing high rate of unemployment as an indication that the stimulus did not work. We think the facts imply the very different conclusion that the stimulus was too small.

constructed. With more than one-third of the $787 going for tax cuts and less than one-third going to protect the vulnerable and as relief to state and local governments, it provided much less stimulus than would have been possible with this amount of cost to the federal government and it did so much more slowly than would have been possible. Tax cuts to individuals, as we have explained in our discussion of the 2008 rebates, are in large part saved during hard times. Less than half of the 2008 rebates to individuals were spent, and there is no reason to think that the rebates provided in the stimulus package would be spent at a higher rate. As to the provision for tax reductions for business, they too are likely to have limited impact. The problem for businesses is not that the cost of new activity—new hiring or new investment—is too high, but that they are skeptical that the demand for their products will be there. Indeed, if the problem were cost, the low interest rates would generate new activity. Under the existing circumstances, tax incentives to business will probably simply offset the costs of some activity that business would have taken anyway, and thus they will provide very little stimulation.

More funds going to protect the vulnerable would have provided a greater stimulus impact (and also would have been desirable because they would help those most in need). Extended unemployment benefits (which were somewhat provided outside the ARRA) would be spent at a much higher rate than general tax rebates, as would funds spent on other programs to aid those who have been most severely affected by the worsening economic conditions.

Also, more funds going to state governments (and through the states to local governments) would have not only provided a greater stimulus to economic activity, but also would have been spent more quickly. The budgets of state governments have been severely disrupted by the economic crisis. Because the tax revenues of state governments have dropped precipitously in the crisis and because virtually all state governments are prohibited by their constitutions from borrowing in order to cover current expenses, they have been forced to cut spending a great deal. According to a February 2010 report by the Center on Budget and Policy Priorities: "Counting both initial and mid-year shortfalls, 48 states have addressed or still face such shortfalls in their budgets for fiscal year 2010, totaling $196 billion or 29 percent of state budgets—the largest gaps on record."[10]

Many of the services paid for by state governments—schools, public safety, road repair, much of public medical care—cannot be cut except by doing harm to vital programs, including those that serve the most needy members of society. Channeling more stimulus money to the states would yield its relatively quick and full expenditure to serve these programs; it would mean the continuation of programs and the maintenance of employment, without the need for planning and implementing new activity. Moreover, these programs at the state and local levels tend to be most visible and widely valued. (While many people argue that there is a great deal of waste, and perhaps a good deal of corruption, in these government programs, there is no reason to think that the rapid reductions that have taken place in state and local spending would reduce either waste or corruption.)

Regardless of how the money is spent, opponents of the stimulus maintain that the resulting deficits place an undue burden on future generations. Our grandchildren, it is said, are the ones who must pay back, through taxes, the loans that the government takes out to finance the deficit. However, a larger deficit now is likely to lead to a smaller deficit over the long term and therefore a smaller burden on future generations. As we pointed out earlier in this chapter, one of the main reasons that the deficit became so large is the Great Recession itself, which resulted in lower tax revenue and greater expenditures (e.g., more unemployment compensation). The best way to reduce the burden on future generations is, then, to reestablish economic stability, income growth, and a higher rate of employment. The slower growth that would take place without the stimulus package would automatically generate a larger deficit, as tax revenue would be lower and payments for unemployment insurance and other such programs would be higher—and slower growth would fail to generate the capacity to pay back the debt.

Loans taken out by the government should be evaluated on the same principles as are any other loans—that is, whether or not the gains obtained by taking the loan are greater than the costs of paying them back (with interest). For example, individuals frequently take out loans to finance a college education, believing (often correctly) that the higher incomes they obtain by having that education will put them in good position to pay back the loan—that is, on net, they will gain. Can the same be said of the impact on future generations of government loans to finance the deficit?

For the stimulus package, the answer to this question, based on past experience, is almost certainly "yes." The huge deficits of the World War II years accumulated to create a federal debt that was 109 percent of GDP in 1946. These deficits, however, fueled the growth of the postwar era. By 1960, the country's output had grown by 132 percent and the total federal debt had shrunk to 46 percent of GDP. (These federal debt figures include only the debt held outside the government. A significant portion of the total federal deficit is held by various departments within the federal government.) In other periods, such as the period following the recession at the beginning of the 1980s, substantial deficits also fueled growth, reducing the burden of the deficit. The point is that it is better to have a larger income with a substantial debt to pay off than a much smaller income with a not-so-much-smaller— maybe even a bigger—debt to pay off. (In the 1980s, while deficits pushed up the economy, the growth was not especially strong. The budget deficits in that period were created in large part by tax cuts for the wealthy, which, as we have explained, tend to have limited impact on growth.)

Still, those who argue against deficit finance often claim that on net it does not stimulate economic growth. They argue that each dollar that the government spends comes at the expense of private activity, which would have accomplished at least as much. This phenomenon is called "crowding out," as the spending by the federal government is alleged to "crowd out" spending by the private sector. Leave aside the fact we noted earlier that the stimulus package, and even the combination of the stimulus package plus the cost of TARP, are responsible for a relatively small part of the deficit. And leave aside that most of those people who have opposed the stimulus package appeared to have had no objection to the Bush-era tax cuts and war spending that generated a larger share of the deficit. The main point is that there is no basis to believe that deficit spending fails to create jobs and stimulate growth in a recession. While many economists have developed elaborate theoretical scenarios to support such claims, reality works in a different manner. In circumstances where resources—both labor and capital—are sitting idle and private firms are not investing (or investing at low rates), then the government's deficit spending is taking nothing away from the private sector. This is certainly the situation that has developed in the United States since the end of 2007; as we noted back in Chapter 2, in March of 2010 nonfinancial corporations were sitting on $1.8 trillion in cash, 7 percent of all their assets. Similarly, in prior recessions and the Great Depression, government deficits were not depriving the private sector of investment funds. In each of those cases, deficit spending played a major role in reestablishing economic growth. Ironically, the recessions did more to create a federal deficit than did the government's spending to overcome the recessions—as was the case in 2009 and will surely be the case in the years to come. (Furthermore, as we discussed in Chapter 8, a great deal of the financing for the federal budget deficit in the early 2000s came from abroad, as foreign governments and private firms and individuals bought U.S. bonds. While this may create some problems in its own right, it belies the concern for "crowding out." Also, crowding out is supposed to have its impact by pushing up interest rates; yet interest rates since 2008 have been quite low.)

Finally, some critics of deficit spending as a means to stimulate the economy raise the specter of inflation. They point out that the government, through the Federal Reserve, may finance its debt by increasing the money supply. An increased money supply would tend to generate price increases (i.e., inflation), and thus the government would be paying back its debt with dollars that were worth less in terms of their buying power. This has happened at previous times in U.S. history. Wartime spending, in particular, has often been followed by periods of inflation. There is, however, little reason to be concerned about this problem in the current era, as the Federal Reserve has shown a strong inclination—perhaps too strong—to regulate the money supply to avoid inflation, and there is little doubt that it could and would do the same were significant signs of inflation to begin to arise. There is, furthermore, no indication in the decisions made by operators in financial markets that inflation is a substantial concern to them. If they did have such a concern, long-term interest rates would be higher and rising.

Box 9.3

Burying Bottles and Building Monuments:
Keynes on the Gains from "Waste"

Some critics of the economic stimulus program have maintained that many of the particular expenditures in the American Recovery and Reinvestment Act of 2009 (ARRA) are wasteful and do not create jobs. For example, Senator Susan Collins of Maine, one of the few Republicans who ended up supporting the bill, described the changes that made the bill acceptable to her: "We worked hard to cut out wasteful, bloated . . . not programs that had anything to do with stimulating the economy."[11] Collins's Democratic partner in scaling back the bill was Senator Ben Nelson of Nebraska, who stated that several of the programs in the stimulus bill were unnecessary and would not create jobs.

Of course it is always better to spend on "useful" programs than on "wasteful" programs, but—leaving aside what is "useful" and what is "wasteful"—in terms of stimulus it doesn't really matter what the money is spent on. Here is what John Maynard Keynes had to say about this issue in his 1936 classic *The General Theory of Employment, Interest and Money*, Book III, "The Propensity to Consume":

> . . ."wasteful" loan expenditure [deficit spending] may . . . enrich the community on balance. Pyramid-building, earthquakes, even wars may serve to increase wealth, if the education of our statesmen on the principles of the classical economics stands in the way of anything better.
>
> If the Treasury were to fill old bottles with banknotes, bury them at suitable depths in disused coalmines which are then filled up to the surface with town rubbish, and leave it to private enterprise on well-tried principles of laissez-faire to dig the notes up again (the right to do so being obtained, of course, by tendering for leases of the note-bearing territory), there need be no more unemployment and, with the help of the repercussions, the real income of the community, and its capital wealth also, would probably become a good deal greater than it actually is. It would, indeed, be more sensible to build houses and the like; but if there are political and practical difficulties in the way of this, the above would be better than nothing . . .

Whether the issue is crowding out or inflation, during a recession, especially a severe recession of the sort that emerged in 2007, deficits do not create a problem. In fact, experience indicates that federal government deficits are an essential mechanism to bring the economy back to stability and growth. Deficits during periods of economic growth, however, can be a different matter. When the economy is expanding strongly and the government fails to cover its expenses by taxation, choosing to borrow instead, then the consequence can be negative. Deficits in the late 1960s, for example, contributed to the emergence of inflation, and in the late 1980s and early 2000s growing deficits engendered domestic and international instability. The same thing (running a deficit) has very different impacts depending on the context (recession or growth). This is a simple truth that seems to be ignored in much of the discussion of economic policy.

Reining in the Finance Industry?

In Part III, we pointed out how the deregulation and lack of regulation of the finance industry formed a central part of the foundation of the economic crisis. This is of course a widely shared view, and as the crisis unfolded many people, including political figures, called for the establishment of new regulations as a means to help prevent another crisis. Some meaningful steps have in fact been taken. An early step was the Credit Card Accountability, Responsibility and Disclosure Act (or simply the Credit CARD Act) enacted in May 2009, which provided significant new protections for credit card holders. Although credit card debt was not a central factor in the financial crisis, it played a role in the general buildup of consumer debt and has long been the source of many abuses of cardholders by financial institutions. Certainly the events of the crisis gave a strong impetus to the enactment of the Credit CARD Act.

Broader reform directly related to some of the factors that generated the crisis was enacted in July 2010 as the Wall Street Reform and Consumer Protection Act, the Dodd-Frank Act. This legislation has been touted by some as a substantial response to those operations of the finance industry that were so important in bringing about the crisis. Indeed, Dodd-Frank contains some positive provisions. While it may not prevent the emergence of another crisis, the act reduces the likelihood that another crisis will emerge in the same way. Nonetheless, the basic structure of the financial industry will remain unchanged, and the act addresses important financial issues in an insufficient and often vague manner. Thus a great deal of detail—and of course enforcement—is left to regulators. With the power of the large financial firms still intact and with the continuing impact of leave-it-to-the-market ideology, it is likely that regulators will exercise a light hand in their dealing with the financial institutions. From our perspective, without altering power and ideology, and the great economic inequalities that lie at their foundation, the impact of any legislation will be limited. Still, it is important to examine the provisions of Dodd-Frank to obtain further insights on the issues we have been addressing.[12]

A substantial reform of the finance industry would require effective actions along at least the following five lines:

- Protection of consumers from sorts of predatory lending practices that characterized the mortgage industry in the early 2000s.
- Limiting and managing risk.
- Prevention of financial institutions from being and becoming too big to fail.
- Elimination of the conflict of interest that operates in the rating agencies.
- Regulation of the compensation system (the bonus and salary system) in the financial sector to remove the incentives for excessive risk taking (and simply to eliminate the obscenity of these compensation packages).

Consumer Protection. Perhaps the most clearly positive feature of the Dodd-Frank Act is its creation of a Consumer Financial Protection Bureau (CFPB) that is charged with writing and enforcing rules for mortgages, credit cards, student loans, and other instruments of consumer finance. Along with the creation of this new agency, the act requires all mortgage lenders (including mortgage firms that were not previously regulated to a significant degree) for the first time to ensure a borrower can repay a loan by verifying income, credit history, and job status; if effectively enforced, this provision will halt the NINJA, NINA, and other de facto fraudulent loan practices. Furthermore, Dodd-Frank bans payments to brokers for steering borrowers to high-priced loans. As the consumer loan practices of many financial firms were a major element in the inflation of the housing bubble and its subsequent bursting, effective regulation of these activities could make a difference. (Also, the impact of the CFPB is likely to be strengthened by President Obama's appointment of Elizabeth Warren as a special presidential assistant to lead the initial development of the new bureau. Warren came up with the idea for the CFPB and is known as a strong advocate for consumer protection.)

There are, however, reasons to be skeptical. The new consumer protection agency will be formally within the Federal Reserve, and the Fed completely failed to handle consumer protection in the years leading up to the crisis. Nonetheless, though "housed" in the Fed, the CFPB will be formally independent of the Fed. A potentially more serious limitation is that the actions of the CFPB will be subject to veto by Dodd-Frank's Financial Stability Oversight Council, the super-regulator chaired by the Secretary of the Treasury and charged with maintaining the stability of the financial system. The close relationship of the Treasury to the largest financial institutions does not generate confidence that the CFPB will be able to operate most effectively. As *The New York Times* financial reporter Gretchen Morgenson noted: "Given that financial regulators . . . often seem to think that threats to bank profitability can destabilize the financial system, the consumer protection bureau may have a tougher time than many suppose."[13] In spite of these limitations, the consumer protection aspects of Dodd-Frank are potentially its most positive and effective provisions.

Moreover, further indication of the positive consumer protection aspects of the bill is the provision that allows states to enforce stronger consumer protections on financial institutions than provided for at the federal level, largely reversing the 2004 action by the Office of the Controller of the Currency that pre-empted state authority on these matters (see Chapter 6). On the other hand, the exclusion from the CFPB's purview of loans made by automobile firms to finance auto purchases casts a stain on the consumer protection features of Dodd-Frank.

Limiting and Managing Risk. The provisions in Dodd-Frank regarding limiting and managing risk in the financial industry are a significant, though limited, reversal of the deregulatory trend of the decades leading into the crisis. At least they move away from the hands-off principle that guided passage of the Financial Modernization Act of 1999, the Commodity Futures Modernization Act in 2000, and numerous other deregulations (described in Chapter 5). Dodd-Frank will not solve the problems associated with derivative trading and other risky operations, but it may be a first step. Some of the act's potentially positive provisions include:

- Establishment of the Financial Stability Oversight Council (FSOC). The FSOC, with nine members and chaired by the Secretary of the Treasury, will have oversight responsibility, monitoring for risks that might endanger the financial system. It would direct the Fed to supervise the largest banks and most of the other interconnected financial institutions. In principle, this more intense degree of oversight could lead to early action to prevent a financial crisis.
- Restrictions on derivative trading. So-called over-the-counter (OTC) trading of derivatives will be substantially limited. That is, the private buying and selling of a derivative between two parties in a fully opaque manner is to be largely replaced by a more transparent system of trading on exchanges. (OTC derivative trading is to be permitted for limited categories of trades.)
- Increased capital requirements. Dodd-Frank provides for higher capital, leverage, and liquidity standards and more extensive oversight of the large financial firms, including the so-called "shadow banks" such as AIG and mortgage financers.

- Separation of activities. Financial firms will be restricted in making investments (essentially "bets") on their own account that put their customers' deposits at risk and will be restricted in their investments in private funds (e.g., hedge funds).
- Resolution authority. Dodd-Frank provides procedures for dissolving a large financial institution that has become insolvent, much like the authority that the FDIC holds over smaller banks. The procedures are designed to prevent the "need" for a bailout of failing banks. Moreover, if the procedures were carried out in the same way that the FDIC handles smaller banks that have become insolvent, the executives and stockholders would not be protected in the dissolution of their institution (i.e., no bailing out of the bankers).

We emphasize that these are *potentially* positive provisions of Dodd-Frank because their impact will depend upon rigorous enforcement and the extent to which the financial firms can find new ways—not restricted by the act—to undertake activities that are substantially the same. For example, it is not clear how regulators will determine which derivative trades will be required to take place on open exchanges. Whether the new regulations will prove to be minor inconveniences for the firms or first steps in a serious limitation of their activities will depend on how power relations evolve in the coming years. Without a shift toward a more democratic system of power and a corresponding ideological shift, these provisions are likely to have little impact.

Too Big to Fail. The new financial regulations do virtually nothing to deal with the too-big-to-fail phenomenon. The position of the country's small group of very largest banks will not change because of Dodd-Frank. The resolution authority that would formally allow for the dissolving—in an orderly failure—of one of these institutions is unlikely to be implemented if the institution is too big to fail. This is a problem in that it allows such firms to place the costs of their failure on society. Also, it involves an implicit subsidy to the firms. Knowing that the government will not allow them to fail, investors will be willing to provide them with capital at a lower cost than would be available to other institutions where real risks of failure exist. (Furthermore, Dodd-Frank does nothing to deal with the problems of Fannie Mae and Freddie Mac.)

Rating Agencies. Dodd-Frank includes a number of provisions establishing greater oversight of the credit rating agencies and greater transparency of their operations. On the important issue of conflict of interest, whereby the agencies have been paid by the firms whose securities they were rating, there is a great deal of wiggle room in the act's requirements. On the one hand, the Securities and Exchange Commission (SEC) is mandated to create a mechanism to prevent issuers of asset-backed securities from picking the agency that they believe will give them the best rating. Unless the SEC identifies an alternative mechanism, an independent, investor-led board will assign rating agencies to provide initial ratings for asset-backed securities. On the other hand, the SEC will have two years to study the conflict of interest issue before the assignment of rating agencies would begin.

Compensation. The 2010 financial regulation legislation requires some very limited provisions regarding compensation in the financial industry. The provisions focus more on transparency than actual change. While transparency can of course bring about change, there is virtually nothing in the legislation that would directly alter the system of incentives that led to the sorts of practices that played a major role in generating the crisis. Worth mentioning here, however, is the requirement in Dodd-Frank that firms disclose the ratio between the CEO's compensation and the median compensation of all other employees. This is one step, albeit a small one, toward recognizing that economic inequality had a role in creating the financial problems of recent years.

In spite of its positive features, the Dodd-Frank bill remains a very limited piece of legislation, inadequate as a means to address many of the important characteristics of the financial industry that contributed to the emergence of the crisis. One of its basic problems is illustrated by the fact that, according to one analysis of the bill, it would require 67 new studies and at least 243 new rule-makings.[14] (As more than one person has quipped, perhaps the bill should have been entitled the "The Full-Employment for Lawyers Act of 2010.") Thus much of the act remains vague, and consequently the precise meaning of many parts of the act will be up for grabs—subject to the exercise of power by the financial institutions.

Indeed, the limits of the bill—its failure to deal with several important issues, and its vagueness on many other issues—have resulted in large part from the exercise of power by these institutions. One direct aspect of this exercise of power was the extensive lobbying effort by the financial firms in the period leading up to the passage of Dodd-Frank. As Americans for Financial Reform noted, "The forces arrayed against us were spending $1.4 million a day to chip away at what we won piece, by piece, by piece. They were successful far too often. They carved loopholes that will make the protections less effective than they should be. They won special-interest carve-outs that defy logic. They stood in the way of structural changes we need."[15]

Power, however, has not operated through money alone. It has also shaped an ideology that provides particular arguments against the sorts of regulations that are contained in Dodd-Frank and against the more extensive regulations that would have been contained in a more effective piece of legislation. For example, one argument heard over and over is that regulation of the financial firms would inhibit financial innovation, which is supposedly good for economic growth. Yet it was financial innovation that was a central feature in generating the crisis. Moreover, the era of greater financial regulation and less opportunity for innovation was generally an era of more rapid economic growth than the more recent period of unrestrained innovation. Then there is the argument—trotted out especially in opposition to any restriction on the size of financial institutions—that regulation would place U.S. banks at a competitive disadvantage in the global economy. Left unspecified in this argument is how the global gains of U.S.–based financial institutions provide benefits to the U.S. population in general. Perhaps more important, the U.S. government is by no means powerless in bringing about regulations on banks based abroad—both by its leadership in world affairs and by limits it could readily place on foreign-based firms that do not comply with U.S. regulations. These objections to the arguments against regulation, however, have little impact while the ideology of leave-it-to-the-market continues to be a major force. (For more on the operation of power in relation to these issues, see Appendix A.)

Opportunities?

It would be easy to look at the various actions that have been taken by the U.S. government and reach pessimistic conclusions about the prospects for curing what ails the U.S. economy (and the global economy). The bailout of the financial firms under TARP—initiated in the Bush administration and continued in the Obama administration—may have avoided a more severe economic downturn, but it reinforced those institutions whose practices created the crisis (to say nothing of its impact on income distribution and power). The fiscal stimulus that began in 2009 and the financial regulation of 2010 both had positive aspects, but both were very limited. The limits of these actions mean that poor economic performance—slow growth and high unemployment—will continue for years and that new crises are likely to develop. It is not a pretty picture.

Yet, at the same time, as we have tried to emphasize, an economic crisis creates opportunities for change. As we have also pointed out, various actions by the U.S. government have been sharp departures from the practices of recent decades. They have been taken in conflict to principles of the ideology that has guided and justified much government policy, and they have not simply served the interests of the most powerful private groups—the provisions of the TARP notwithstanding. It is, we think, quite reasonable to interpret these actions as indicating the opportunity for more extensive change.

If the argument we have developed is correct, however, this change will require more fundamental departures from the economic and political trends of the last several decades. None of the economic policy measures that have been undertaken by the U.S. government do anything substantial about the underlying factors that we have identified as the foundation for the crisis—economic inequality, the concentration of political power in the hands of the wealthy, and the perverse free-market ideology that continues to define the role of the government in the economy—in spite of the obvious failure of that ideology. The nastiness of the boils on the surface has been somewhat reduced, but the underlying infection has not been treated; indeed, it has been ignored.

So what might be done to change things, to deal with the underlying infection and create a foundation for real economic progress? How might the opportunities created by the crisis be used most effectively? What might be done to move things in a different direction?

Notes

1. The month-by-month federal funds rates are available in the *Economic Report of the President, 2010,* Table B-73.

2. Congressional Budget Office, "Did the 2008 Tax Rebates Stimulate Short-Term Growth?" Economic and Budget Issue Brief, June 10, 2009, www.cbo.gov/ftpdocs/96xx/doc9617/06—10—2008Stimulus.pdf.

3. Testimony by Federal Reserve Chairman Ben S. Bernanke, "Federal Reserve programs to strengthen credit markets and the economy," Before the Committee on Financial Services, U.S. House of Representatives, Washington, D.C., February 10, 2009, www.federalreserve.gov/newsevents/testimony/bernanke20090210a.htm.

4. Krishna Guha and Edward Luce, "Greenspan Backs Bank Nationalization," *Financial Times,* February 18, 2009, www.ft.com/cms/s/0/e310cbf6-fd4e-11dd-a103-000077b07658.html?nclick_check=1.

5. On the PNC takeover of National City, see TradingMarkets.com, "PNC profit falls 28 percent in first quarter: Repaid U.S. bailout of $7.6 billion," April 23, 2010, www.tradingmarkets.com/news/stock-alert/ncc_pnc_pnc-profit-falls-28-in-first-quarter-repaid-u-s-bailout-of-7—6-billion-932960.html. For a list of institutions receiving TARP funds and the amounts received, see Pro-Publica, "Bailout Recipients," bailout.propublica.org/main/list/index. Wells Fargo press release "Wells Fargo and Wachovia Merger Completed," www.wellsfargo.com/press/2009/20090101_Wachovia_Merger.

6. "Overview of Funding," Recovery.gov, www.recovery.gov/Pages/home.aspx?q=content/investments, and Committee on Appropriations, "Summary: American Recovery and Reinvestment: Conference Agreement," February 13, 2009.

7. Congressional Budget Office, *The Budget and Economic Outlook: An Update,* August 2010, Summary Table 1, p. XI, http://www.cbo.gov/ftpdocs/117xx/doc11705/08–18-Update.pdf; also Budget Office, *Monthly Budget Review, Fiscal Year 2010,* October 7, 2010, www.cbo.gov/ftpdocs/119xx/doc11936/September-MBR.pdf.

8. This accounting of the different factors contributing to the 2009 federal budget deficit is based on John Irons, Kathryn Edwards, and Anna Turner, "The 2009 Budget Deficit: How Did We Get Here?" Issue Brief #262, Economic Policy Institute, August 20, 2009, http://epi.3cdn.net/0974dad8645a9d3216_5tm6bnxqd.pdf. The calculations in this study were completed based on an early estimate of the deficit, which was larger than the final figure; the actually figures here are not a precise description of what actually occurred. However, the qualitative conclusions are not affected.

9. This calculation has been carried out in similar fashion by others, sometimes with different assumptions and some different basic figures but with similar results. The calculation here owes a great deal to that of Paul Krugman, presented in his blog of January 6, 2009, under the title, "Stimulus arithmetic (wonkish but important)," online at http://krugman.blogs.nytimes.com/2009/01/06/stimulus-arithmetic-wonkish-but-important/. Regarding the length of time it has taken to spend the money, see Louise Radnofsky, "White House Under Fire for Unspent Infrastructure Cash," *Wall Street Journal,* August 18, 2010, http://online.wsj.com/article/SB10001424052748704532204575397061414483040-search.html.

10. See Elizabeth McNichol and Nicholas Johnson, "Recession Continues to Batter State Budgets; State Responses Could Slow Recovery," Center on Budget and Policy Priorities, www.cbpp.org/cms/index.cfm?fa=view&id=711.

11. "GOP's Susan Collins Bucks Party in Senate's Stimulus Battle," *Point of View,* February 2, 2009, www.wowowow.com/post/sen-susan-collins-takes-stand-against-party-economic-stimulus-bill-202464.

12. A useful and detailed description of the provisions of Dodd-Frank is provided by Americans for Financial Reform at http://ourfinancialsecurity.org/2010/06/what-happened-on-wall-street-reform/.

13. Gretchen Morgenson, "Strong Enough for Tough Stains?" *The New York Times,* June 25, 2010, http://dealbook.blogs.nytimes.com/2010/06/28/strong-enough-for-tough-stains/.

14. The analysis is that of the law firm Davis Polk and Wardwell LLP, www.davispolk.com/files/Publication/7084f9fe-6580—413b-b870-b7c025ed2ecf/Presentation/PublicationAttachment/1d4495c7—0be0—4e9a-ba77-f786fb90464a/070910_Financial_Reform_Summary.pdf.

15. Americans for Financial Reform, "What Does Wall Street Reform Mean?" at http://ourfinancialsecurity.org/2010/06/what-happened-on-wall-street-reform/.

10

Moving in a Different Direction

In telling the story of the first economic crisis of the new millennium, we have described the machinations of the financial operators and the support they have received from government officials over an extended period. The details of this story are important. As we have also tried to make clear, however, there is a deeper story. Underneath the particulars of the banks' actions and the government policies lie great economic inequality, extreme concentration of power in the hands of large corporations and the very wealthy, and a perverse ideology avowing that unregulated markets—"free markets"—generate the most desirable economic and social outcomes.

This deeper story did not begin in the late 1970s, though it certainly took on greater force in last quarter of the twentieth century. Inequality, elite power, and free-market ideology have long roots in U.S. history. Slavery, one of those roots, played no small part in the longer story, but the deep economic, social, and political divisions in the society were by no means confined to the South. The industrial and commercial North was also characterized by wide gaps between those at the top, the so-called captains of industry, and the great majority of the population. During the early part of the twentieth century, the divisions in the United States showed up in extreme economic inequality. As we have noted, for example, in 1928 the 1 percent of families with the highest incomes obtained nearly a quarter of all income.

Yet there have been contending forces in U.S. history. Some of these forces have been based in the objective conditions—or the seemingly objective conditions—that have shaped life in the United States and shifts in the nature of the economy. Through the nineteenth century, the availability of land gave some people an option that enhanced their incomes and their power and, not incidentally, created upward pressure on wages. Also, in the first half of the twentieth century, the move of many African Americans from the rural South and out from the subjugation of southern share-cropping to the urban north, created opportunities and laid the basis for significant income and power shifts. These changes, however, were not based simply in objective conditions, but were brought about in large part by political phenomena. The availability of land had depended on the dispossession of the Native

Americans, and the movement of African Americans had depended on the struggle against slavery and the post-slavery restrictions on their mobility. (As we explained in Chapter 7 and will comment more on shortly, globalization, which often appears as an objective condition, is similarly shaped by political phenomena.)

Furthermore, among the contending forces that have countered the economic, social, and political inequalities, there have also been active political struggles based in a variety of social movements. As we pointed out in Chapter 3, the Great Depression and World War II set the stage for a period of substantial social progress in the quarter century following the war, and political action played a substantial role in that progress. A major pillar of progressive change was the growth and rising influence of the labor movement. Certainly the objective conditions of the Depression had given a powerful impetus to the advance of organized labor, but the impetus was extended by the National Labor Relations Act. Most important, workers themselves, the organizers of unions and the rank and file activists, built the labor movement and brought about major changes in economic conditions, political power, and people's outlook on economic organization—that is, people's ideology. Not only did unions directly affect the conditions of their members and indirectly the conditions in many nonunion workplaces, but they also contributed to progress in civil rights and the development of improved social welfare programs (though of course not all unions always play positive roles in these advances).

The civil rights movement was also at the center of change in the post–World War II period. The movement is often identified with the challenges to Jim Crow restrictions (e.g., the Montgomery bus boycott) that appeared in the late 1950s and the struggle for voter rights in the 1960s. Civil rights struggles, however, began to emerge right after the war and had much longer roots. The 1954 Supreme Court decision declaring the illegitimacy of racial segregation in the schools was both a product of the longer political struggle and a catalyst to the struggles of subsequent years. And there were other important social movements that contributed to the changes of the years following World War II, which were marked by the slow shift toward greater economic equality of the era. The women's movement, the welfare rights movement, the student movement, the antiwar movement, and, somewhat later, the environmental movement, the gay and lesbian rights movement, and the disability rights movement are all examples of an intertwined set of political struggles that affected power, ideology, and the distribution of income and wealth. These movements did not solve all the problems of our society. As we stated earlier, the 1950s and the 1960s were not the "good old days," as they are sometimes portrayed. But they were different from the current period, both in terms of social, economic, and political conditions and in terms of economic stability.

The point of this brief reminder of the impacts of political struggles in our recent history is to stress that in fact such movements can make a difference. Also, they can make a difference because seemingly objective conditions are often not all that objective, but are shaped by political decisions. Conscious political action is of course affected by the context of larger economic and social forces, but it also affects those forces. In the face of the extreme power that resides in the hands of those who own and run large firms and obtain a disproportionate share of the fruits of economic activity, it is easy to believe that popular struggles can have little if any impact. Similarly, with the globalization of economic activity, where economic forces operate beyond political boundaries and seemingly beyond political control, efforts to bring about meaningful change can sometimes seem pointless. History, however, belies these reactions. It may not be possible to do everything, but it is possible to do something—sometimes a great deal. It may even be possible to alter the forces that are at the root of the current economic crisis.

There are many ways to challenge the inequality and the power arrangements and ideology that have dominated economic and political life during recent decades in the United States and that have generated so much instability and hardship. At the beginning of this book we pointed out that inequality, elite power, and market ideology form a vicious circle, with each component supporting the others. For example, inequality enhances the power of those at the top, and they can use that power to both enhance their incomes and generate an ideology that justifies their position. So the problem of how to bring about progress becomes the problem of how to break into this vicious circle, to undermine its components, and transform it to a virtuous circle. With a move toward a more equal distribution of income and wealth, for example, elite power is weakened. Likewise, when the perverse market ideology is undermined, social movements can be strengthened, enhancing democratic power and leading toward more economic equality.

The thrust of what we have to say may appear a bit odd in the context of the debates regarding what should be done about the economy. We are not proposing steps to solve housing problems or to regulate banks or to provide more effective stimulus. These are all important, but we are after something deeper. So our proposals—really just examples of what needs to be done—are directed toward shifting the distribution of income and wealth, power, and ideology in a progressive direction.

Any review of the impact of social movements in U.S. history indicates that a variety of seemingly disparate movements have at times had a common and combined impact on advancing social progress. Our purpose here is simply to present some components of a broad effort to bring about progressive change. In doing so, we hope not only to promote that change but also to extend our analysis of central problems in the U.S. economy. In promoting universal social programs, the redevelopment of the labor movement, and the reshaping of globalization we want to show how these efforts, useful in themselves, can also alter the roots of economic instability. For example, expanded social programs and a redeveloped labor movement would tend to strengthen the ideological support for greater government regulation of the economy, a regulation that should be able to at least temper the instability inherent in markets (especially financial markets). Likewise, stronger social programs and stronger labor unions tend to generate greater democratic power, power that can limit the ability of elite groups to shape economic policies in ways that enhance their incomes and generate instability. A different approach to globalization also holds out the promise of both reducing instability and enhancing the power of workers in their relations with employers—both in the United States and elsewhere. All of these steps—and there are certainly others as well—tend to support one another, creating in effect a virtuous circle of change.

However, we need to make one thing clear, a feature of our approach that distinguishes it from the usual policy proposals of economists. Our intended audience is not policy makers in Washington or other centers of political authority. We are, instead, directing our analysis toward a much larger and potentially more powerful audience: the people and organizations that are engaged in popular struggles to bring about progressive change. Our aim is to give some support, and perhaps some focus, to those struggles. Much of what we say might be interpreted as advice to the formal policy makers, but, at this point in history, the policy makers, certainly the policy makers in Washington, are not about to implement our proposals. If we were speaking to them, we would be wasting our breath. In order to obtain progressive changes, changes of the sort we discuss here, it will take a lot of pushing. That pushing has to done by a broad, popular set of movements. Our intent is to support the push.

It is a push for greater democracy. Democracy is fundamentally about expanding effective engagement in political decisions. The openings for effective popular engagement are small, and they have become smaller as power has become increasingly concentrated—along with income—in the hands of the very wealthy. However, there are openings. So our goal is to help people struggle for progressive change to take advantage of those openings, to help build popular organizations that increasingly involve people in having a say in the economic and social programs that affect their lives. We believe that, ultimately, these organizations and the people in them can bring about positive change.

Universal Social Programs

One way to attack the roots of the current economic crisis while at the same time pushing for concrete, direct gains for the great majority of the populace is to develop the struggle for universal social welfare programs. Both the struggle for and the implementation of universal social welfare programs can favorably affect income distribution, power, and ideology. Compared to other high-income countries, the United States has relatively limited social welfare programs; this is not a "welfare state." The social welfare programs that do exist in the United States are usually "targeted" programs—that is, programs for which a person or family is eligible on the basis of having a low income. The Temporary Assistance for Needy Families program (TANF), Section 8 housing subsidies and public housing, food stamps, day care subsidies, school meals programs, Medicaid and the subsidies provided in the health care legislation enacted in early 2010—these are all examples of targeted social welfare programs. To take part in these programs, a person or family must demonstrate low income, usually low in relation to the official poverty line.

There are, however, some important social welfare programs in the United States that are universal; eligibility for the benefits of these programs is not connected to economic need. Social Security and Medicare, programs for the elderly, are the well-known examples. (One must contribute to these programs while working or be married to someone who has contributed in order to be eligible, but economic need is not an issue.) Although not usually viewed as a social welfare program, the public education system should be included as an example of a universal social welfare program. No one views these programs as perfect. The public school system, in particular, is fraught with problems and characterized by great inequities—though there are many very good public schools. Nonetheless, these universal programs have wide popularity and are responsible for major social gains. Social Security and Medicare have dramatically reduced poverty and insecurity among the aged. Even those who are harsh critics of public education do not challenge the idea that all children should have access to schooling at the expense of society.

The wide support that exists for these universal programs is one of the reasons they provide a useful focal point for progressive political movements. Efforts to create new universal programs—for example, health care and with early child care (day care)—should be able to garner similar support. Indeed, opinion polls indicate that a substantial majority of the population favors the creation of universal child care programs and universal health care—that is, programs available to all and paid for by general revenues.

(Such a health care system is usually referred to as "Medicare for all" or as a "single-payer" system. And we should emphasize that by universal child care programs, we mean available programs, not compulsory programs.) While this potential for support makes the advocacy of universal programs politically opportune, it is their potential contribution to altering the root causes of economic instability that makes them most relevant here. Targeted social welfare programs have some positive aspects, but they lack several important characteristics of universal social programs. These characteristics make universal programs more effective in meeting people's needs and valuable components in effecting changes in income distribution, power, and ideology.

- **Income Distribution.** Social welfare programs in general—whether targeted or universal—can generate greater income equality. Any program that provides benefits to the poor (a targeted program) and is paid for out of general revenues has an equalizing impact. But universal programs also promote equality because they provide the same absolute benefits to people regardless of income, thus providing proportionally more to those with lower incomes. (Of course the overall impact of either type of program depends on how the general revenues are raised: the equalizing impact of the benefits is diminished when the revenues are collected by a regressive tax, as is the case with Social Security and Medicare. With public education, a large share of funding in the United States has come from local property taxes, a practice that has introduced "savage inequalities," to use education critic Jonathan Kozol's term, into this universal social program.)

  Universal social welfare programs, however, have an important advantage over targeted programs with regard to their impact on income distribution—namely that they do not tend to preserve the status quo. Targeted programs tend to keep people in poverty and therefore maintain inequality over the long run. Conservative critics of social welfare programs have long argued that these programs tend to keep people in poverty by creating a "culture of dependence." According to this view, when the poor receive various supports these "free handouts" undermine their initiative. People supposedly learn they can get something for nothing and therefore accept a life of nonachievement. In reality, there are very practical reasons that targeted programs keep people in poverty. If people are receiving support from various targeted social welfare programs, then efforts to improve their incomes will be self-defeating since those income gains will be offset by the loss of eligibility for the targeted support programs. For example, an analysis undertaken by the

Center for Social Policy at the University of Massachusetts Boston and the Crittenton Women's Union shows that in Massachusetts a single mother with two children who obtains training and thus moves from an $11 an hour job to a $16 an hour job could suffer a net loss of effective income because she would lose so much in targeted support (see Box 10.1). This feature of targeted social welfare programs—that is, of most social welfare programs in the United States—tends to keep people in poverty and tends to maintain the status quo income distribution.

Universal social welfare programs offer a way to assist low-income people without perpetuating their low incomes. Under existing circumstances, low-income families that are able to raise their incomes do not worry about losing access for their children to the public schools. But what about access to health care? And what about access to day care vouchers for their younger children? Were health care and day care also handled, like the public schools, as universal programs, significant negative incentives would be removed, incentives that inhibit these families from improving their positions.

Universal programs create a "social wage," a share of people's income that comes to them as members of society and is not tied to their particular employment. A larger social wage, a share of income that is the same for everyone and is not directly tied to employment, contributes to greater income equality and greater economic security.

- **Power.** The implementation of more universal social programs would serve to create a more equitable distribution of power because they would provide the great majority of the population, not simply low-income people, with a higher degree of security. Perhaps the clearest example is universal health care. Today many people fear the loss of their jobs because they obtain their health insurance through their employers, and loss of one's job means either loss of insurance or much higher insurance premiums. A universal health care system would open up options. A person would not be faced with the dilemma: Do I keep my current, undesirable job with health insurance or switch to a more desirable job and lose my health insurance? Instead, regardless of a person's employment status, health care would be available.

Greater options mean greater power. And power at the workplace is often a foundation for wider power in society. A substantial social wage thus not only contributes to a more equitable distribution of income, but also to a more equitable distribution of power. Workers would gain power in their workplaces (which, of course, means a reduction of the power of their employers). Also, to the extent that people have greater economic security, their political as well as their economic power is enhanced.

Box 10.1

One Step Forward, Two Steps Back

Social welfare programs targeted at the poor and thus dependent on recipients having low incomes can undermine incentives for people to attempt to improve their economic conditions. This perverse situation is well illustrated by the following example from *Fits & Starts: The Difficult Path for Working Single Parents*:[1]

". . . consider the hypothetical situation of a low-income single mother with two children, ages eight and three, living in Boston. To meet her family's basic food, housing, healthcare, childcare, and transportation needs, she would have to earn $58,133 per year (pre-tax) or $29 per hour in a full-time job. With only a high school diploma, she is able to earn $11 per hour ($22,000 annually) cleaning rooms full time at a local hospital. At this wage, she is able to meet her family's basic needs only if she receives all work supports for which she is eligible (child care assistance, Food Stamps, MassHealth, EITC, CTC, WIC, and Section 8 housing assistance), when, in fact, most eligible families do not receive child care and housing supports because of lengthy waiting lists. With all eligible supports and after paying her essential expenses each month, our single mother is left with about $538 to pay for "nonessential" expenses, such as her children's school supplies, medical copayments and debts, emergency expenses, credit card bills, and tuition and fees for education or training that will enable her to attain a family supportive wage . . ."

"In the hopes of moving ahead, this mother invests her small monthly savings to enroll in a medical assistant training program. Upon completing the program, she finds a medical assistant job paying $16 per hour, about $32,000 annually. Although she is proud to have earned this substantial leap in wages, after several paychecks, this mom finds that she is actually less financially secure than when she was cleaning rooms for $11 per hour. The $5.00 per hour raise resulted in a marked decrease in the family's monthly child care subsidy, Section 8 rent allowance, and their state and federal Earned Income Tax Credits. Plus, her family is no longer eligible for WIC and Food Stamps benefits. Her $833 per month wage increase resulted in a loss of $863 in monthly work supports. In the end [when tax changes are also factored in], the raise resulted in her net monthly resources falling from $538 a month to $391, a reduction of $147."

Indeed, it seems that the power that workers would gain through a universal health care program is one of the reasons that employers outside of the health care field do not support "a single payer system," even though it would seem to be in their direct interest to have such a system. For example, U.S. car makers have long had a competitive disadvantage in relation to their foreign competitors because the U.S. firms pay a large amount for their workers' health insurance while their competitors generally operate in countries with public, universal programs. For General Motors in the early 2000s, health care costs amounted to approximately $1,500 per car, but for Toyota in Japan, the health care costs were about $100 per car.[2] (Of course with a single-payer plan there would still be costs—for example, the taxes that would pay for the public health care program. But however these costs were financed, they would not be spread unequally across employers and they would be more in line with the costs of foreign firms.) Yet, while U.S. automakers would obtain direct gains from a public, single-payer health care system, they would lose power in relation to their workforces.

- **Ideology.** In addition, universal social programs can contribute to a more democratic structure of power by the way they affect ideology. To begin with, existing, targeted social programs tend to create a division between low-income families, who receive support, and middle-income families, who do not. Middle-income families, struggling to meet their expenses (among which health care accounts for an increasing share) and worried about job security, often resent the fact that low-income families are receiving support that they themselves could use. They not only resent the fact; they resent the families. This resentment is all the more divisive because it often appears along racial lines. The resentment readily translates into a particular opposition to the role of government in providing social welfare programs and into a general opposition to government's role in the economy. By contributing to these sorts of divisions among the majority of the population and to an antigovernment ideology, targeted social programs—however otherwise desirable—tend to undermine the political power of the majority, leaving greater power in the hands of the economic elite (for power is always a relative phenomenon).

Universal social programs, however, can have a very different ideological impact, tending to generate solidarity rather than division. The material basis for resentment of "welfare recipients" by middle-income families is removed because the basic benefits embodied in the social wage are received by all segments of society. We do not hear, for example, expressions of resentment toward low-income families because their children receive education in the public schools. Nor is there resentment toward low-income people as beneficiaries of Medicare or Social Security. Not only does the universal nature of these programs generate an ideology of solidarity, but the solidarity has become quite practical (and an expression of power) when these programs have come under attack.

Moreover, when social programs are universal, there is no stigma associated with participation in them. It is not degrading to apply for Medicare or Social Security or to register one's children for public school. One neither has to declare oneself poor nor go through the degrading process of proving one's poverty. Participation in these programs is viewed as a right. What's more, because there is no need for the bureaucratic process of income verification to participate in universal programs, administrative costs are greatly reduced—not a trivial matter.

The broader ideological impact of universal social programs lies in that they establish the importance of meeting many of society's basic needs outside of the market. When we establish universal public schools or Medicare, we as a society are saying that what these programs provide is a right—a service not provided by one's ability to pay, not provided through markets, but provided by all of us to all of us. If we extend universal social programs, we are extending this view, this ideological outlook. Many of us consider universal health care, Medicare for all, as a right as well. Also, there is increasing recognition that universal provision of early childhood programs is necessary to ensure equal education, another generally accepted right. With the extension of universal programs, with the wider acceptance of social responsibility for the provision of basic economic well-being and security, ideology is altered. The idea that things should be "left to the market" loses a good deal of its force.

While universal social programs are good in themselves (in that they provide for fundamental needs of society in a most effective manner), our emphasis here has been on how they have long-term impacts on income distribution, power, and ideology. These impacts are also good in themselves, but, in the context of the larger story we are telling here, they have great value in contributing to long-term economic stability. They alter the "deeper story" we have been telling about the foundations of the current economic crisis. However, there is also a way in which the existence of universal social programs would have a direct favorable impact on economic stability were another serious economic downturn to emerge. In the same way that in the current economic downturn Social Security and Medicare expenditures have been maintained and therefore have provided some stability to aggregate demand, other universal social programs would also contribute to stability. At the beginning of 2010, under pressure to restrain the expansion of the federal budget deficit, President Obama declared a spending freeze on discretionary spending. But Social Security and Medicare were excluded from the freeze (as was military spending, but for rather different political reasons). As universal programs, it would not have been politically viable to reduce Social Security and Medicare, even in the face of mounting attacks from "deficit hawks."

Finally, on the issue of universal programs, we have used the examples of health care and day care to make our case. It is easy to understand how such programs could be established—and indeed, health care and day care do exist as universal programs in many other high-income countries. Also, there are already substantial movements to establish universal health care and universal day care. Nonetheless, the concept of universality can be applied in other social welfare realms. For example, in the realm of housing, a universal program would not provide public housing to everyone, but could assure everyone of support for their basic housing expenses. At present, we provide substantial housing subsidies through the tax deduction for mortgage interest payments. This tax deduction system, while formally universal, works very much in favor of people with high incomes: it is only available to those who itemize deductions on their tax returns; and the benefit is greater for those people who have larger mortgages and who are in higher tax brackets. Were we to create, instead, a universal housing tax credit (analogous to the earned income tax credit), it could provide much greater support for low-income and middle-income families, including renters.[3] Another example of potential universal social programs is provided by adult education and training (or retraining) programs that could be especially important as parts of a general policy to deal with the impacts of international trade (as we will point out below). Universal adult education and training programs would be distinguished from programs for the retraining of people displaced from their jobs by imports precisely by the fact that they would be *universal*—and would thus avoid many of the problems associated with the more narrowly provided, targeted programs.

Redevelopment of the Labor Movement

We have no magic formula for the redevelopment of the labor movement. Measured in terms of the percentage of the labor force that is in labor unions, organized labor has been in decline for decades. The redevelopment of the labor movement will also take decades. What we would like to do here is first point out the importance of the labor movement for establishing a more democratic structure of income distribution, power, and ideology. Second, while "objective" forces have been involved in the decline of the labor movement, we want to underscore that the decline has also been brought about by political decisions; and, to a degree, the "objective" forces themselves have been shaped by political decisions. Therefore, to at least some degree, political action should be able to reverse the decline.

It is strongly suggestive that since early in the twentieth century periods of a rising labor movement have been associated with shifts toward greater income equality, and periods of labor movement decline have been associated with rising income inequality. This relationship is illustrated in Figure 10.1, which shows for the 1917 to 2008 period union membership as a share of the civilian labor force and the share of income going to the highest-income one percent of families. (The line showing income inequality is the same as in Figure 3.1.) Equally important, there is a similar association with the changing position of organized labor and the changes in ideology regarding the roles of government and markets, changes that we described in Chapters 3 and 4.

In the latter half of the twentieth century, the declining role of unions was an important factor setting the stage for the current economic crisis. Union membership as a share of the civilian labor force peaked at 26.9 percent in 1953 (up from 15.7 percent in 1940 but changed only slightly from the 26.6 percent of 1945), and then fell off slowly. In 1979, however, union members still made up more than 20 percent of the civilian labor force. From that point onward, union membership declined sharply, just as inequality rose sharply. As the crisis emerged in 2007, unions accounted for only 10.2 percent of the workforce, and the highest-income one percent of families were obtaining 23.5 percent of all income. (Again, see Figure 10.1.)

It is well established that unions raise the pay and benefits of their members. For example, in a 2010 study at the Center for Economic and Policy Research using data for 2003 to 2009, John Schmitt showed that in every state "unionization substantially improves the pay or benefits of workers . . . In the typical state, unionization is associated with a 15 percent increase in hourly wages (roughly $2.50 per hour), a 19-percentage-point increase in employer-provided health insurance, and a 24-pecentage-point increase in employer-sponsored retirement plans." These increases were computed after the impact of other factors such as age, gender, and education of the workers and the industry of occupation were accounted for.[4]

Yet in terms of the impact on the distribution of income, the important issue is how unions affect the level of wages in general, not just the wages of their own workers. It is theoretically possible that in obtaining improve-

200

Figure 10.1   **Union Membership and Income Inequality, 1917–2008**

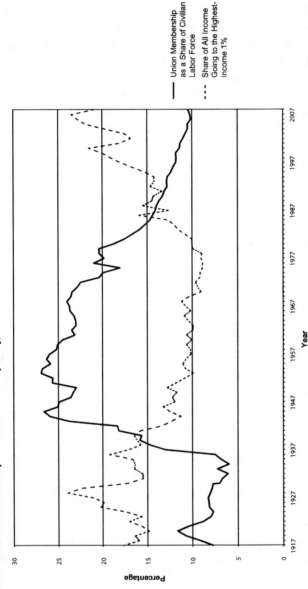

Sources: Civilian Labor Force: post-1970, *Statistical Abstract of the United States* (SAUS), various years; pre-1971, *Historical Statistics of the United States* (HSUS), D4 and D14. Union Membership: post-1970, SAUS, various years; unreported years, G. Mayer, "Union Membership Trends in the United States," Congressional Research Service, 8-31-2004, online at digitalcommons.ilr.cornell.edu/cgi/viewcontent. cgi?article=1176&context=key_workplace; 1930–1970, HSUS, D948; 1917 to 1930, L. Troy and N. Sheflin, U.S. Union Sourcebook, 1st Edition, W. Orange, NJ: Industrial Relations Data and Information Services, 1985, Table A1. Income data: see Figure 1.
Note: Data for 1917 to 1930 and data from 1930 to 2008 are from different sources and are not fully compatible. A union membership figure for 1982 could not be obtained; the number there has been taken as halfway between the 1981 and 1983 figures.

ments for their members, unions are contributing to greater disparities among workers generally and thereby possibly increasing overall income inequality. Experience, however, suggests strongly that unionization has a positive impact on the general level of wages. In fact, ironically, one of the explanations often offered for the decline in union membership is that unions have succeeded in improving conditions for workers generally and therefore many workers do not see a great need to form unions. Much of this union success has come through obtaining legislation that protects workers' rights. For example, legislation limits the hours of the working day, guaranteeing premium pay for overtime work. Also, workers no longer need to rely on unions to secure health and safety protection because those protections have been secured by legislation (that operates, for example, through the Environmental Protection Agency and the Occupational Safety and Health Administration)—though even with legislation there often remains a problem of enforcement.

Unions have this broader impact in two ways. First, as economist David Gordon described the phenomenon in his analysis of the corporate squeeze of working Americans: "[U]nion contracts have always had a 'spillover' effect on wages in the nonunion sector. Nonunionized employers have often felt the need to match, at least in part, union wage gains in order to continue to attract the workers they want. Perhaps more crucially, they have sought to emulate union wage gains in order to help scratch whatever unionizing itches their otherwise less satisfied employees might conceivably develop."[5] In other words, in pushing up the level of wages of some workers, unions tend to push up the wages of workers in general. Second, unions affect the overall level of wages and working conditions through the political process, as illustrated by the overtime and health and safety provisions just noted. A further important example is that unions have been strong supporters of increases in the minimum wage, not simply out of an altruistic concern for those at the bottom, but also seeing a higher floor on wages as placing upward pressure on wages in general (including those of their members). Indeed, the movements of the minimum wage (adjusted for inflation) correspond well with the movements of average wages in recent decades. Also, unions have generally supported stronger social welfare legislation, again not simply for altruistic reasons, but because improved conditions for those at the bottom tend to lift the well-being of all workers—and during difficult economic times unionized workers themselves are often in need of social welfare supports. Success in these political efforts has generally been associated with the strength of unions, and failure with their weakness. Thus, though no one would pretend that unions speak with a single voice, they are an instrument of power, not only within firms, but also within the political process. And their power is closely associated with the material well-being of most working people.

The power of unions is also an ideological matter. Free-market ideas and individualism have always been significant components of general ideology in the United States. Yet, in an earlier era, the concept of social solidarity, a recognition of the importance of group responsibility as embodied in collective bargaining, and a recognition of the validity of collective action—all epitomized by labor unions, in principle if not always in fact—were also important parts of that general ideology. As these aspects of ideology have been eroded and increasingly dominated by the free-market individualistic ideology, unions have declined. It is relatively clear that the connection between the ideological shift and the power of unions works in both directions. The shift undermines unions' power, and the decline in unions' power furthers the shift. It is hard to imagine that the ideology could shift back in a more democratic direction without an associated change in the role of unions.

The overall potential of the redevelopment of the labor movement is evident in the widely cited study undertaken by economists Richard Freeman and James Medoff, in which they examined the question that became the title of their book, *What Do Unions Do?* Freeman and Medoff saw an emerging picture of unions that tended to be confirmed by their own extensive quantitative research: "[I]n the economic sphere, unions reduce wage inequality, increase industrial democracy, and often raise productivity, while in the political sphere, unions are an important voice for some of our society's weakest and most vulnerable groups, as well as for their own members."[6]

It is, however, widely believed that the decline of unions is not a phenomenon that can be reversed easily if at all. In this view, the decline has been a consequence of objective factors, factors that cannot be altered by changes in union strategy or even through the political process. In particular, in this view globalization and shifts in technology have undermined union organization. Globalization has placed U.S. workers in competition with much more poorly paid (and poorly protected) workers in other parts of the world, eviscerating, it seems, the ability of U.S. unions to improve, or even maintain, the position of their members. People over forty—and many who are younger—are aware that everything from T-shirts to computers to auto parts that now bear the "made in" label of Mexico, Bangladesh, or, especially, China, used to be produced by workers in the United States. In the 1960s, as we pointed out in Chapter 7, total imports each year amounted to about 5 percent of GDP; in the first eight years of the new millennium this figure had tripled to about 15 percent.[7]

Also, and connected to globalization, the dramatic decline of employment in manufacturing—the site of great union concentration and advances in the post–World War II era—has decimated unions' membership and greatly reduced their strength. Whereas at the beginning of the 1960s manufacturing accounted for 30 percent of total nonagricultural employment, this figure fell steadily in subsequent years and stood at only 10 percent in 2007.[8] The decline in manufacturing employment, while connected to globalization, has in large part been a consequence of technological change—which has, ironically, been in part a consequence of union strength. As unionized workers gained wages and benefits, their employers had a rising incentive to find technologies that would reduce labor costs, including especially technologies where the advances were embodied in the machinery (e.g., robotics) rather than in the skills of the workers. (The process has often been referred to as the "deskilling" of work.) This not only reduced the number of employees per unit of output, but also made it easier to move production to sites around the world where labor was less costly (because the technology was embodied in the machinery, not in the skills of the workers).

There is no doubt that globalization and the decline in manufacturing have been important factors in weakening organized labor. Moreover, the argument claiming that the redevelopment of the labor movement is futile is given some strength by the fact that in virtually all high-income countries, organized labor has been in decline during recent decades. This decline has involved a self-propelling character. As the "objective" forces have led to the shrinking of unions as a proportion of the workforce, their political clout—their political power—has also declined; and as their political clout has declined, they have been in a weaker position to organize and rebuild their membership. For example, with waning political clout, unions have seen appointments to the National Labor Relations Board who are often hostile to the unions and their organizing efforts. Yet the very fact that the political power of unions has been an element in their decline demonstrates that it is not simply objective forces that have brought about that decline.

Where there is room for political decisions, there is room for different political decisions. In the past, decisions in Washington have been instrumental in affecting the power of unions. The enactment of the National Labor Relations Act (NLRA) in 1935 was extremely important in positively affecting the terrain for union organizing. And the Taft-Harley Act of 1947 moved things significantly in the other direction. Each of these important pieces of legislation was, to be sure, an outgrowth of its times. Similarly, the decisions of the NLRB that have often allowed workers engaged in union organizing to be fired (noted in Chapter 4) have reflected circumstance of the times. Yet these developments were not simply determined by background conditions. Each involved political decisions.

Furthermore, the background condition of neither globalization nor technological change is a purely objective process that takes place wholly outside of social control. As we emphasized in Chapter 7 and will discuss again shortly, globalization is not one thing. Commerce spreads across international boundaries in different ways, and political decisions can affect the way this geographic spread of commerce has its impacts on workers and their unions. Similarly, the shape of technological change is not preordained by the logic of science. Firms make choices about the direction of their research and development (R&D) and their innovation, and those choices are directed toward enlarging profits. This can mean, for example, choosing a technology that ensures management's most effective control of the production process and that avoids labor conflicts—which can mean choosing a labor-displacing technology even when it is not the most efficient technology. The nature of technology, then, is a function of firms' power to make decisions about R&D and innovation, and those decisions can affect the future power of the firm in relation to its workforce. Also, much technology-oriented research is carried out with public funds, and, at least to some degree, the direction in which those funds push innovation is affected by political power. As a case in point, a significant amount of agricultural research takes place in public universities, and it often has been directed toward labor-displacing technologies. Perhaps more important, the way technological change has its impacts on labor is a contested process, where legal limits play—or fail to play—a significant role. For example, firms will be less quick to introduce labor-displacing technologies when they are constrained in their ability to dismiss workers or required to pay substantial severance packages—reflecting the costs that those dismissals place on the community.

Because the position of labor unions, the impact of objective forces on labor unions, and the nature of those forces are so subject to political processes, there is room for redevelopment of the labor movement. In recent years, for example, there has been an effort to enact the Employee Free Choice Act, which would significantly facilitate union organizing. The act would have the NLRB certify a union as the bargaining representative of the workers in an enterprise when a majority had signed cards requesting the representation; at present, the signing of cards only leads to a vote as to whether or not the union will represent the workers. At this writing it appears that the act is dead for the time being. It is an example, however, of the way that the foundation for union redevelopment can be affected in Washington. We can also conceive of ways in which a broader impact could be brought to bear on the composition and actions of the NLRB. As we said, we have no magic formulas, but we do think that there are possibilities. The important point for our purposes here is that gains for unions embody wider gains, including a more democratic distribution of income and power, a shift in ideology, and, consequently, greater economic stability.

Reshaping Globalization

In addition to globalization's broad impact on economic and political life in the United States, it has also and directly been an important factor in the current economic crisis. While the crisis emerged from U.S. events—most particularly from the housing bubble and from the related government policies and financial shenanigans—it has been an international crisis, both in terms of its causes and consequences. As we have explained, the global economy has evolved in such a way that, on the one hand, economic activities are increasingly international while, on the other hand, systems of economic regulation—political systems—remain thoroughly national. It is therefore quite difficult to regulate economic activity and to reshape the structures of global economic activity. Yet, to the extent that the structures of global economic activity contributed to the crisis, it is necessary to consider them in figuring out how to establish lasting stability.

The problem is not new. At what we might call the dawn of the current era of globalization, in the mid-1970s, U.S. Secretary of State Henry Kissinger made the following comment in an interview with *Business Week* magazine: "One interesting feature of our recent discussions with both the Europeans and Japanese has been the emphasis on the need for economic cooperation . . . How you, in fact, coordinate policies is yet an unresolved problem."[9] More than three decades later, the need for cooperation is no less and the means of coordination remain as elusive. There are international institutions that play some role in charting global economic policy: the International Monetary Fund (IMF), the World Bank, and the World Trade Organization. There is also the United Nations and its various agencies, as well as the regular meetings among the political authorities in various nations (the so-called G-7, G-8, and G-20). Yet these institutions and forums do not have the power to effectively regulate the global economy. They are not without influence, but they cannot play the role internationally that a government can play within its own borders.

There is no great mystery regarding the sorts of changes that are needed to provide greater stability in the global economy. As the current crisis developed, the President of the General Assembly of the United Nations convened a Commission of Experts to make recommendations on reforms of the international monetary and financial system. The commission's approach and list of recommendations are largely consistent with the analysis we have presented in this book. For example, the approach presents loose monetary policy and failures of regulation as central factors in the emergence of the crisis, and the commission also cites weak aggregate demand, "aggravated by increasing income inequality within most nations," as part of the explanation for the loose monetary policy. (The commission, however, seems to give much more emphasis to "inadequate appreciation of the limits of markets" and to "previously fashionable economic doctrines" than to the exercise of power in establishing these conditions.) The commission's many recommendations include, for example:

- Strong and coordinated fiscal simulation by the governments of developed countries.
- Mobilizing development funds by creating a new credit facility.
- Improved coordination of global economic policies—including regulation of international financial activity, which would effectively involve capital controls (i.e., restrictions on the movement of capital in and out of countries).
- Avoiding protectionism and opening of the markets of developed countries to exports from developing countries.
- More representative governance of existing international institutions, particularly the IMF and World Bank.
- Reformation of international tax policy to raise revenue for international development, including such possibilities as a carbon tax, which would help address problems of global warming and impose the real cost of long-distance commerce on traded goods, and a financial services tax (a transactions tax), which would help stabilize international financial markets.
- A host of particular proposals for the regulation of financial markets, including derivative markets, and rating agencies.[10]

By and large, the recommendations of the Commission of Experts are reasonable and useful. (We especially like the proposals for a financial services tax and for a carbon tax; see Box 10.2.) There are, however, two major problems. First, the commission offers no means by which effective international cooperation and policy coordination might be achieved. Second, the commission's advocacy that protectionism be avoided in developed countries is presented without providing ways in which workers in those countries would have their interests—their income and security—protected. Indeed, workers, working conditions, labor standards, and wages are absent from the commission's report.

We too have no solution to the problem of international cooperation and policy coordination. We believe, however, that a significant part of the solution lies with the U.S. government because of the great economic and political power that this country's government and businesses exercise in the world. After all, the terms of globalization have been to a great extent

Box 10.2

Good Taxes

The Commission of Experts on Reforms of the International Monetary and Financial System points out a need for revenues to finance development in low-income countries and to deal with global warming. These revenues might be raised in part, the commission suggests, by a financial transactions tax and a carbon tax. Both taxes would have positive impacts on economic stability and power relations in the global economy.

A financial transactions tax would be a very small percentage tax on short-term international currency transactions—a rate of perhaps one-twentieth of one percent of the amount of a transaction. The tax would discourage speculation in currency trading, which can destabilize the international economy. Longer-term transactions, undertaken to finance international trade or real investment, would not be affected.

A carbon tax would be levied on the burning of fuels in proportion to their carbon content. The use of fossil fuels (coal, oil, gasoline, natural gas) and bio-based fuels (wood, ethanol) would be affected. The tax would reduce carbon dioxide emissions, a major factor in global warming. It would encourage energy conservation and reliance on "environmentally friendly" sources of energy (e.g., wind power or solar power). Carbon taxes are already used in the European Union.

Both taxes would affect international commerce. The financial transactions tax would directly reduce international currency speculation and associated instability. The carbon tax would make international trade more costly, as it would require the users of fuels to pay the real social cost of their fuel use. Consumers would shift toward the purchase of more locally produced goods.

There would be complications in collecting these taxes, as there is no international institution in place that could readily accomplish this task. Nonetheless, both taxes could bring prices more into line with the real social costs involved in the affected activities and have the potential to raise significant amounts of revenue. Also, by limiting speculation and increasing the costs of global commerce, these taxes would reduce the flexibility of firms and thereby improve the bargaining power of workers.

shaped by U.S. efforts, and thus it is reasonable to assume that U.S. efforts could go a long way toward effecting reform. Moreover, the other problem we have noted with the commission's recommendations—the lack of consideration of the position of workers in developed countries—is a central problem for the United States. So we approach the changes that are needed in the global economy from the perspective of what needs to be done in the United States.

Our principal point is that globalization is not one thing. If we define globalization simply as the increase of commerce across international boundaries, it can take place in several different ways. The advocates of globalization in the United States and some other advanced countries identify the phenomenon with the elimination of regulation of international commerce—that is, with free trade. Yet the idea that free trade and globalization are one and the same thing has no foundation in reality. Historically, as we explained in Chapter 7, globalization has taken various forms, including most often forms that involve a major role for states. Also—and, again, as we have emphasized—the current era of globalization was shaped by planning and political decisions, largely by the U.S. government. Globalization did not just happen.

Even today as the United States and several other developed counties proclaim the virtues of free trade as the foundation of globalization, they continue to directly protect many particular markets. Moreover, in a time of crisis, the principles of free trade stand as little more than rhetoric, as has been shown by the U.S. government's bailouts of the banks and auto companies. Even in "normal" times, there is no place in either the rhetoric or reality of free trade for the free movement of labor across international boundaries. Yet, when capital is free to move and labor movement is restricted, the power of business is enhanced by its greater options.

Great gains can be obtained from the expansion of international commerce. Those gains are both material and cultural. Yet there is no more reason to think that the international economy can run effectively and stably without regulation than that national economies can operate well without regulation. Likewise, there is no reason to believe that individual countries should involve themselves in international commerce without regulating that involvement. The issue, then, is not whether to regulate, but how. And an important part of regulation—on both the domestic and international level—is how economic gains will be distributed. Once this is recognized, once the perverse ideology of "leave it to the market" is abandoned, it becomes possible to begin to deal with the problems of the global economy. This fundamental change of ideology—linked to changes in power and income distribution—is dependent on the sorts of domestic changes that we have already discussed: the expansion of social programs and the redevelopment of the labor movement. In this sense, changes in the global economy, changes of the sort proposed by the UN Commission of Experts, depend upon domestic changes—within the United States and also within other countries.

Even if these changes were implemented, the problem would remain: how to avoid the waste and inequalities of protectionism while maintaining the well-being of workers within the developed countries. A first step in finding a solution to this problem lies in recognizing that it is part of a more basic problem that is not unique to international commerce. For example, when we impose new regulations to protect the environment, workers in some industries are affected in the same way that workers in other industries are affected by the removal of import restrictions; both groups lose their jobs. The same is often true of new technological developments. Workers who have done their jobs quite satisfactorily pay the price of change. Or when bad managerial decisions bring about the collapse of a firm, again workers who have done their jobs pay the price. (The U.S. automobile industry, especially General Motors in the current period, might be used as an example of all of these phenomena.) The common issue in all of these cases is: How do we regulate economic life without stifling socially desirable change *and* without placing the burden of that change on workers who have made reasonable decisions about which jobs to take and have done their jobs in a reasonable manner?

Which brings us back to universal social programs and the redevelopment of the labor movement. As we have explained, universal social programs provide a foundation of security, and their existence would greatly ease the transition of workers from jobs that have disappeared—due to import competition, environmental regulation, technological change, bad management, or whatever—to new jobs. Furthermore, well-developed universal social programs could provide support for further education and training for displaced workers. Labor unions have often been placed in the position of resisting otherwise positive social change because they must protect their members, who, in the absence of adequate support, are the ones who bear the burden of that change. At the same time, labor unions have often been prime advocates of the programs, the social supports that remove such burdens from their members. So the combination of the expansion of universal social programs and the redevelopment of labor unions offers a possible foundation for resolving the continuing conflict between the socially desirable changes and workers' well-being. Not a panacea, but a possible foundation.

Ultimately, however, the problems associated with globalization are global problems. The vast differences that exist between the economic well-being of most of us living in the high-income countries and our counterparts in the low-income countries create a tension and potential conflicts of interest that cannot be resolved by even the best national policies. While the wages of workers in China, India, and elsewhere are so vastly below those of workers in the United States, the growing interconnectedness of commerce, (globalization) will continue to place pressure on and be a threat to the members of the more privileged group. Their well-being cannot be fully secure until great improvements are attained in economic conditions in the low-income countries. Struggles for improvements of working conditions and labor standards— especially the right to organize independent unions—are an essential basis for obtaining these improvements, and those struggles need to be widely supported. Effective global full-employment programs are also essential, and, in addition, help provide a foundation for workers' struggles. Bringing greater economic stability to the world economy is a step in the right direction. Movement toward greater economic equality and progressive shifts in power and ideology are also positive steps. But they are only beginnings.

A Final Word

A final word is necessary regarding income and wealth distribution. Throughout this book we have dealt with economic inequality as an important force generating economic instability in general and the current economic crisis in particular. For this reason alone, it would be important to bring about greater economic equality.

As we expect our readers have realized, however, our commitment to a more equal society rests on a broader basis. There is something about living in a society with vast differences in people's well-being, where some people have "everything" while others live in severe need, that strikes us as wrong. It is unpleasant and stressful to live in a society with great economic inequalities. It is unpleasant and stressful even for those who stand relatively high up in the social and economic hierarchy. Equality matters to us because, as the philosopher Samuel Scheffler has put it, "we believe that there is something valuable about human relationships that are—in certain crucial respects at least—unstructured by differences of rank, power, or status."[11] Furthermore, the value of reducing inequality goes beyond our particular views—though we believe our views are widely shared. As Richard Wilkinson and Kate Pickett have explained in their important 2009 book, *The Spirit Level: Why Greater Equality Makes Societies Stronger,*[12] it turns out that societies with greater equality in the distribution of income tend to excel in all sorts of practical ways as well—for example, better physical health, lower rates of violent crime, less mental illness, fewer teenage pregnancies, and better natural environments. Some have argued that greater inequality is the necessary price we pay for greater opportunity, for having a more mobile society (i.e., greater opportunity for people to move up from humble origins). The facts, however, tell a different story: greater economic equality and greater mobility tend to go together.

So, yes, we do think that an improvement in the distribution of income and wealth—greater economic equality—is essential for establishing long-term economic stability. But we advocate greater equality for many other reasons. It is, we believe, a foundation of the good society.

Notes

1. From R. Loya, R. Liberman, R. Albelda, and E. Babcock, *Fits & Starts: The Difficult Path for Working Single Parents,* Report prepared by Crittenton Women's Union and the Center for Social Policy at McCormack Graduate School, University of Massachusetts, Boston, 2008, http://www.mccormack.umb.edu/centers/csp/documents/Fitsdocument_000.pdf. Used by permission. Note: In the published version of *Fits & Starts,* the $538 and $147 at the end of the second paragraph were misprinted as $547 and $156.

2. Such figures on health care costs per car are widely quoted, but we are not able to locate the original source. See, for example, Eric Bryant, "What Do Automakers Pay for Healthcare?" The Autoblog, October 20, 2005, www.autoblog.com/2005/10/20/what-do-automakers-pay-for-health-care/, where costs per car for GM and Toyota are reported as $1,500 and $97, respectively. Senator Claire McCaskill (Democrat of Missouri) referred to figures of $1,500 for GM and $110 for Toyota in the Congressional Record of January 25, 2007, www.gpo.gov/fdsys/pkg/CREC-2007—01—25/html/CREC-2007—01—25-pt1-PgS1136—2.htm. And Senator Thomas Coburn (Republican of Oklahoma) referred to the same figure for GM on May 27, 2008, www.beheard.com/records/Detail.aspx?id=11012008052210.

3. A "housing affordability tax credit" along these lines has been proposed and outlined by Michael Stone of the Center for Social Policy at the University of Massachusetts Boston; see his "Reconstructing Housing Policy to Overcome the Manifestations and Causes of Shelter Poverty," www.mccormack.umb.edu/centers/csp/_rppc/presentations/michael_stone_presentation060409.pdf.

4. John Schmitt, *The Unions of the States* (Washington DC: Center for Economic and Policy Research, 2010), p. 18.

5. David M. Gordon, *Fat and Mean* (New York: Free Press, 1996), p. 221.

6. Richard B. Freeman and James L. Medoff, *What Do Unions Do?* (New York: Basic Books, 1984), p. 5.

7. Import and GDP data are from the *Economic Report of the President 2010,* Table B-1.

8. Employment data are from the *Economic Report of the President 2001,* Table B-46, and the *Economic Report of the President 2010,* Table B-46.

9. *Business Week,* January 13, 1975, p. 76.

10. The Commission of Experts on Reforms of the International Monetary and Financial System, Recommendations, March 19, 2009, www.un.org/ga/president/63/letters/recommendationExperts200309.pdf.

11. Samuel Scheffler, "Choice, Circumstance, and the Value of Equality," *Politics, Philosophy, and Economics* 2005, 4 (1), p. 17.

12. Richard Wilkinson and Kate Pickett, *The Spirit Level: Why Greater Equality Makes Societies Stronger* (New York: Bloomsbury Press, 2009).

Appendix A

Brief Notes on Wealth and Power

We argue throughout this book that the power of the wealthy has brought about a high degree of economic inequality and generated a perverse leave-it-to-the-market ideology. The inequality, ideology, and power have worked together as a vicious circle to generate economic instability. Yet the United States is a formally democratic society. We have regular elections and extensive civil liberties. These essential procedures of democracy have been violated many times in our history (not least by provisions of the Patriot Act), and it is possible to point out various flaws in the country's election procedures. Nonetheless, by both international and historical standards, democratic procedures in the United States, while not ideal, are pretty good. So how is it that "the wealthy" have been able to exercise such great power in shaping the way our economy operates?

A full discussion of the operation of power in the United States is beyond the scope of this book. It will nonetheless be useful to say a bit in this appendix to make our meaning clear when we set out claims about what has been happening. In briefly describing how the wealthy exercise their power, we want to emphasize that this power is not absolute. Indeed, if we thought the power of the wealthy was absolute, we probably would not have bothered to write this book! Nonetheless, we think it is important to recognize and understand the existence of this undemocratic power and to recognize how it operates in order to establish a more democratic society and secure a more stable operation of our economic lives. (Of course, not all wealthy people have the same interests, and many business groups have particular interests that are in conflict with one another. However, on broad general issues, such as taxation and regulation, the wealthy share a broad set of common interests. It is in exercising power on these broad general issues that they can, and do, by and large act in concert.)

Money in Politics

The direct use of money to pay for lobbying and to provide donations to political officials is widely recognized and gives the wealthy a distinct advantage. While lobbying is nothing new, there has been a substantial growth of lobbying expenditures in recent years. Between 1999 and 2009, lobbying expenditures grew from $1.45 billion to $3.49 billion. The leading business sectors have been the so-called FIRE sector (finance, insurance, and real estate) and the health care sector (including pharmaceuticals, hospitals, and other health care firms). The FIRE and health care industries spent $4.2 billion and $4.1 billion, respectively, on lobbying in the 1998 to 2010 period. In 2009 the FIRE sector spent $467 million on lobbying and used 2,663 lobbyists, while heath care firms spent $545 million and used 3,432 lobbyists.[1]

Although labor unions are often lumped together with business as spending large amounts of money for political influence, unions' lobbying expenditures are dwarfed by business spending. Over the entire 1998 to 2009 period, unions spent a total of $416 million, and in 2009 their lobbying expenditures were $44 million—that is, about one-tenth of what was being spent by firms in either the FIRE or health care sector. As further contrast to the role of unions, in 2009 the U.S. Chamber of Commerce spent $144.5 million on lobbying, more than three times as much as all of organized labor; and several individual firms—ExxonMobil, General Electric, Pfizer, and Blue Cross/Blue Shield—each spent more than $20 million.

The impact of lobbying rests in part simply on the pressure that lobbyists apply by their regular contacts with legislators, regulators, and other policy officials. Perhaps more important, they are able to supply information, analyses, and arguments to the officials who make and implement policy. Indeed, legislators often rely on lobbyists to write legislation, accepting that the lobbyists are highly knowledgeable about the issues of the industry they represent and ignoring the obvious fact that they are there to obtain legislation that is favorable to their employers' interests. Indeed, the effectiveness of business lobbyists is tied closely to and rationalized by an ideology that asserts a congruence between the interests of business and the general interest.

Behind the lobbyists are both contributions to political campaigns and the "revolving door," whereby politicians, top aides to politicians, regulators, and other policy makers move from their positions in government to often high-paying positions with private firms. Regarding contributions, the Center for Responsive Politics has compiled a list of 136 individuals who "contributed at least $50,000 to federal candidates and parties during one or more election cycle [since 1989]" and identifies the organization with which each was affiliated when making the contribution. Few of the names on the list are well known, but their organizations are a familiar roster of large firms. Among the 136 individuals are 17 affiliated with Goldman Sachs and an equal number affiliated with Time Warner. Eleven on the list are connected to Comcast and 10 to Microsoft. Examples of other firms on the list include Walmart Stores, Citigroup, Walt Disney, General Electric, and the now-defunct Enron Corporation.[2]

Contributions also come directly from corporations and other organizations. Among the top twenty-five donors in the 2007–2008 period are AT&T, the National Association of Realtors, Goldman Sachs, Citigroup, UPS, and the American Bankers Association. However, this list of the top twenty-five organizational donors in those years also includes a dozen labor unions. Examples are the National Education Association, $56.2 million, and the Service Employees International Union, $30.4 million. Still, though unions are not without clout in the use of money to influence political outcomes, their overall role does not match up with that of the corporate sector.[3] (In early 2010, in the Citizens United case, the U.S. Supreme Court struck down limits on corporations' political spending. This will surely have a major impact, leading to great increases of the figures cited here for the pre-2010 period.)

With the "revolving door," the corporate sector has unchallenged dominance. In recent years, two well-known figures stand out as prime examples of this revolving door and, thus, of the pay-off that comes to politicians (and other policy officials) who are friendly to business. One is Phil Gramm, a Republican U.S. Senator from Texas from 1985 to 2002 (and a congressman from 1975 through 1985). Gramm was a leader (as we note in Chapter 5) in the effort to deregulate the financial industry, and upon departing from the Senate became a vice chairman of UBS Americas, the large Swiss-based financial firm. Another is Tom Daschle, a Democratic Senator from South Dakota from 1987 to 2004, and Minority Leader (and briefly Majority Leader) of the Senate from 1995 to 2004. Leaving the Senate, Daschle became a consultant to InterMedia Advisors, a private equity firm, and chairman of its executive advisory board; he then took up a highly paid position with a Washington lobbying firm.[4]

The Gramm-Daschle combination illustrates the fact that both major parties are involved in the revolving door and, more generally, in the direct use of money to influence politics. Many firms, contributing to political campaigns, give to both parties. While the Republicans are generally viewed as the party more friendly to business, many large firms lean toward the Democrats. For example, the contributions associated with Goldman Sachs, the firm that had such a prominent role in dealings that precipitated the financial crisis of 2007–2008, have gone largely to the Democrats.[5]

Shaping Ideology

The direct use of money, however, is only a part of the story of how the wealthy exercise power. The control of wealth is also of considerable importance in influencing how people think—that is, in shaping ideology, the framework that affects how people interpret particular situations and make decisions. One example of a place where the process is both important and readily apparent is in school reform. School reform has been and continues to be greatly influenced by philanthropic foundations, established (and generally controlled) by very wealthy individuals. Not only does this role directly demonstrate the power of the wealthy in affecting an important social structure (the schools), but in addition the particular direction in which these foundations have pushed reform carries with it a strong ideological message.

While major foundations have long been involved in efforts to influence the direction of school reform (the Rockefeller, Ford, Annenberg, and Carnegie foundations, in particular), a number of relatively new foundations have come to play large roles in recent years; examples include the Gates, Walton, and Broad foundations. These foundations have pushed a variety of changes in the schools, some of which have received support from a broad political spectrum of school activists; a prime example is the effort by the Gates Foundation to promote smaller schools. However, many actions of these new foundations have shared the common theme of advocating reform that is outside the traditional public school system. These actions emphasize charter schools (and sometimes school voucher programs) and build on the idea that teachers' unions and excessive constraints of public "bureaucracy" are The Problem. It is an approach that moves toward privatizing the educational system, and often incorporates for-profit companies as the operators of schools. The ideology that both informs this approach to school reform and is generated by this approach is one that sees the The Market, unfettered by social controls, as the solution to society's problems. (Some older foundations have also pushed in this direction—for example Scaife, Olin, and Bradley.)[6]

Moreover, the approach to school reforms generally pursued by wealthy foundations and sometimes more directly by wealthy individuals posits a one-way causation from the problems of the schools to the problems of society. It largely ignores the impact of our society's great economic inequalities on what happens in the schools. A prime example is provided by the support of Wall Street billionaires for the much-heralded Harlem Children's Zone. One need not question their desire to support this holistic approach to improving the lives of children in Harlem to recognize, first, that they apparently ignore their own role in generating the economic problems that contribute to the plight of so many of those children (a role we discuss in various chapters). Second, good or bad, these efforts of wealthy financiers in Harlem are a prime illustration of the way they can exercise power in shaping both social institutions and influencing the way people think about social reform.[7]

Another example of wealthy individuals affecting school reform—operating directly or through foundations or through some other forum—is provided by the activities of the Commercial Club of Chicago. The Club, "an organization of the city's top corporate, financial and political elites," promoted a plan that, in its first phase, would close 60 of Chicago's existing schools, replacing them with 100 new schools, "two thirds of which will be charter or contract schools run by private organizations and staffed by teachers and school employees who will not be [union] members. The schools also will not have Local School Councils . . . elected school governance bodies composed primarily of parents and community members . . . [that] have power over a school's discretionary budget, approve the School Improvement Plan, and hire the principal."[8]

The point here is not that the support of wealthy individuals, corporations, and foundations for school reform always leads in the wrong direction—though that is often the case. Instead, as these examples illustrate, the wealthy are able to use their position effectively to influence social policy and spread an ideology that supports their interests. (We should also note that when the wealthy endow foundations or donate directly to school reform programs, then for every $10 they give, the government loses about $4 in taxes. They are, in effect, giving away the public's money without public control.)[9]

In spreading an ideology that supports the interests of the wealthy, the schools have a strong partner in the mass media. Indeed, the mass media are prime generators of that ideology. Of course we have a free press in the United States, in the sense that there are very few legal limits on people disseminating information and propagating their ideas. So how is it that the media in general and the press in particular are dominated by the interests of the wealthy?

The answer to this question was implicitly supplied in 2002 by the then president and CEO of The New York Times Company, Russ Lewis. Lewis was addressing the failure of the press to fully examine the implosion of the Enron Corporation and other "corporate disasters" and also the reason why the press focused so much more attention on government misbehavior than on corporate misdeeds. Lewis wrote:

> Historically, the press's ability to act as a check on the actions of government has been helped by the fact that the two institutions are

constitutionally separated, organizationally and financially. The press does not depend on government officials either for its standing or its resources.

But it has a much more intricate relationship with big business. Today's news media are themselves frequently a part of large, often global corporations dependent on advertising revenue that, increasingly, comes from other large corporations. As public companies themselves, the news media are under the same kind of pressure to create "shareholder value," by reducing costs and increasing earnings, as are other public companies. And they face numerous potential conflicts of interest as they grow larger and more diversified.

The First Amendment makes it difficult for government to impede or financially threaten the work of the press. But no such constitutional provision applies to the intersection of the press and big business.

It is both impractical and unrealistic to expect news media companies, including newspaper firms, to retreat from their positions as increasingly large, diversified business enterprises. To do so would not only undermine their financial strength; it would also deprive them and their staffs of the resources needed to perform their increasingly difficult and demanding roles.[10]

Lewis's statement is useful, first, because it makes clear that press enterprises—and the same is true of other media enterprises—are themselves large corporations and are enmeshed with, and to a large extent dependent on, other large corporations. The owners of the press are, correspondingly, among the very wealthy. It is therefore hardly a great leap to assert that the press (and the media generally) are dominated by the interest of the wealthy.

The Lewis statement also underscores an aspect of the ideology that is so important to corporate interests—namely the idea that government is corrupt and inefficient while private firms are efficient and the high incomes obtained by their executives and owners are in some sense deserved. The press, as Lewis points out, focuses on the problems of government, while tending to ignore the scandals in the operations of large corporations. (The fact that events of recent years have created at least a partial shift, with the press giving more attention to the outrages committed by large firms that led us into the current economic crisis, is a hallmark of the way a crisis can change many well-established practices.)

There is of course the principle espoused by most news organizations that the editorial page is separated from the news pages, and the latter is based on professional (not ideological) judgments of highly qualified journalists. Without impugning the integrity of journalists, it is not difficult to understand how over time, regardless of formal separation of editorial and news pages, the interests and ideology of owners have great impact on the outlook and decisions of those preparers of the news pages. The choices of topics on which to focus and the implicit slant of reporting will tend to conform to—or at least not sharply challenge—the interests of the owners on fundamental issues. The process is more a matter of self-censorship than of any overt censorship, as journalists generally internalize the ideology that they disseminate.[11]

The Foundation: The Function of Owners and Executives

Ultimately, however, the power of the wealthy is not based simply on the direct role of money in political affairs and on the shaping of ideology, though both are surely important. The foundation of business power lies in the function of owners and executives of business—that is, in our society's reliance on their private decisions to determine investments and job creation. Political authorities at all levels believe that if they are "unfriendly" to business interests, they will run the risk of slowing business activity, reducing employment, and thus alienating voters. When firms ask (or demand) tax incentives, looser regulations, or some other favors that will increase their profits, they argue that increased profits will generate more investment and more jobs—and that a failure to grant their requests will do the opposite. Similarly, tax breaks for the wealthy are supported with the argument that putting more income in their hands will lead to more investment and more jobs. To a large extent, money in politics and ideology have their impact in buttressing this argument, this basic power of business and the wealthy.

This argument—the claim that policy makers must do what businesses and the wealthy want in order to maintain a high level of economic activity— has an element of truth. If it is not sufficiently profitable for firms to make investments and employ more people, the economy will falter and hardship will be widespread—and the political authorities may well join the growing ranks of the unemployed. This element of truth gives a great deal of power to the wealthy. It has allowed them to propagate the idea of trickle-down economics, the theory that if benefits are provided to those at the top, everyone else, including those at the bottom, will share in the gains.

But "an element of truth" is by no means the whole truth, and "sufficiently profitable" is certainly a vague term. Clearly some taxes on the wealthy and some regulation of business are possible without stifling business activity. During periods of successful economic growth—for example, during the post–World War II years—tax rates on business and on the wealthy have been much higher than now and regulations have been much more extensive. Policies that are of immediate benefit to business and the wealthy are often not good for society. Indeed, much of this book is devoted to demonstrating how what has been good for business, for the financial firms in particular, has not been good for the rest of us. Other periods in recent decades—the 1980s, for example, and the early 2000s—demonstrate the ineffectiveness of trickle-down economics. Cutting taxes for the rich and adoption of policies favoring business did not lead to rapid economic growth and provided little if any economic gains for most people. Yet it is the emergence of the crisis in 2007 and 2008 that best demonstrates the fallacy of the claim that giving business and the wealthy what they want is good for all of us.

Notes

1. These data and data noted below on lobbying and political contributions are from the "Open Secrets" website of the Center for Responsive Politics, www. opensecrets.org.

2. The list is available on the "Open Secrets" website at www.opensecrets.org/orgs/indivs.php.

3. Again, the data are from the Center for Responsive Politics at www.opensecrets.org/orgs/list_stfed.php?order=A.

4. The Gramm and Daschle details are provided at www.opensecrets.org/revolving/index.php, and Daschle's involvement with InterMedia Advisors has been widely reported; for example, by ABC News at blogs.abcnews.com/politicalpunch/2009/01/bumps-in-the-ro.html.

5. Once more, the "Open Secrets" website, www.opensecrets.org/orgs/summary.php?id=D000000085.

6. See Barbara Miner, "Who's Behind the Money?" and "The Gates Foundation and Small Schools," *Rethinking Schools* 19 (4), Summer 2005, pp. 24–25 and 21–26.

7. See Paul Tough, *Whatever It Takes: Geoffrey Canada's Quest to Change Harlem and America* (Boston: Mariner Books, 2009).

8. Pauline Lipman, "We're Not Blind, Just Follow the Dollar Sign," *Rethinking Schools* 19 (4), Summer 2005, pp. 54–58.

9. This parenthetic point is made by Richard Rothstein, former education columnist for *The New York Times* and analyst on the educational system, as quoted by Barbara Miner, "Who's Behind the Money," *Rethinking Schools*.

10. Russ Lewis, "The Press's Business . . . ," *The Washington Post,* January 30, 2002. Cited by Robert W. McChesney, in *The Problem of the Media: U.S. Communications Politics in the Twenty-First Century* (New York: Monthly Review Press, 2004), pp. 92–93.

11. The brief statement of this point is usefully elaborated by both McChesney as cited in the previous note and Edward Herman and Noam Chomsky, *Manufacturing Consent: The Political Economy of the Mass Media* (New York: Pantheon Books, 1988). There is of course much more to the role of the media in affecting ideology than we deal with in this brief account, and the media include much more than the press, which we have focused on here. McChesney and Herman and Chomsky are good sources for more comprehensive analyses.

Appendix B

What's Wrong with the Case
for Free-Market Globalization?

During the current phase of globalization, a period we can date as beginning sometime in the late 1970s or early 1980s, the world economies have grown more slowly than in the preceding post–World War II era. These recent decades are the years in which "free trade," or deregulation, has been the guiding ideology of globalization. The slower economic growth of this period might lead one to conclude that the merits of free-market globalization are oversold.

But the advocates of globalization—who see free-market globalization as the only globalization—are not dissuaded. They remain convinced that market-driven globalization has in fact accelerated economic growth and poverty alleviation without worsening global inequality and, on top of that, contributed to better government. World Bank economists David Dollar and Aart Kraay, for example, claim:

> Well over half the developing world lives in globalizing economies that have seen large increases in trade and significant declines in tariffs. They are catching up [with] the rich countries while the rest of the developing world is falling farther behind. . . . The increase in growth rates leads on average to proportionate increases in incomes of the poor. . . . Globalization leads to faster growth rates and poverty reduction in poor countries.[1]

And a report by the global economic consulting firm A.T. Kearney asserts:

> Overall, countries integrating rapidly with the world economy have fared better than those integrating more slowly . . . because the fastest globalizing countries have enjoyed rates of economic growth that averaged 30 to 50 percent higher over the past 20 years. The same countries also enjoyed greater political freedom, benefited from more social spending, and received higher scores on the United Nations Human Development Index, an indicator of longevity, literacy, and standard of living.[2]

While powerful weapons for spreading the faith of free-market globalization, these studies are fundamentally flawed, as is the general argument they represent. They uniformly rely on slight of hand to reach pro free-market results that fly in the face of the historical record of economic development.

Poor Methods, Misleading Results

A simple comparison of growth rates before and after the current phase of globalization is misleading, according to these advocates of free trade, because it lumps together countries that pursued globalization policies and enjoy its benefits with those that did not. The first task in each of these pro free-market globalization studies, therefore, is to sort out the globalizers from the nonglobalizers.

But that is exactly where the problems begin: the criteria for selecting globalizers rely on a slight of hand. Each study substitutes *performance* variables that reflect the degree of engagement with the global economy for *policy* variables that reflect the degree to which that engagement was market-driven. The Global Business Policy council of A.T. Kearney ranks 34 developed and developing countries from "globalizing slowly" to "globalizing rapidly" based on their score on ten different indices. It then passes off the greater integration of the economies around the world measured by their globalization indices as the equivalent to free-trade. This method alone predetermines the pro free-market globalization outcome of these studies.

The globalization debate, however, is not about economic isolation versus integration into the world economy. Instead, the debate is about what policies allow a developing economy to successfully engage with the world economy. For the authors of these studies, that engagement requires the free-market or free-trade policies promoted by internationally operating firms, the International Monetary Fund, other international agencies, and the U.S. government. For the opponents of free-market globalization, more national control, protections for workers and the environment, and limits of the movement of foreign and domestic capital are polices for engagement with the world economy that are more likely to produce a widespread and equitable economic development.

These pro free-market studies fail to distinguish between the two different strategies for economic development in today's international economy, let alone assess the success of each. In the Kearney measure of globalization, one way or another, fully seven of the ten variables that comprise their globalization index are measures of a country's degree of engagement with the world economy, but not of the degree of openness of the policies that determine the manner of engagement.

One of these indices, the level of trade, shows exactly how these studies mislead. Kearney specifies the level of trade by the combined value of exports and imports as a percentage of gross domestic product (GDP) and then reports a positive correlation between the level of trade and economic growth (measured by the increase of GDP per capita). But this correlation does not tell us that openness to trade (lower tariffs and nontariff barriers to trade) causes economic growth. It simply attempts to answer a related but very different question: Does international trade raise economic growth rates?[3]

On top of that, even a positive correlation between economic growth and the level of trade does not tell us that trade "causes" faster economic growth. One might conclude that higher levels of trade are caused by more rapid rates of growth, and that other economic policies are responsible for the rapid growth. The Kearney study does not tell us which is the proper reading of the correlation.

Perhaps nothing better could be expected from a report produced by a for-profit research company "established in 1926 to provide management advice concerning issues on the CEO's agenda," as Kearney touts itself.[4] But the study conducted by World Bank economists Dollar and Kraay does no better. Employing a method similar to that of the Kearney report, this World Bank study uses "decade-over-decade *changes* in volume of trade as an imperfect proxy for *changes* in trade policy." (emphasis in original)[5] Their method alleviates some of the problems that arise when looking at the volume of trade across countries. However, it suffers from the same flaws as the Kearney globalization index: it measures the change in a country's degree of engagement with the world economy, but not of the change in the degree of openness of the policies that determine the manner of engagement.

Alternative Views

When economists do properly address the current policy debate about globalization, the evidence fails to endorse the pro free-market globalization position championed by these studies. For instance, in their critique of Dollar and Kraay's work, economists Howard Nye, Sanjay Reddy, and Kevin Watkins found that when "the performance of globalizers and non-globalizers [is] selected on the basic of reductions in average tariffs (from 1985–89 to 1995–97), non-globalizers actually *outperformed globalizers* in terms of increases in the growth rate of GDP!" (emphasis in the original).[6]

In their exhaustive survey of the major studies of trade policy and economic growth, economists Franciso Rodriguez and Dani Rodrik found, "little evidence that open trade *policies*—in the sense of lower tariff and non-tariff barriers to trade—are significantly associated with economic growth" (emphasis added).[7] By weighting down their globalization measures with trade performance variables that say little about the policy issue, the pro free-trade globalization studies manage to obscure the findings against free-trade that otherwise would have resulted.

Yet Another Problem

The correlation between rapid economic growth and globalization claimed in these pro free-trade studies is highly misleading in yet another way. The studies do not claim that rapid growth is associated with their measure of the *level* of globalization, no matter how flawed. Instead they claim that rapid growth is associated with *changes* in that measure. The contradictions introduced by relying on changes in trade volumes or even changes in tariff levels are numerous and plaguing. As Nye, Reddy, and Watkins report in their critique of Dollar and Kraay, countries that undertook the greatest cuts in tariffs still on average had higher tariffs after the cuts than most countries. And those *higher levels* of average tariffs were associated with *higher levels* of growth. Likewise, countries with large increases in trade volumes often begin with lower levels of trade than most countries, casting doubt on whether they can really be characterized as "globalizers."[8]

These same contradictions are evident in the Kearney globalization study, which also ranks countries not by their level of globalization but by the change in their globalization index. For instance, the Kearney study classifies China as an "aggressive globalizer" because it has recently liberalized its trade policies. But Singapore, the most globally integrated economy on the Kearney list (in terms of the ratio of trade to GDP), is only a "strong globalizer"—one rung down.[9]

Most damagingly, levels of globalization, as opposed to the changes in the level of globalization, are *negatively,* not positively, correlated with economic growth. For the period from 1988 to 2005, the "less" and "least" globalized economies in the Kearney study grew on average 4.1 percent and 4.0 percent a year respectively, while the "most" and "more" globalized economies with the supposedly better government performance grew just 3.1 percent and 3.2 percent a year respectively.[10]

Free Trade and Poverty Alleviation

Parallel criticisms apply to Kearney and Dollar-Kraay claims that free-trade globalization alleviates poverty. The correlation between their measures of globalization and poverty alleviation tells us little more than that economic growth is associated with lower poverty rates. But even this evidence contradicts much of what the globalizers have to say about the benefits of free trade. Over the last fifty years, the most dramatic reduction in poverty has occurred in East Asia among countries such as South Korea, Taiwan, and China, all of which have had extensive trade restrictions and relied on heavy government intervention into their economies.

Ironically, the authors of these studies (and other cheerleaders for free-market globalization) often use China and India to support their claims. But India and China do more to reveal the problems with these studies than to confirm their results. India and China are more open to international trade than in the past, but they hardly make good poster children for free-market globalization. The more successful of the two, China, remains a country that does not have a convertible currency, maintains state control of its banking system, allows little foreign ownership in equity markets, and has inflexible labor markets.

The Historical Record

In his *New York Times* column, Thomas Friedman, an advocate of free-market globalization, once challenged the critics of globalization to name "a single country that has upgraded its living or worker standards, without free trade and integration."[11] An accurate reply to Friedman's challenge is that *every one* of today's developed countries has relied heavily on government control of its international commerce. Britain came to its advocacy of free trade only after its industry had been well established in the eighteenth century on the basis of protectionism, and continued to maintain its colonial empire as it touted free trade. During its rapid development in the half century following the Civil War, the United States imposed tariffs on imports that averaged around 40 percent, a level higher than those in virtually all of today's developing economies. Development in both Germany and Japan during the second half of the twentieth century presents a compelling brief for managed trade, not free trade, as the key to rapid economic growth. Even the World Bank in its 1993 *East Asian Miracle* report acknowledged as much for the Japanese postwar boom.[12] And South Korea and Taiwan, two other East Asian countries with their most formative growth period during the 1960s and 1970s, faced a world economy with far less capital mobility and engaged that world with policies antithetical to free trade—export subsidies, domestic-content requirements, import-export linkages, and restrictions of capital flows, including direct foreign investment.

So it turns out that neither the historical record nor the studies by advocates of free-trade globalization support the claims that the policy agenda of lower barriers for trade and the movement of international capital bring about faster economic growth, greater poverty alleviation, or better government. One might think that would be enough to put the kibosh on the pro free-market globalization hype. But not so with the cheerleaders for globalization. That crowd is prepared to believe that "the world is flat"—the title of Thomas Friedman's paean to current phase of globalization—if it fits their worldview.[13]

Notes

1. David Dollar and Aart Kraay, "Trade, Growth, and Poverty," *The Economic Journal* 2004 *114* (493), p. F22, http://onlinelibrary.wiley.com/doi/10.1111/j.0013–0133.2004.00186.x/full.

2. A.T. Kearney, "Globalization Ledger," Global Business Policy Council, April 2000, p. 1. This paper is available online by clicking on the link "Globalization Index 2000" at www.atkearney.de/content/servicekompetenz/globalbusinesspolicycouncil_global.php.

3. See A.T. Kearney, "Globalization Ledger," p. 18.

4. A.T. Kearney Press Release, "Hong Kong, Jordan, and Estonia Debut Among the Top 10 in Expanded Ranking of the World's Most Globalized Countries," www.atkearney.com/index.php/News-media/hong-kong-jordan-and-estonia-debut-among-the-top-10-in-expanded-ranking-of-the-worlds-most-globalized-countries.html.

5. See David Dollar and Aart Kraay, "Trade, Growth, and Poverty," p. F26.

6. Howard Nye, Sanjay Reddy, and Kevin Watkins, "Dollar and Kraay on 'Trade, Growth, and Poverty': A Critique," August 24, 2002, p. 5, www.maketradefair.com/en/assets/english/finalDKcritique.pdf.

7. Francisco Rodriguez and Dani Rodrik, "Trade Policy and Economic Growth: A Skeptic's Guide to the Cross-National Evidence," revised May 2000, www.hks.harvard.edu/fs/drodrik/Research percent20papers/skepti1299.pdf.

8. Howard Nye, Sanjay Reddy, and Kevin Watkins, p. 7.

9. See A.T. Kearney, "Globalization Ledger," p. 4.

10. See A.T. Kearney, Foreign Policy Magazine Globalization Index 2005, www.atkearney.com/index.php/Publications/globalization-index.html.

11. Thomas Friedman, "Parsing the Protests," *The New York Times,* April 14, 2000.

12. *The East Asian Miracle: A World Bank Policy Research Report* (Oxford: Oxford University Press, 1993), pp. 5–9.

13. See Thomas L. Friedman, *The World Is Flat: A Brief History of the Twenty-First Century* (New York: Farrar, Straus, and Giroux, 2005).

Index

About the Authors

Arthur MacEwan is Professor Emeritus in the Department of Economics and Senior Fellow in the Center for Social Policy at the University of Massachusetts Boston. Educated at the University of Chicago and Harvard University, he has written extensively on international economic issues, economic development, and U.S. economic affairs. Among his books are *Neo-Liberalism or Democracy? Economic Strategy, Markets, and Alternatives for the 21st Century,* and *Debt and Disorder: International Economic Instability and U.S. Imperial Decline.* Professor MacEwan writes regularly for *Dollars & Sense* magazine.

John A. Miller is Professor of Economics at Wheaton College. Educated at Washington and Jefferson College and the University of Pittsburgh, he has published academic articles about sweatshops and globalization, government spending and tax policy, economic crises, and gender and unemployment. Professor Miller writes regularly for *Dollars & Sense* magazine and edits the magazine's classroom reader *Real World Macro.*